Christopher Madden was born in the north of England in 1952.
He is a cartoonist, with work appearing in numerous publications
including Philosophy Now magazine and the BBC's
science magazines Focus and Knowledge.
He lives in London.

Where Are We
What Are We
Why Are We

And Why Do We Want To Know

?

INKLINE PRESS

Where Are We, What Are We, Why Are We?

Copyright © 2009 Chris Madden

ISBN: 978-0-9548551-4-7

Published by Inkline Press
www.inklinepress.com

Preface

This book is an attempt to explore the underlying reasons why people feel the urge to give meaning to life.

It approaches its task by looking at our perception of our place in the universe, and it speculates on how this perception may give rise to such phenomena as spiritual and religious sensibilities.

In recent years there has been a veritable deluge of books published on the subjects of religion, belief and atheism – a genre to which this volume is a modest contribution. The first draught of the book was written in 1998, predating this mushrooming of titles. Since then much has changed in the world, and indeed in the author's head: the book has evolved and expanded accordingly.

For the purposes of religious classification the author categorises himself as a "non-believer". Despite this fact, the book that you now hold in your hands is not so much a criticism of religion but rather the distillation of the author's attempts to understand its existence. The book contains practically no mention of religious dogma or doctrine, and the world's principal monotheistic religions are only mentioned by name once. The word atheism only appears twice, with both of those occurrences being in the preface that you're reading now (So that's got that over with).

The author's only qualification for writing this book is that he is a cartoonist: a profession that encourages him to stand back and look at life from unusual angles and to think about things in slightly skewed and unconventional ways. While the core of the book is based on current understanding of the topics involved, some parts are purely the product of the author's own speculation. He would like to apologize in advance for any inappropriate lapses into humour that may occur in the following pages.

Contents

Introduction

It's a common feeling. The one that you get when you look up at the night sky with its countless stars, or when you stare at the ocean with its seemingly endless expanse of water, or when you gaze at the view from the top of a mountain with its awe-inspiring panorama of majestic peaks: the feeling that compels you to ask "What's it all about?" "What's the meaning of life?" "Why am I here?"

Well, if you're standing on the top of a mountain you may indeed ask "Why am I here?" Climbing to the top of a large and dangerous mound of rock purely so that you can go down again is an activity of seemingly lunatic pointlessness (especially as the summit is probably shrouded in cloud so that you can't get a glimpse of the awe-inspiring panorama anyway).

Think about those questions though: "What's it all about?" "What's the meaning of life?" "Why am I here?"

I have another question to add to them: "Why do I ask?"

Maybe you need to answer *that* particular question before you can attempt to answer the others. After all, before you can answer a question you need to know why you ask it in the first place.

Why do you want to know what the meaning of life is?

This book is to some extent an attempt to answer that question.

In the following pages I try to explain how we perceive the world around us and how we react to what we perceive. I try to describe how we see our position in the wider universe, and I delve into the subject of how we came to be in that universe in the first place. And I explore the issue of why some people think that there are spiritual or supernatural forces behind these things.

You're probably reading this book because you're interested in the meaning of life yourself. You're intrigued to know more about the greater, deeper truths that define existence: you're gripped with fascination about life, the universe and everything. Hopefully the book will shed a small amount of light on these subjects.

Intriguingly, you're reading this book because you want to know why you're reading this book.

Part I

Where Are We

?

Chapter 1

The Flaws of Perception

Before you can answer the question "What am I here for?" you need to try to work out exactly where this place that you call "here" is to begin with.

To answer that question it would seem obvious that the first thing that you need to do is to take a good look around yourself, and while you're at it, maybe listen out for any noises in your immediate vicinity and perhaps sniff the air for any smells. Place your hand on some nearby objects to get a feel for their textures, their forms and their temperatures (and if any of those objects turn out to be food, try tasting them too). This should give you a good overall impression of where you are.

What you've just done, as I'm sure you realise, is gather information about your surroundings by using your senses.

What's the Sense?

All well and good. But what exactly *are* those senses? Surely, in order to know where you are in the world you really need to have some knowledge of the equipment that you are using in your attempt to get to know what you know?

You no doubt don't need telling that we have five senses, and that they all function by utilising specialised biological information gathering receptors. Four of our senses have receptors that are conveniently arranged in various positions on our heads: these are our eyes, ears, noses and tongues. The fifth sense receptor, our skin, is positioned not only on our heads but extends over the whole of our bodies.

1

These receptors provide the input for our five senses – sight, hearing, smell, taste and touch – with which we make *sense* of the world.

With their truly amazing powers they allow us to be aware of the world in all of its astonishing glory.

Or so we think.

Unfortunately it isn't quite true.

When it comes down to it, our senses are surprisingly limited in their ability to actually sense very much of what's going on around us at all, so as a result we don't see the world in anything approaching *all* of its astonishing glory. Despite their role as information gatherers our senses actually give us the most sparing amount of information that they can get away with. They supply us with just sufficient knowledge about the world around us to allow us to function efficiently within it. They operate very much on a "need to know" basis.

To illustrate this, let's look more closely at what many people think of as our primary sense: vision. This is a sense that, as we'll see, is riddled with inherent, though partly hidden, limitations.

The Vision Thing

Early last winter I was strolling in the local park with a friend when we came across a berry-laden holly bush.

My friend commented on the profusion of berries, expressing surprise that the branches didn't collapse under the weight.

I stared at the bush. "What berries?" I asked.

I, unfortunately, am red-green colour blind, and I find it difficult to distinguish between certain shades of those two colours. Colour blindness in various forms affects about 10% of men (but less than 1% of women).

I see those lovely berries as a colour that's more or less

indistinguishable from the bush's foliage, so they don't jump out at me in the way that they are supposed to. It's only when I get close to the bush, so that the berries appear larger and more prominent, that I can tell that the berries are not the same colour as the leaves.*

It's obvious that I have a vision deficiency when compared with my friend, because she can see something that I can't – the holly berries.

But just imagine what it would be like if *everyone* on the planet was red-green colour blind.

No-one would know that they had defective vision because everyone's vision would be the same.

There'd be all of those beautiful red berries on the holly bushes (and other red berries on other bushes, not to mention red flowers, red ladybirds and so on) and people wouldn't be giving them a second glance. When you consider that many things that are red are that colour specifically in order to get a second glance – in order to draw attention to themselves – that would be a real shame.

(Not everything that's red is red for attention grabbing purposes, of course. Blood, for instance, is red purely as a side effect of its chemistry. It certainly draws attention to itself when it's spilt, but it'd do that no matter what colour it was, purely by virtue of the gruesome nature of the event. Equally, a ruby isn't

---

* If you want to check whether or not you're colour blind yourself there's a simple test that's available at your local opticians or on the internet (just type "colour blindness test" or similar into a search engine). The test involves looking at groups of coloured dots that create an image, usually in the form of a number, on a differently coloured background. If you can't tell the difference between the colour of the image and the colour of the background - and thus can't see the image - you're colour blind.

red to make itself get noticed, although it is the reason that it's turned into jewellery.)

If everybody was red-green colour blind then we wouldn't know that we were red-green colour blind, because no-one would be aware of the difference between the colours. However, while it's true that we're not all red-green colour blind we *are* all colour blind in other parts of the spectrum. There do indeed exist colours that no-one can see at all.

For instance there's a lovely colour called ultraviolet, which you will be unfamiliar with (other than by name).

And there's infrared too.

These are the colours at either end of the visible spectrum – colours that are just beyond our range of perception (Figure 1). You might argue that therefore they're not really colours, but many insects and birds can see them, so they'd disagree.

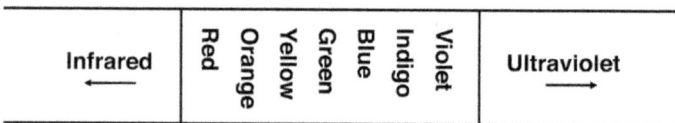

Infrared ←	Red	Orange	Yellow	Green	Blue	Indigo	Violet	Ultraviolet →

Figure 1: The colours of the spectrum, bounded by infrared and ultraviolet

These colours – ultraviolet and infrared – are out there in the world, but our eyes just aren't equipped to pick them up.

But as I said, some creatures can. And they make full use of the fact.

Many birds are clothed in vivid colours, as you may have noticed. Especially the males. However, many of them have an even wider range of colours in their wardrobe than we're aware of, due to the fact that they are clad in hues that are invisible to us: hues that are there only for the appreciation of other birds.

Take blue tits. To us, male and female blue tits look almost exactly the same, but to blue tit eyes the males have bright patches of ultraviolet in their plumage, in visually important areas such as their crests. In blue tit aesthetics the males that have the brightest and biggest patches of ultraviolet are the most attractive (surprise, surprise).

Pigeons are similarly decked out in colours that we can't see. Look at a male pigeon in springtime as it struts in front of a female, puffing out its chest and generally showing off, and you'll notice that its colours shimmer slightly in the sunlight. What you're seeing is the tiniest hint of how that male pigeon looks to the female pigeon that he's so relentlessly pursuing. To the female pigeon's eyes he's possibly almost as gaudy as a peacock.

It's not only some birds that can see in the ultraviolet region of the spectrum: many insects can too.

They can see the colour in the petals of flowers. Many flowers appear brightly coloured to us, it's true, but you should just see what some of them look like through the eyes of insects.

A flower that appears as a plain (but lovely) white to our eyes may to an insect have shimmering rings of vibrant ultraviolet around its centre – creating a visual effect that plant breeders would love to harness if only they were aware of its existence. These colours are there to guide the insects to the flower's supply of nectar (and thus to get the insects to brush against the flower's sepals and stamens to ensure pollination). The colours are the natural world's equivalent to the seductive packaging that we wrap around sweets, chocolate bars, and other temptations of the palate.

Flowers are brightly coloured purely for the purpose of tempting insects – they only look good to we humans as a happy by-product. (Intriguingly, it's still not understood precisely why humans find flowers so appealing, although it's possibly linked to the fact that bright colours, being unusual in a world full of greens and browns, are generally a sign of something remarkable.)

While some insects can see the colour ultraviolet, others can see infrared – the colour that's just beyond the other end of the visible spectrum. Infrared is a colour that's radiated by hot objects (just as very hot objects such as the metal rings or hotplates on electric cookers radiate the "ordinary" red that we can see). People are relatively hot objects, being warm-blooded creatures (at a temperature of about 37°C or 99°F), so we radiate infrared light ourselves. If you've ever sat outside in the open air at dusk on a summer's evening and wondered how the mosquitoes manage to find you so annoyingly easily in such dim lighting conditions, it's partly because you're a veritable beacon that's glowing in the infrared region of the spectrum – the mosquitoes can see you as easily as you can see the glowing embers of a campfire at night. Essentially, they use thermal imaging.

Thus it is that some insects can see ultraviolet and are attracted to flowers, while other insects can see infrared and are attracted to humans (Which type of insect do you prefer?).

Why is it then that *we* can't we see the colours ultraviolet and infrared? They're colours after all, so it seems a bit silly that we can't see them – if only to be able to enjoy such things as the sight of multicoloured shimmering pigeons and more variety in the hues of flowers.

The answer is very simple – the reason that we can't see them is because we don't *need* to see them. We can survive quite happily without them.

THE FLAWS OF PERCEPTION

It's not all Black and White

Our sense of vision developed to its present state of usefulness over time. A very, very long time. It developed and changed by the process known as evolution by natural selection (a process that is covered in much more detail in Chapters 12 and 14).

Millions of years ago our very early mammalian ancestors (whatever they were – possibly some sort of mouse-like creatures) could probably only see with monochrome vision, similar to black and white, which they would find very useful for helping them to get around.

The ability to see in black and white is perfectly adequate for many purposes – after all, until quite recently most television and newspaper images were in black and white and people were more than happy with those at the time.

However, with monochrome vision there are some things that you just can't see particularly well, so the ability to differentiate between different colours was gradually acquired.

Full-blown colour vision didn't come about overnight. Different colours were probably added to our ancestors' sense of vision one by one, in a logical order: it's more useful to be able to recognise some colours than others, so the most useful colours were probably added first.

For instance, when our monochrome-visioned ancestors wanted to eat fruit it would have been useful for them to be able to tell the difference between unripe and ripe fruit. Unripe fruit tends to be green while ripe fruit is often red, so the ability to recognise red as being different to green would certainly have been a useful early advance on monochrome vision.

The visual effect produced could be likened to a black and white photograph in which a single object is in colour.

(It may be argued that the relationship between the evolution of colour vision and of coloured fruit was the other way round: that fruit evolved to become red on ripening because it signalled the fruit's ripeness to creatures that already had colour vision: however it seems to me to be more probable that the basic chemical processes of ripening made the colour of the fruit change irrespective of whether or not there were creatures around that could appreciate the colour difference. Ripe fruit is probably red for the same reason that blood is red: for no reason other than its chemical composition. The same applies to autumn leaves, which I think it's safe to say don't go red for our benefit but because of the change in the balance of chemicals as the trees wind down for the winter. Once the colour red became a significant signal colour however, various life-forms such as flowers and ladybirds evolved to utilise the colour as such.)

There's something interesting about the colours of ripe and unripe fruit. They're red and green – which just happen to be the colours involved in the most common form of colour blindness. I'm only speculating here, but the reason may not be entirely unconnected.

The human eye is wired to be sensitive to red, green and blue light, creating other colours by combining the sensations of these three primary colours. As described above, it's possible that the eye evolved the means to differentiate between red and green quite early on, because of its usefulness in a predominantly green environment (with red highlights). The eye may have then developed a means of recognising the colour blue much later. The ability to register blue would be a lower priority to being able to register red and green – after all, how useful is it to know what colour the sky is? The result of this is that the red/green recognition system in the eye is slightly different to the system that later developed in order to process blue, and happens to be more prone to error.

This is only my own theory I have to point out, and it may be rubbish. To find out whether it may have a germ of truth in it I really ought to do some scientific research. Until then, it's just a theory (as some people mistakenly say about the whole subject of evolution by natural selection).

So it was that we developed eyes that could see red and green (usually) and blue, but we never got round to developing eyes that could see ultraviolet and infrared.

As I've mentioned, this was because being able to see ultraviolet and infrared is unnecessary for us, because we could survive quite adequately without them. Being able to see colours that are superfluous to our requirements would be nice, but would be a bit of a luxury and would require extra processing power in our brains, so we just never developed the ability.

Our vision works on a practical, utilitarian basis, where it processes the information that's necessary in order for us to stay alive and nothing more. It isn't there to make everything look nice just for the sake of it.

All we need of our vision is the ability to find our way around the world, and to survive in it, which we get with the visual range that we've got.

The Nature of Colour

At this point I think it's time to change tack slightly and to say something about the nature of colour. After all, I've been talking about colour without explaining what it actually is: as though it's so obvious that it doesn't need saying.

In truth the actual nature of colour is much more bizarre than you may think – it's only because we are so used to it that we don't normally question it.

Colour is a quality that we experience when light that's

emitted from glowing objects or that is reflected from surfaces enters our eyes and forms an image in our brains. It's important to realise that the light itself isn't "coloured" as such. The colour that we experience is an effect that's completely *inside* our heads.

To understand what colour actually is you have to first understand something about the light that gives rise to it.

Light is a form of energy that radiates from objects in which the atoms are in a state of high excitation, such as when they are hot (Atoms are covered in greater depth later, in Chapter 8). Typical light-emitting objects include such things as the Sun and electric light bulbs. The excitation of the atoms in these objects is intimately linked to the phenomena that we're familiar with as electricity and magnetism, so the energy that's emitted is known as electromagnetic radiation.

The energy of light is best thought of as a number of waves radiating out from the source that's generating it (Figure 2). The source usually emits lots of different waves of various wavelengths simultaneously, with each different wavelength being the result of different activity at an atomic level.

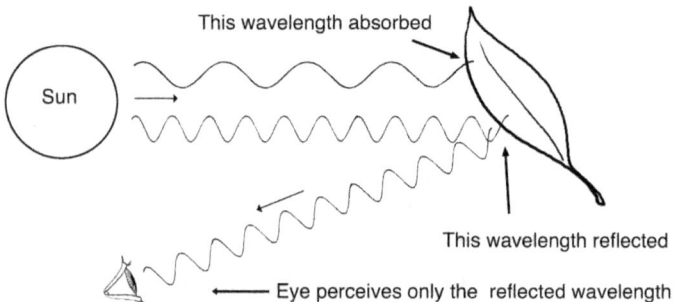

Figure 2: Why objects are one colour rather than another

These energy waves travel away from the source that's emitting them (such as the Sun), and eventually some of them hit other objects.

When the waves hit an object, the object absorbs some of the energy into its surface and reflects the rest. Precisely which wavelengths are absorbed and reflected is determined by the molecular structure of the object.

If you happen to be looking in the direction of the object some of the reflected energy that has bounced off the object enters your eye. This energy is simply a stream of waves with varying wavelengths, and would be pretty indecipherable if your eye didn't then process it in order to make a meaningful image out of it. To do this your brain generates a subjective effect that makes sense of the different wavelengths – it creates an image *within* your brain. To oversimplify madly, your brain essentially "dyes" or "colours in" the areas of the image that correspond to different wavelengths, creating the coloured effect that we know as vision.*

Think of the process involved in creating a coloured image in the brain as being somewhat analogous to the process of creating an image on paper using the technique of painting by numbers (Figure 3).

Imagine that when you're looking at an object in the real world, such as a flower, the object itself is totally devoid of colour. The painting by numbers image in Figure 3 is analogous to this real world flower as it actually exists, before your eyes process and "enhance" it by adding colour.

---

* The constructed, subjective sensations that we experience via our senses - such as colour, sound and flavour - that are created within the brain in order to give meaningful form to the external stimuli that provoke them are referred to in philosophical circles as *qualia*.

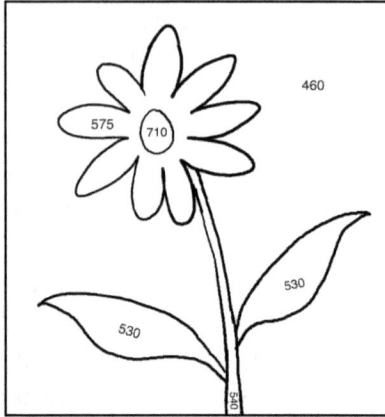

Figure 3: Add colour in your brain

Also imagine that every object that you can see in the real world has a number written on it to represent the wavelength of the light that the object reflects. For example, in my figure, a leaf has the number 530 on it, while the petals of the flower are labelled with the number 575 and the sky with the number 460 (Most objects reflect many different wavelengths of light from each area of their surface, but for simplicity in my example each area reflects only one). On the version of the image that's inside your head your eye and brain then "add pigment" to each of these numbered areas – a different pigment for each different number – to create a coloured image, just as colour is added to a painting by numbers picture. For instance, for the number on the leaf your brain adds green, for the number on the petals it adds yellow and for the number on the sky, blue.

The numbers that I've used to represent the wavelengths of light that are bounced off the objects (such as 530 for a leaf) were not picked at random – they are actually the wavelengths of the light itself, measured in nanometres (A nanometre is a billionth

– or 1/1,000,000,000 – of a metre). So the number 530 on a leaf shows that the leaf reflects waves with a wavelength of 530 nanometres, which we perceive as a particular shade of green.

The actual "greenness" of leaves is generated totally inside your head – thus it isn't actually a quality of the leaves but of your mental "reconstruction" of the leaves. However, to say that "leaves are green" is much nicer than saying that "leaves are reflecting light waves that have a wavelength of 530 nanometres", even though it may be scientifically, or at least philosophically, less accurate.

Our brains only apply colour to the electromagnetic energy that is bounced off objects when the energy has a wavelength between about 380 nanometres (violet) and 750 nanometres (red). We completely ignore the wavelengths that correspond to ultraviolet and infrared, stretching out from either end of the visible spectrum, so when these wavelengths enter your eye you don't register the fact.

I've glibly mentioned that the visible part of the spectrum has wavelengths that are between 380 - 750 nanometres (or about 4 to 7 ten millionths of a metre). Those dimensions actually take some taking in when you realise the actual lengths involved. Translated into everyday terms the wavelengths of visible light are about a two thousandth of the width of the lines that form the letters of these words.

But there's more.

Many objects emit electromagnetic radiation at wavelengths other than those of the visible spectrum and the infrared and ultraviolet that bound it. The visible spectrum that we're familiar with, that gives rise to the colours from red to violet, is just a miniscule part of the full range of the electromagnetic spectrum.

And I really mean miniscule.

WHERE ARE WE?

To give you some idea of just *how* miniscule, let's consider another part of the electromagnetic spectrum – the part that consists of what we know as radio waves. You can see it in Figure 4. These waves are exactly the same as light waves in their nature except that they have much longer wavelengths. These wavelengths range from lengths that you could easily measure on a ruler or tape measure to ones that are the diameter of a planet or more (making them the longest waves in the spectrum).

So, radio waves can have wavelengths that are longer than the earth's diameter while visible light has waves that are about a two thousandth of the diameter of the full stop at the end of this sentence.

But that's not the half of it.

Light waves are obviously incredibly short, especially compared to radio waves, but there are other waves such as X-rays, gamma rays and cosmic rays that are even shorter. Some of these waves have wavelengths that are of a shortness that we find impossibly hard to comprehend – in the region of fractions of the diameter of an atom.

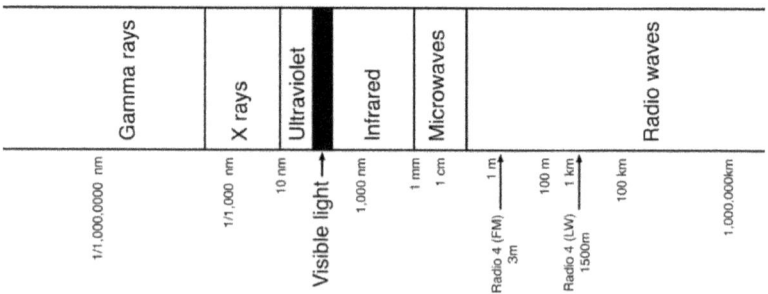

Gamma rays	X rays	Ultraviolet	Visible light	Infrared	Microwaves		Radio waves	
1/1,000,0000 nm	1/1,000 nm	10 nm		1,000 nm	1 mm	1 cm	1 m (Radio 4 (FM) 3m)	100 m, 1 km (Radio 4 (LW) 1500m), 100 km, 1,000,000km

Figure 4: The spectrum of electromagnetic radiation

THE FLAWS OF PERCEPTION

A cursory glance at Figure 4 may give you a false impression of the scales involved, due to the fact that the visible part of the spectrum is quite significant in the figure. It's deceptive though, because the scale that's used in the figure isn't linear: it becomes more compressed as you go from left to right – a centimetre at the left end covers a billionth of a metre, while a centimetre at the right end covers a billion metres. If a normal linear scale had been used the figure would have been undrawable.

All of the types of radiation that I've mentioned above, from radio waves, through visible light, to X-rays and so on, are essentially the same apart from their wavelength – their separate names are just convenient labels to differentiate between different wavelengths that are produced in different ways or that interact with the world in different manners (such as in the case of X-rays by having the ability to pass through people and to affect photographic emulsion).

Although radiation with all of these different wavelengths is out there in the universe, being emitted by stars and other cosmic sources of energy, very little of it reaches us here on Earth (fortunately, as some of it is very dangerous). This is because the Earth's atmosphere prevents it from penetrating to the surface of our planet (just as to some degree clouds prevent visible light from reaching us). The only wavelengths that can travel unhindered through our atmosphere are visible light (when it's not cloudy), parts of the infrared and ultraviolet spectrum and some radio waves.

The energy in radio waves is such that when the waves strike certain types of metal they energize the atoms in the metal. This phenomenon is exploited in telecommunications, where pieces of metal are deliberately placed in the paths of radio waves: the energy in the excited metal is then harnessed and is converted into another form of energy – sound. You'll be familiar with these pieces of metal under their technical name of aerials, and you'll also be familiar with the sound producing apparatus- radios (What else would you listen to radio waves on?). This substituting of sound for the energy of the radio waves is somewhat analogous to the way that the energy of light waves is converted into something else – colour – in the brain.

These radio waves are all around us: streaming down from outer space and (at certain wavelengths) being transmitted from radio transmitters here on earth. In fact radio transmitters are positively glowing like beacons in the regions of the spectrum that they are transmitting at – so why can't we see them glowing, rather than seeing them as simply dull grey metal objects?

Why can't we *see* radio waves?

Because it's totally unnecessary when it comes to the everyday task of staying alive.

Everything that we absolutely need to see reflects light that's in the visible part of the spectrum. There's nothing out there that's important to our survival (such as food and predators) that only reflects radio waves. So detecting them is surplus to requirements. On top of this, when our ancestors started to evolve eyes (a topic that's expanded on in Chapter 14) they lived underwater, as did all early life on Earth. Radio waves can't travel through water, unlike light waves, and thus the underwater world is "dark" in the radio part of the spectrum. Our aquatic ancestors therefore developed the ability to detect the light waves that permeated their medium rather than the totally unknown radio waves that did not: thus the ability to see in the visible portion of the spectrum gained a march on any possible ability to see in the radio portion. After the creatures emerged from the water to pursue a life on dry land they could probably have started to evolve a degree of vision that operated in the radio part of the spectrum if it had been useful, but by that time they could see as well as they needed to in the visible portion of the spectrum, making "radio-vision" unnecessary.

So it is that from the whole spectrum of wavelengths of the electromagnetic spectrum, from those that are longer than the diameter of a planet to those that are shorter than the diameter of an atom, we can only see those that have a wavelength of about a two thousandth of the diameter of a full stop.

What are the implications of the fact that we can only see in such a tiny portion of the electromagnetic spectrum?

It means that when we look at the universe we only see a miniscule part of it. It's as though rather than looking at the universe itself we're looking at a screen that's in front of it that's blocking our view. Imagine that the screen is untold thousands of miles long, corresponding to the length of the electromagnetic spectrum. The only place where you can see through the screen is at an extremely narrow slit the width of a razor blade, at the point along its length where visible light occurs.

Amazingly, with the ludicrously limited amount of information that we glean by looking through this slit we try to make sense of the universe beyond.

Over the past hundred years or so we've managed to widen the slit somewhat by devising ways of detecting some of the electromagnetic radiation that is beyond our visual range (such as by using antennae to detect radio waves). This has to some extent extended our ability to perceive the universe, but the whole thing is quite an effort, to put it mildly.

You're probably expecting me to now say that with our absurdly narrow window onto the universe how can we possibly hope to understand our place in the cosmos? Indeed, this argument concerning the narrow window, highlighting the poverty of our vision, is frequently put forward to show the absurdity of our predicament and the hopelessness of the task of trying to understand very much at all about anything. But I think that this is an unnecessarily pessimistic way to look at things – and is in fact a somewhat flawed way too.

There are two factors in the metaphor of "the razor-thin slit in the preposterously long screen" that are apt to throw us off balance.

These factors are:

1) That we have a natural tendency to over-inflate the importance of scale (incredibly long screen; incredibly narrow slit).

2) That we are at the mercy of inappropriate metaphors.

To some extent the power and appeal of the slit metaphor comes from the dramatic impact of the scales involved. A few pages ago I went to some pains to emphasize that the full gamut of wavelengths of the electromagnetic spectrum spans an ungraspable range, from subatomic to superplanetary in scale, and that the tiny band of the spectrum that we can see – in the form of visible light – is incredibly narrow. It's easy to be seduced by these scales, and to thus think that we're on a hiding to nothing when trying to use our incredibly narrow visual range to make sense of things. But these staggering scales may be leading us astray. The huge and tiny sizes involved are, by and large, irrelevant.

The thickness of the razor slit and the length of the screen are factors that would be significant if they existed in the world of real, physical, day-to-day objects with which we, as creatures that are generally around five to six feet tall, interact at our personal corporeal level. But they don't. The slit and the screen stand in as metaphors for things that exist at the level of electromagnetic radiation – and at that level an incredibly narrow slit is all that you need in order to gain access to the other side. The limitations of the metaphorical slit are nothing like as great as they seem.

Also, the length of the screen is in some ways irrelevant, just as the length of a wall is irrelevant as long as you are right next to the door. (We are inevitably, and not at all by chance, born right next to the "vision" slit in the screen, as I explain in Chapter 14 concerning the evolution of the eye, so there's no problem there.)

As a result, even though our slit in the cosmos-obscuring screen seems to be distinctly narrow, it's actually perfectly wide enough for us to get a half decent view of what's on the other side. We can, so to speak, poke our heads through it.

The practical, real-life outcome of this is that simply because we can't detect a particular wavelength of radiation doesn't mean that we can't detect the object that's radiating it. The Sun, for example, emits electromagnetic waves at a huge variety of wavelengths, but it only takes the ability to detect a tiny number of those wavelengths to allow us to realise that the Sun's there.

(This doesn't mean that that there aren't many things that we can't detect of course. I can't mention these things by name, needless to say, as I obviously don't know what they are. Such stuff as the mysterious substance known as "dark matter" springs to mind though – this being an undetectable material that may possibly pervade the cosmos, the existence of which is postulated in order to make the figures in the current mathematical models of the universe add up.)

The truth is that the amount that we can learn about the universe by utilising the narrow range of radiation in the visible spectrum is vastly greater than the range's width suggests.

That's a pleasantly optimistic conclusion to come to.

I'll come back to the subject of the use and abuse of metaphors later, but for now let's move on to consider another restriction to our sense of vision that has a more immediate impact on how we see the universe: the restriction of the amount of detail we can see when we look at things.

It's all in the Detail

The amount of detail that you can see when you look at things is the factor that governs such matters as the size of the smallest letters that you can read on a page, or the amount of detail that can be put onto a map without it being too small to see. It affects how much information you can extract from something.

If something is too small to be seen clearly, it's lost (Figure 5).

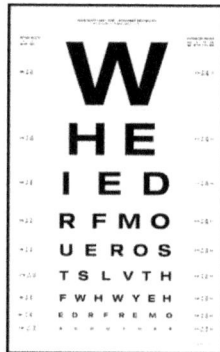

Figure 5: What's in the small print?

The fact that we can only discern detail down to a particular size is so familiar to us that we hardly give it a moment's thought (until the failing eyesight of middle age starts to make the small print on packaging too difficult to read). It has however, for most of human history, profoundly influenced the very way that we see our place in the universe.

Take a look upwards at the sky to see what I mean.

THE FLAWS OF PERCEPTION

When we look at the sky we see what for all the world looks like an inverted bowl arching from horizon to horizon. In daylight the bowl is light blue with a fiercely bright, fiery disk of light – the Sun – crossing in front of it, while at night it's black, with pin-pricks of light – the stars – somehow attached to its surface, and with an interesting silvery disk – the Moon – moving in front of it.

Looking at this sight it would seem reasonable to assume that the earth was at the centre of the universe, with the huge canopy of the sky encircling it. (This doesn't necessarily entail a flat earth concept of the world by the way. The idea that the earth was a sphere at the centre of this canopy was being toyed with long ago. It wasn't too difficult a theory to formulate – apart from anything else it seemed probable that the earth was curved because it could be seen that ships at sea disappeared over the horizon once they were about three miles away.)

This well-ordered dome of the heavens with its interesting and manageable array of accompanying lighting arrangements in the form of the Sun, Moon and stars helped foster a view of the universe as a rather parochial place, with the comings and goings on Earth as the most important and significant events that were happening anywhere.

Then, at the beginning of the 17th century, in what is now Italy, Galileo Galilei pointed a telescope at the night sky.

Galileo didn't actually invent the telescope, as is often mistakenly believed. The instrument had been developed by the Dutch, and several examples of the device were in circulation in Europe when Galileo came to hear of it.

It was clear that the telescope was a splendid device for making distant landscapes look bigger and for observing ships that were far out at sea – a very useful function in a world that was dominated by maritime activity. Galileo however, rather than looking at sailing ships in the distance pointed the device heavenward – and what he saw changed our concept of the workings of the universe forever.

Galileo, by the way, as well as not being the person who invented the telescope, was not necesarily the first person to point one at the sky, contrary to popular belief (again). Other people aimed these novel contraptions in that direction, especially at the Moon. For instance, while Galileo was peering at the sky in Italy the celestial realm was also being studied from Wales. In Carmarthenshire, Sir William Lower (a Cornishman who had settled in Wales) and John Prydderch (or Protheroe) looked at the Moon and made the following observation, described in a letter from Lower to the distinguished scientist Thomas Hariot (or Harriot), who had constructed the telescope and given it to Lower:

> "… and the whole brimme along looks like unto the description of coasts in the Dutch books of voyages. In the full she appears like a tart that my cooke made me last weeke; here a vaine of bright stuffe, and there of darke, and so confusedlie all over. I must confess I can see none of this without my cylinder."*

Observers such as Lower and Prydderch didn't publish their observations. Galileo on the other hand, realising the implications of what he saw, and being a consummate self-publicist, rushed into print to announce his discoveries.

Telescopic observation showed that the Moon, rather than being the smooth (though somewhat blotchy) object that it was assumed to be before Galileo's day, was actually covered in extremely large numbers of "confusions" such as craters and mountains.

Galileo didn't only point his telescope at the Moon, which

---

* Henry C King, *The History of the Telescope*. (Courier Dover Publications, 2003), p 40.

was an obvious thing to look at: he also aimed it at the stars. He chose to point it at one of the handful of stars that were known to move mysteriously through the sky relative to the other "fixed" stars (which all retained the same positions relative to each other, as though glued to the sky's canopy). These peripatetic stars were known by the Greek word for wanderers: planets.

To his surprise he saw that the planet to which he'd turned his attention, Jupiter, wasn't just a pin-prick of light like the other stars but was a distinct disk, like a tiny version of the full Moon. This fact was fascinating in its own right, but what was equally astounding was that the planet seemed to be accompanied by four tiny dots of light strung out in a line on either side of the disk (Figure 6).

Figure 6: Jupiter as seen through a telescope, with its accompanying four dots

On observing the planet over a period of time Galileo noticed that these companion specks moved relative to the planet, but never strayed far from it (Figure 7). He deduced that they were orbiting the planet. Jupiter, it seemed, had satellites.

Needless to say, at about the same time that Galileo was making this observation, other observers such as Lower in Britain were probably noticing the moons of Jupiter too, but without publicising the fact or possibly without immediately realising their significance.

Figure 7: And yet they move! Jupiter's attendant dots turn out to be satellites

Prior to the time that Galileo made this observation of Jupiter's satellites it was generally assumed that all celestial objects rotated around the Earth, which was thought to be at the centre of creation, quite naturally. On discovering the moons of Jupiter Galileo had found that some celestial objects revolved around other celestial objects. It was a revelation.

The door was now open for it to be argued that the Earth may revolve around the Sun rather than the Sun around the Earth. This theory was not new. Incredibly, it had been postulated eighteen centuries earlier in ancient Greece by Aristarchus of Samos. It was a concept that was very much in circulation in intellectual circles in Galileo's time, following the ideas of the Polish polymath Copernicus in the previous century. Copernicus's idea hadn't caught on when he first published it seventy years earlier, but here was evidence that there may be something in it.

Having the Earth rotating round the Sun rather than vice versa demoted the Earth from its position at centre stage in the cosmos. This didn't go down very well at the time as you can imagine, but it's a state that many of us now prefer, on sober reflection.

One of the most remarkable, though little remarked upon, aspects of the story of Galileo (and the other telescope users) is that the things that they saw through their instruments – the sight of which changed forever the way we see the universe – are things that are *just* beyond the range of unaided human vision. If our eyes were capable of seeing with only a *smidgen* more detail we'd be able to see the craters on the Moon and the satellites of Jupiter just by looking at them (The Jovian satellites are of a brightness where they are actually teetering on the edge of visibility to the naked eye, although the glare from the planet itself contributes to making seeing them well-nigh impossible). I would speculate that a hawk, with its hunter's eye, or even more so an owl, with its excellent night vision, can see the craters on the Moon and possibly the satellites of Jupiter (if they can get around the glare problem) quite easily just by glancing casually at them. But they know not the implications of what they see.

Think how different the history of our awareness of our place in the universe may have been if we'd only had very slightly better eyesight.

Or conversely, try imaging how much *less* aware we would be of our position in the universe if we didn't possess vision at all. Imagine how we would perceive things if we were totally blind, and instead of using vision as our means of registering the world we used something akin to the sonar that's used by bats.

Sonar, or echo location, operates by sending out a pulse of sound and then analysing the echo that's bounced back from objects. It seems like a crude way to sense things to us, but that's possibly only because our own sense of hearing is relatively underdeveloped. It's theoretically possible for echo location to be sensitive enough to be able to build up an "image" of the world that's in many ways as realistic as that obtained by vision. In fact, if the echo is routed appropriately within the brain the resulting sensation could easily be a three-dimensional model of the world that's not a million miles from the three-dimensional model of the world that we obtain using vision. Although probably not in colour.

It would reveal to us the position and form of all of the everyday objects around us, such as tables, chairs, trees, hills and animals, simply by analysing the echoes of the sound waves that these objects reflected.

However, things would be different when we shifted our attention away from the objects here on Earth and turned it instead towards those in the sky.

Any sound waves that we sent upwards into the sky would not be returned as echoes. Sound waves need a medium such as air for them to travel through – as a result sounds sent upwards would simply fade away as they approached the vacuum of space, never to return.

Using echo location to look upwards would reveal nothing but an empty void (Not necessarily in an existentially worrying sort of way – perhaps more like a cloudy-sky-at-night sort of way, when there's just nothing up there to bother paying attention to).

We would have no awareness of the Moon or of the stars. (Although we may wonder what the intriguing source of heat was that passed over our heads each day: the Sun.) We wouldn't know that there was such a thing as outer space, with other objects in it.

It's pure luck that, because we have an ability to detect light, we can see the Moon and the stars and the planets spread out before us when we look up at the sky. It's pure luck because we don't need to see those things at all – but we can.

Although we can see the cosmos beyond our planet there are however still whole aspects of the nature of the universe that are beyond our senses, purely because of the chance consequences of how our senses work.

THE FLAWS OF PERCEPTION

It would be extremely useful if we happened to have an extra sense that could somehow allow us to peer into otherwise hidden aspects of reality (whatever they might be), just as our sense of vision allows us to peer outwards at the Moon and stars. If we had such a sense then we may have a much better appreciation of our place in the universe. But we don't – because peering into hidden aspects of reality is something that we don't need to do for the purposes of staying alive.

We just have to buckle down and make the most of the senses that we've got, by trying to extract extra meaning from the predominantly electromagnetically relayed information that we receive about the universe around us. But it's not easy.

And it isn't helped by the fact that when it comes to analysing the information that we receive we're in some ways rather second rate in the interpretation department.

This can be very clearly seen by looking at a few examples of visual misinterpretation. Exploring this topic is extremely enjoyable because it gives you the perfect excuse to play around with a few optical illusions.

For example, have a look at Figure 8. What do you see when you look at this arrangement of lines?

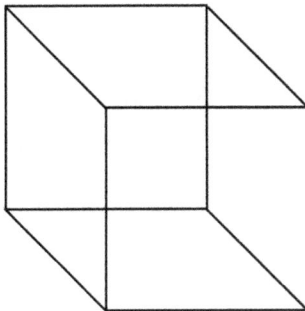

Figure 8: What do you see?

You probably see a cube.

When you first look at it you may see a cube from slightly above (as shown on the left in Figure 9 with the aid of shading). Look at it for a short time however, and you will probably notice that the lines could equally well be of a cube viewed from below, as on the right in Figure 9.

Figure 9: The cube flips between two views

It's impossible to pin the shape down to only one cube, as it keeps spontaneously flipping between the two possibilities.

This image, famous in the field of the interpretation of perception, is known as a Necker cube.*

There is however something that's fascinating about the Necker cube illusion that usually goes unremarked upon.

Take another look at the original image in Figure 8.

What do you see again?

A cube that flips between above and below, yes.

Interestingly, that's probably all you see.

The chances are that you haven't registered the fact that it isn't a cube at all.

---

* Necker was a chemist who worked with crystals in the first half of the nineteenth century. He was looking at cubic crystals through a microscope when he noticed that he couldn't tell which way round they were, so he then reproduced the effect as a line drawing which he published in 1832.

THE FLAWS OF PERCEPTION

Look again. It's just a flat arrangement of lines on a page.

Of course you know that, but you can't see it that way. You see a cube.

Strangely it takes an almost superhuman degree of effort to see the image as a flat pattern instead of as a flipping cube.

It's marginally easier to see it as a flat arrangement of lines when it's rotated so that it no longer "stands" with the faces of the cube horizontal and vertical (Figure 10). It then takes on something of the look of a corporate logo or car badge.

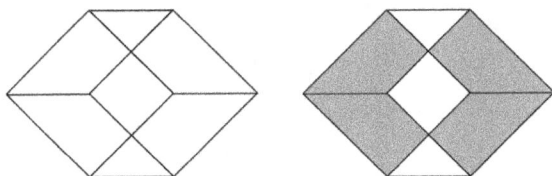

Figure 10: The Necker cube on its side (left), and shaded to try to disrupt the tendency to see a cube (right)

The point of this demonstration is to show that you've got to be *very* careful about the way that you interpret things. With the Necker cube you spend your time trying to interpret whether the cube is being looked at from above or below, when in reality you're almost blind to the fact that there's no cube there at all. You're seeing something that isn't there. (This trap is very significant, and will be encountered later, in Chapter 3.)

In case you're thinking that optical illusions are all very well, but that they are a little irrelevant to real world situations because they are essentially "party tricks" that only work because they exist in the physically impoverished state of a two-dimensional image on a flat page or screen, think again.

Figure 11 (overleaf) is a photograph of a real-world situation.

I know that it's a photograph of a real situation because I took the photo myself. (Of course, being a photograph, what you've got here is an impoverished, two-dimensional representation of a real-world situation, but take it from me that the phenomenon that I'm going to demonstrate works with the real thing too).

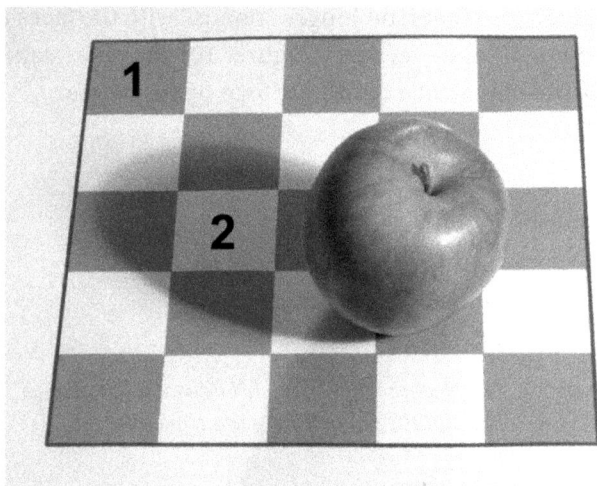

Figure 11: A real-world optical illusion. Which square is darker: 1 or 2?

All that I ask you to do is to look at this image and decide which square is the darker: square one or square two (The numbers have been added to the photo later – apart from that the image is undoctored).

A no-brainer?

Now look at Figure 12 on the next page, where I've superimposed a uniform gray strip across the photo.

Figure 12: Can you believe your eyes? Squares 1 and 2 are the same shade

As you can see, squares one and two are exactly the same shade of gray.

This illusion is known as Adelson's checker shadow illusion, published by Edward H. Adelson, Professor of Vision Science at the Massachusetts Institute of Technology in 1995.

Our inability to interpret even these simple images with any degree of accuracy shows that when it comes to trying to appreciate and understand our place in the universe it's a very dodgy idea to believe the evidence of our eyes.

And perhaps of our brains too.

Chapter 2

Progress is a Snowball

The Snowball Effect

Trying to fathom out the true nature of the universe and of our place within it can seem like a decidedly uphill struggle sometimes.

The information's out there in the endless, tractless vastness of space, but here we are, insignificant little creatures a few feet tall practically glued to the surface of our tiny planet, incapable of even seeing the craters on the Moon without artificial aid, and woefully inadequately equipped mentally to understand what's going on. After all, we can't even see optical illusions for what they are.

It's almost enough to make you throw in the towel and just get on with life.

But don't despair. Progress can be made. And one of the great things about progress is that it can take you a lot further than you expect.

This is because progress tends to follow a principle called the *snowball effect*.

The snowball effect works like this: when a person who is standing at the top of a snowy slope rolls a hand-sized snowball down the slope the snowball picks up more snow as it travels, so that by the time it reaches the bottom of the slope it's a massive object that's the size of a large boulder.

So it is with progress. As progress rolls onwards through time new ideas stick to it, which in turn pick up more ideas, making the ultimate result much more impressive that the small and tentative bundle of ideas that first started rolling (and often making the result more dangerous too, in very much the same way that a boulder-sized snowball is more dangerous than a hand-sized one. But that's another subject).

In this book we're primarily interested in intellectual progress regarding our quest to understand the cosmos and our position in it, but we can draw some relevant conclusions about the nature of progress by looking at a few examples of much more prosaic and down to Earth advancement – examples selected from the realms of the mechanical and the technological.

Take, for example, the progress of writing .

Writing is the slightly bizarre though incredibly useful phenomenon whereby a series of odd-looking marks are lined up in different combinations as a symbolic representation of language, which itself is a slightly bizarre though incredibly useful phenomenon whereby a series of sound effects issued from a person's mouth are made to symbolically represent objects and ideas. You can see some examples of writing on this very page.

Our prehistoric, pre-literate ancestors probably started making marks on cave walls, on the ground, on animal skins and on themselves by dipping their fingers in some form of coloured medium such as mud, ash or blood. The original creator of "the mark" probably wasn't actually seeking to invent the mark as such: it's much more likely that he or she casually dragged a dirty finger across a surface and noticed that it made a blotch or smear – and then realised that this was a phenomenon that was worth exploiting. The invention essentially presented itself – all it took was someone with the insight to appreciate the implications.

From there it was a small step to noticing that a similar

marking effect could be obtained by using a stick instead of finger, which had the advantage of avoiding the painful wear and tear on the digit's tip.

The earliest forms of mark-making would involve the creation of self-contained symbols and images, such as representations of mammoths, but over time some of these marks would be appropriated for use in language, either to represent words or individual parts of words such as letters. (To this day some of our letters still bear the fossilised form of simplified images: the letter A for example is an inverted ox's head – ∀ – based on *aleph*, an early eastern Mediterranean word for ox.)

The stick (or possibly bone) mark-making implement sufficed for all writing needs for untold thousands of years, only to be superseded in the relatively recent past by the use of cut reeds, feathers (in the form of quill pens) and brushes. Only in the *very* recent past have the writing implements that we're familiar with today been invented.

Pencils, for instance, were initially developed in the first half of the sixteenth century, in Borrowdale in the English Lake District. The local people, who reared sheep as a living, discovered in their hills a seam of unusually pure graphite – a form of very high-grade coal – which they found to be extremely useful for marking their sheep. To this day the seam is still the purest graphite deposit known to man (and sheep). The raw mined graphite was wrapped in sheepskin or string to create a marking implement. The mineral was called graphite because of its qualities as a graphic marker.

The pencil as we know it, made from a mixture of graphite and clay held in a wooden sheath, was patented in 1795 by a French army officer and inventor named Nicolas-Jacques Conté. He had been asked to come up with an alternative to the pure graphite pencils that had until then been imported into France from Britain, but which were at that time unavailable due to the inconvenient fact that Britain and France were at war. It only took him a few days to come up with his idea once he'd put his mind to it.

Moving on to ink-based implements, the fountain pen was developed during the nineteenth century, with a version being patented in France in 1827. The design of the fountain pen was improved on by insurance broker Lewis Waterman in the USA in the 1880s – he developed a pen that provided a much smoother supply of ink to the nib by exploiting the phenomenon of capillary action. His desire to improve the design had been prompted due to the experience of having his previous, inferior fountain pen leak ink all over an important document that was being signed.

The ballpoint pen was invented in the 1930s by Hungarian journalist László Bíró, with the aid of his brother Georg, a chemist. They invented it as a means of using quick drying (and therefore very convenient) newspaper printer's ink in a pen, as this type of ink dried too quickly to be used in a fountain pen.

So there we have it, a brief history of writing implements, from the bronze age to almost the present day. Almost 6,000 years of writing with sticks and only 70 years of writing with ballpoint pens. Notice the time scales.

(I myself was possibly among the last generation of British schoolchildren to have gone to school when it was still necessary to use pens that were dipped into inkwells set into the desks, and when new-fangled ballpoint pens were actually banned because they were thought to encourage bad handwriting. By the time I left school everything had changed and the inkwells had been assigned to the dustbin of history. Ballpoint pens were by then so cheap, ubiquitous and disposable that there were many of them in the dustbins too.)

All of the writing instruments that I've described here have been hand-held writing implements that dispense a pigment or dye from their tips. They all require the user to move a hand across a surface in order to form the letters.

In the relatively recent past there has of course been a massive development of mechanical and electrical type-based writing instruments, starting with typewriters and moving through to the computers of today. Significantly more advanced as these mechanical and electrical machines are in comparison to hand-held writing instruments such as the quill and the ballpoint pen, it's important to realise that none of them would ever have been invented if people hadn't previously used the simpler hand-held implements to develop the medium of writing for which the machines were applied.

In other words, machines such as computers wouldn't exist if earlier people hadn't written down their ideas using burnt sticks, quills, ballpoint pens or whatever relatively primitive instruments were available to them at the time.

This is a very good example of the snowball effect in action: new inventions adhering to older ones as they roll through history (and with the newer inventions frequently burying the earlier ones deep within the rolling ball as they are rendered obsolete).

I'll come back to typewriters and computers later, in a different context, but for now let's just go back to those hand-held writing devices for a moment.

I'd like to point out something about the way that they were each invented.

Several were invented as a result of necessity: the familiar (wood-bound) pencil was devised due to the fact that English (sheepskin bound) pencils weren't available in France thanks to hostilities, while the capillary action fountain pen was developed because of the fact that earlier pens blotted important documents. It would seem to be true that in many cases necessity is indeed the mother of invention.

However, there's another factor at work in the creation of some of the inventions. Several of them were invented to a large extent as a result of the resources that just happened to be to hand at the time: the prehistoric stick with its coating of ash/mud/blood (or even more so the prehistoric finger, which was nothing if not *to hand*); the first (sheepskin bound) pencil with its graphite (and sheepskin) from the hills; the ballpoint pen with its quick-drying ink from the printing presses. In these cases the usual mother of invention, necessity, took the passenger seat, and the driving seat of innovation was occupied by another concept – the realisation that there was a resource or idea that could be exploited.

This factor, that inventions, and thus progress, are influenced by what is immediately available has quite a profound influence on human development, and possibly more importantly, on human thinking.

It works like this.

Imagine that you're a prehistoric person and that you have a problem that needs addressing.

Imagine, for example, that you need to build a shelter or a dwelling in order to protect yourself from the elements.

If you lived in a forest you'd look around, see all of the wood that was surrounding you, and you'd almost automatically start collecting lengths of branch with which to build the shelter.

If you lived somewhere rocky (and treeless) things would be different. You'd look around, see all of the rocks everywhere and you'd almost automatically start to pile them on top of each to build your shelter.

PROGRESS IS A SNOWBALL

You wouldn't choose your building material, wood or stone, by virtue of whether or not the material was the best one to use to build a shelter: you'd choose it simply because it was the material that was available.

In fact your choice of building material wouldn't really be a matter of choice at all. If you happened to live in a place where the landscape was totally devoid of objects other than, for some bizarre reason, snails, you would no doubt devise an ingenious way to make a shelter out of snail shells.

If you lived in a forest and you were totally unaware of the existence of rocks the idea of building with rocks simply would never present itself to you, and you'd never find yourself thinking along the lines of "If only I could find a hard mineral substance that exists in handy sized blocks (or that could be chiselled to such shapes) then I could build a dwelling that's a lot more permanent than the relatively flimsy wooden structures that I've managed to construct so far."

You solve practical problems such as how to build a shelter by creating solutions based on what materials are to hand, and linked to this, your thoughts about how to solve these problems tend to be shaped by what's to hand too.

To solve any immediate problem you often look around not just for materials but for an idea about how to go about your task. People very rarely think too deeply about problems or approach them from first principles.

This doesn't only apply to basic practical problems such as shelter building: it applies to cutting-edge technological advances as well. Such advances often occur because they simply present themselves as basic modifications to already existing technologies. Even radical innovations often consist of taking existing ideas or principles and applying them in novel ways or to different fields or disciplines.

Here's an example.

The city of London lies on the River Thames, close enough to the sea for the river level to rise and fall with the tides. From time to time when there's an exceptionally high tide (known as a surge tide) the water coming up the Thames estuary threatens to flood the low-lying parts of the city. To prevent this undesirable occurrence a moveable barrier was built across the river a few miles downstream of central London in order to hold back the rising tide. The barrier, which was completed in 1984, had to be designed in such a way that it was only moved into position when it was needed, as it was important that it didn't interfere with the normal flow of the river or of the boats and ships that used it.*

Imagine that you were given the task of designing such a barrier. How would you go about it? You'd probably think about the structure of other barriers and related mechanisms that you were aware of and you'd adopt or modify one of them to fit your needs (Figure 13).

Figure 13: Different types of barrier: portcullis, checkpoint and gate. The water has been removed from the illustrations for clarity

---

* When the barrier was first built it was raised once every few years: now, due partly to the fact that the south east of Britain is sinking and partly to the effects of global warming, it is raised about twenty times a year.

You may for instance think of a portcullis type barrier, where the barrier would be suspended on a gantry above the river and would drop vertically down into the water, or you'd think of a road checkpoint type barrier, where the barrier would hinge down from one side. A gate type barrier, similar to those used in canal locks might be another option, where the barrier would swing out horizontally from the riverbank.

The chances are that you probably wouldn't think of the design that was conceived of by the barrier's designer, Charles Draper. He used none of the previously mentioned tried and tested concepts. He devised a barrier that lay flat on the riverbed and that rose up when it was in use. You may now be imagining something along the lines of a flat, door-like barrier that's hinged along one edge, with the hinged edge remaining on the riverbed while the other edge swings upwards like a drawbridge, not unlike Figure 14.

Figure 14: A barrier design in which the barrier lies on the riverbed when not in use

You'd be wrong. The design is much more innovative than that. You can see it on the next page, in Figure 15.

41

Figure 15: The concept behind the Thames Barrier

To understand how the barrier works, imagine a gigantic, long metal drum lying on its side (Figure 16) and mounted between two piers so that it can revolve. Then imagine that most of the drum is cut away, apart from the ends, so that there's only a thin slither of about a quarter of the circumference left. That remaining sector is the barrier.

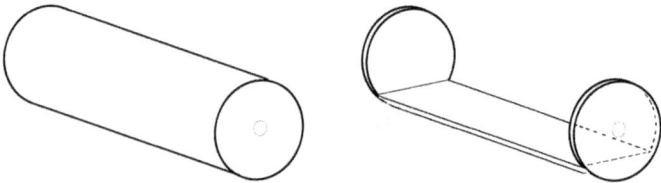

Figure 16: The drum that forms the barrier

Normally this sector lies flat on the riverbed, but when it's needed the drum (or rather what's left of the drum) is rotated so that the barrier rises upwards, slicing through the water with minimal resistance.

How was it that Draper came up with such an ingenious idea?

PROGRESS IS A SNOWBALL

I actually worked on the development stage of the barrier, in a *very* junior capacity, and this is the story that I heard in the office. He thought of the idea while he was at home one day doing a few jobs in the garden. He looked at the outside tap, and the concept came to him in a flash. He knew that some types of tap worked on the principle of blocking the flow by rotating a cut-away cylinder, and he realised instantly that this technique could be used for the barrier.[*]

The barrier's design is known as a rising sector gate. It's interesting is ponder whether or not Draper would have devised such a mechanism if he hadn't by chance looked at that tap. If he hadn't done so would he have created a design using one of the more obvious methods such as the lock gate method or the dropping portcullis method?

It's probably significant that Draper was not technically speaking a professional engineer, which may have helped him to steer clear of conventional solutions to his design problems. He was certainly a lateral thinker.

The Thames Barrier is a good example of how we formulate concepts based on examples that are presented to us in the world around us. Here's another water-based concept that was supposedly conceived in a similar manner, and that will re-emerge later in this book under different circumstances: Archimedes' famous principle that when an object is immersed in liquid the object is buoyed up by a force equal to the weight of the fluid that's being displaced by the object (meaning that if the upward force that's buoying up the object is greater than the downward weight of the object, the object floats).

---

[*] Other than the word at work, I have no confirmation of this story that he hit on his design while pottering around at home - although it's generally accepted that he got his inspiration from the principle of a tap.

WHERE ARE WE?

Legend has it that Archimedes conceived of this principle after he got into a bath of water and noticed that the level of the water rose as he got in. He was thus presented with the evidence that when an object is put into water the water is displaced. One has to ask: how would Archimedes have got on if the ancient Greeks had been in the habit of taking showers rather than baths? In fact, do *eureka moments* ever occur in showers?

This dynamic by which experiences in the real world give rise to concepts in people's heads brings me to a social trend that is causing me some anxiety at the moment. I'm extremely worried that in future such avenues towards inventiveness will be in short supply, due to the way that people now experience the world more and more through the screens of their computers and televisions. As a result of our increasing tendency to gain experiences through electronic media our stock of real life experiences is becoming worryingly impoverished, giving us depleted mental libraries of concepts to call on when the need to be inventive arises. The stimuli that are supplied through electronic media are fantastic in their own way of course, but you can only get out of such media what someone else has already thought to put into it.

The Thames Barrier design probably wouldn't have been conceived had Charles Draper been staring at a computer screen rather than at a tap.

Similarly, if computer generated virtual worlds (such as Second Life) had been available in ancient Greece, and Archimedes had been having a virtual bath in a computer simulation rather than a real bath (because he was so immersed in his Second Life that he neglected bodily hygiene in his real one), it's quite possible that the water level in the virtual bath wouldn't have risen, because the programmer of the simulation may have neglected to add code to incorporate it, and thus

Archimedes' principle would have remained undiscovered. On top of this, the fact that Archimedes wouldn't even have experienced the feeling of lightness that one gets on entering a bath, which is another clue to the buoyancy principle, wouldn't have helped either.

So there you have it.

One of the ways that people solve practical, material problems such as how to construct a shelter or a writing instrument is by exploiting any potential that's inherent in the materials that are to hand (such as wood or stone for shelters, or ash, mud, blood, sticks or bones for writing instruments). The materials provide prompts as to their potential usefulness, and they are then either accepted or ignored.

It's not only the materials have to present themselves – the concepts and ideas have to present themselves too. They do this by having some link to experience (the tap that prompted the concept for the Thames Barrier; the bath water for Archimedes' principle). Concepts and ideas don't come out of thin air. We are incapable of thinking of things that are completely alien to our interactions with the world, as we simply don't have the conceptual models with which to comprehend them. This has implications beyond the developing of ideas that are of practical use, such as the design of shelters or of barriers across rivers. It has implications for our desire to understand the deeper workings of the universe, as it means that we are incapable of formulating concepts that function in ways other than those that we come across in our day-to-day lives.

However, as we progress, courtesy of the snowball effect mentioned earlier, we find that we have new day-to-day experiences that we can call upon with which to model our view of the world.

For instance, nowadays it's conventional to think of the brain as working by using electrical impulses, and of being some kind of organic computer. In earlier centuries electricity was completely unknown (apart from static electricity), and computers were inconceivable, so such a theory would have been impossible to contemplate. It would have been impossible, for example, for Thomas Willis (1621 – 1675), an Oxford physician, to devise such a theory. For his time, however, Willis developed very advanced ideas about the brain, even coining the term *neurology*. Being a citizen of the seventeenth century he thought of the brain as a form of alembic – a type of device composed of bottles and tubes that alchemists used for the distillation of substances. To him, the brain's activity was the result of "spirits" carrying messages through the brain's substance. He devised the theory that people of low intelligence (especially peasants) were mentally slow because their spirit messengers had a difficult time travelling through their brains due to the fact that the substance of their brains was especially thick or dense. Notice those adjectives. Thick and dense. Terms that are still in use today as derogatory descriptions of people of below average intelligence.

Willis's views of the brain were ahead of his time, but were obviously firmly rooted in the attitudes of the era.

We have a tendency to scoff at some assumptions from bygone days – especially, and ironically, the ideas of people such as Willis who actually made an effort to think about things in original ways (I wonder what people in 400 years' time will think of the attitudes of our own age). At the same time that we deride some assumptions from times gone by we positively take on board other beliefs from the past – ones that happen to chime with our contemporary preoccupations. These ideas we elevate to the ranks of "ancient wisdom".

Chapter 3

Anthropomorphic Projection

Anthropomorphism: it's Only Human

The previous chapter mentioned our tendency to derive or extract ideas from what presents itself to us in our surroundings. Now let's look at another aspect of our interaction with our surroundings – our tendency to project human qualities into the things that are in it.

People, you may have noticed, have a seemingly inexhaustible propensity to project human characteristics onto objects around them that aren't human.

It almost goes without saying that we anthropomorphize animals, especially pets such as cats and dogs and any baby creatures that look in the slightest bit cute.

We also anthropomorphize creatures with which the empathic link seems much more tenuous or even nonexistent. Insects are a good example. We endow these arthropods with personalities far beyond the capabilities of their few brain cells – you won't be alone if you've thought that ladybirds are friendly, adorable little things while cockroaches are creatures that have just crawled up from the domain of Hades.

When we project a personality onto an animal we take for granted the fact that we are bestowing the creature with a degree of mental capability or *consciousness* from which this personality can arise. That's perhaps understandable. However, we also have the seemingly odd habit of projecting human-like personalities onto completely inert and inanimate objects too, in which mental capability is patently nonexistent.

Children have an innate tendency to give human personalities to their toys. You undoubtedly did it as a child yourself with your dolls (if you were a girl) or your killer robots from the planet Zarg (if you were a boy). Of course dolls and robots are human-like toys that are specifically designed to have personalities projected onto them – usually one appropriate to the gender of the person playing with them – however children project personality onto many other toys too, such as plastic dumper trucks and bikes. Maybe there's no point in playing with most toys unless they have been assigned personalities.

The act of projecting personality onto these inert objects means that we endow them with a degree of consciousness – not dissimilar to the way that we endow creatures such as ladybirds, cockroaches and pet guinea pigs with consciousness. Indeed, how can a toy railway engine with a face painted on the front of it, called Thomas, *not* be in possession of consciousness?

As maturity eclipses our childish ways we stop seeing toys as semi-sentient entities and transfer our anthropomorphic projections onto grown-up objects instead.

Such as cars.

It's possibly not an accident that the fronts of cars look vaguely like faces (and is it just me, or are they being designed to look more aggressive these days?).

Some people even giving their own car a name.

Sometimes, when a car (particularly one with a name) refuses to start for some reason the owner may feel that the vehicle is acting up because it hasn't been treated with the respect and love that it deserves. The car has gone into a huff.

Personally, I don't have a car that's got a personality (or a name), but I do have a computer that's very temperamental. I often curse it under my breath (which I suspect it hears, thus encouraging it to become even more stroppy).

People have probably projected personality and consciousness onto the things around them, both animate and inanimate, since the dawn of the human race. For instance, you can well imagine a primitive human, tending a fruit tree in the early, tentative days of agriculture, establishing a "relationship" with the tree. And you can imagine how, if the tree were to fail to produce fruit one year, the person caring for the tree would possibly explain it as being because he or she must have offended the tree in some way.

As well as our propensity to project human-like consciousness into nonhuman objects we also have an almost irresistible tendency to see the *shapes* of humans (and of other living things) where they don't exist.

Look at clouds for instance. Only the day before I wrote these words I saw a cloud that looked so much like a human head that it could hardly be a coincidence. There was a perfect chin, mouth, nose, prominent brow and wonderfully bouffant hairstyle. Then I looked at another cloud and amazingly saw another head (although not quite as perfect as the previous one, I have to admit). Then another! It seemed as though the clouds were gathering for a convention. Interestingly, although I could see lots of clouds that looked like human heads, I could see none that looked like human feet or other anatomical extremities. One of the clouds had a head that looked suspiciously like a rhinoceros. Why, I don't know.

Not only did the clouds look like heads, they also looked angry and threatening – they had personalities.

Later that day they rained all over me – they were callous.

We see human and animal forms in all sorts of objects, and thus we give those objects a degree of semi-consciousness – even clouds (which can be angry and callous as I've just mentioned, but which can also be quite pleasant, in a light and fluffy sort of way). On top of this we also see human and animal forms in visual environments where there is nothing more to be perceived than a random conglomeration of colours and shapes, where no real object of any type exists at all. We see animal and human forms in the random splatters of Rorschach inkblot tests such as the one in Figure 17. In these tests a symmetrical shape is formed by folding a piece of paper on to a blob of wet ink, which spreads the ink out in haphazard directions – the interpretation of this random blot by the viewer is supposedly a clue to their psychological make-up. What do you make of Figure 17?

It's some sort of man-insect, isn't it?

Figure 17: A Rorschach inkblot test, depicting whatever you want to see

The same detection of nonexistent animal and human forms frequently happens with abstract paintings. This can be an irritating problem for the painters of such works, who often find that the carefully crafted and deliberately non-representational forms that they have created are transformed in the minds of the audience into humans, animals or birds.

I, along with a fair number of other people, have a tendency to see the heads of giant insects when I look at certain types of kitchen tap. Fortunately I find insects fascinating, so as a result I find taps fascinating too. Look at the tap in Figure 18. If that's not some sort of weird giant insect head I don't know what it is.

Figure 18: A fascinating tap

And here's the whole insect, just to prove it.

Figure 19: An insect with a fascinatingly tap-like head

Although it's animals' heads that are most commonly discerned in objects (such as taps), whole animals can sometimes be observed. I have an ironing board which when folded flat could easily be mistaken for a gargantuan cockroach squatting up against the wall. Insects again. The ironing board is very rarely used, so spends most of its time leaning in the corner looking disturbing. (It isn't only me who sees the ironing board as a cockroach, thankfully, so you can't accuse me of some sort of personality disorder here. Or maybe I should be more careful when choosing friends.)

In the same way that we tend to give animals human-like personality traits (such as thinking that ladybirds are nice), when we see animal forms in inanimate objects such as taps or ironing boards we give those objects human-like personality traits too. Which is why my ironing board is sinister – if only it looked more like a ladybird than a cockroach. Perhaps a cheery red and black spotted cover would do the trick.

So it is that due to our tendency to see animal and human forms almost everywhere we look, in the clouds, on the front of our cars, in kitchen taps, we find ourselves totally surrounded by objects onto which we project human-like personality – and from there, by extension, human-like consciousness.

Have you ever been on the coast at a spot where cliffs drop down into the sea, where some of the cliffs protrude out into the ocean creating ranks of separate headlands?

It's often easy to see the jagged profiles of human faces in such cliffs, the faces gazing eternally out across the water. Maybe that's why they are called headlands.

It's tempting to imagine that the cliffs are somehow acting as sentinels, perhaps keeping a lookout for storms caused by the angry and callous clouds that I mentioned earlier.

The cliffs actually seem to have some sort of consciousness. But why stop there? It's not hard to imagine that if cliffs can have consciousness then surely, by extension, the very Earth itself can have consciousness too. Perhaps *everything* has consciousness.

The notion of endowing the whole world of non-living things with consciousness is a feature of animistic or shamanistic philosophies, which we in the western world tend to associate with "primitive" peoples. However the tendency is closer to the way that we see things than we sometimes care to acknowledge.

ANTHROPOMORPHIC PROJECTION

The consciousness that's presumed to be possessed by non-human entities such as trees and cliffs is given a name other than consciousness, so that the whole idea doesn't sound too odd – it's given the name *spirit*. Thus it's possible to conceive of trees as being the harbourers of tree spirits, cliffs of cliff spirits, the ground of earth spirits, rivers of river spirits and so on.

The whole idea sounds as though it has a definite element of the *supernatural* to it. However it doesn't have to be so.

We presume that there's a supernatural aspect because in English the word spirit is frequently used in the context of the otherworldly (as in referring to ghosts as spirits, the spirit world, the Holy Spirit, or indeed anything that's *spiritual*).

But the word can also be applied to things that are as familiar as the human spirit or even high spirits. The word has a very wide spectrum of meanings, and herein lies a potential trap.

As soon as the word spirit is applied to something non-human such as a river or a rock the meaning is cut loose from its anchor and can slide from one part of the spectrum of meaning to another. A river that started out as possessing something akin to consciousness can end up with the properties of a supernatural entity, simply because the same word is used for both.

So it is that the natural can easily slip into the supernatural.

I'll come back to this, and the implications of the mobile meanings of concepts such as spirit later.

The imprecision of meaning of the word spirit can, amongst other things, cause misunderstandings in translation between languages. For instance, if a primitive animistic people's word for the consciousness that a tree supposedly possesses is translated as "spirit" it's automatically assumed that there is a religious dimension to their attitude to trees, where there may indeed be none. A world-view may be mistranslated into a religious view.

Face Recognition Software

Why do we see the shapes of people and animals where there aren't any: in inkblots, in clouds, in cliffs, in taps?

It could be because our brains are wired to prioritise human and animal forms in the visual environment. Basically, we're obsessed with such forms. Our brains devote a huge amount of circuitry to the recognition of them, with a special emphasis being put on human faces. Here's an explanation of how our brains do it, followed by the reason why they bother.

Firstly, it's important to realise that the brain doesn't see the world around it simply as though the scene was projected onto a cinema screen on the inside of your skull. Before a scene can be observed "in your head" it has to be broken down into a number of different components for processing, and these components then have to be recombined into the meaningful form that we call "an image". Amongst other things, the scene is broken down into its different colours – red, green and blue – in a way that's analogous to the manner in which a television image or magazine photograph is broken down into tiny dots of primary colours (which are too small to be noticed individually when we look at them, but which when seen collectively give the impression of a continuous full colour image). However, unlike TV and magazine images, the image that we see with our eyes is broken down not only into separate colour components but into other components too. It is, rather incredibly, deconstructed into component parts such as horizontal lines, vertical lines, circles and so on. Each of these component parts is sent to a separate area of the brain for processing, with the different components of the scene only merging again when they are unified into what you perceive as the image.

The degree to which the scene that constitutes the outside

world is split into separate components for processing is quite surprising. Not only are horizontal lines sent to a different part of the brain to vertical lines, but lines that are at 30°, 45°, 60° and so on go to their own individual areas too, and even *movement* is processed in its own discrete areas of the brain by its own dedicated brain cells.

The separate areas of the brain that are used for processing different types of visual information can be detected by the use of brain scanning techniques such as functional magnetic resonance imaging (fMRI). This technique works by probing the brain with the use of powerful magnetic fields. Areas of the brain that are busy processing data have higher blood flow than other areas, and this increased flow is detected by the scanner and shows up as light areas (Figure 20 shows an artist's impression of such a scan).

The resulting image has something of the Rorschach test about it, don't you think? Perhaps you can deduce the personality of the brain's owner from it.

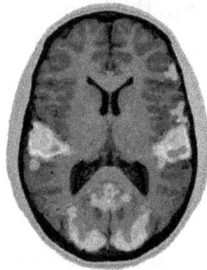

Figure 20: An fMRI brain scan, with the active areas of the brain showing up lighter than the rest

When the person whose brain is being scanned is looking at a horizontal line a particular part of the brain lights up, and when looking at a vertical line a different part lights up. And so on.

If a person suffers brain damage to an area of the brain that deals with a particular type of visual information the ability to process that information may be impaired. For instance if the region that deals with horizontal lines is damaged, horizontal lines may drop out of the final image, while vertical ones and angled ones are still seen with no problem. Thus a person with this condition may be unable to see horizontal objects such as bookshelves but be able to see the books that are resting on them because their spines are vertical.

If you have trouble visualising this selective blindness and you think that it sounds too bizarre to be true, bear in mind that each of your own eyes is selectively blind already, with its own blind spot – an area that is blind to everything – just off to one side of the centre of vision.

This blind spot is caused because there is a portion of the retina at the back of your eye that has no light detecting sensors, due to the fact that the area is occupied by the "cable" that takes the visual information away from your eye and into your brain.

If you're not familiar with the blind spot, here is how to notice its presence – by staring at Figure 21.

Figure 21: Find your blind spot by making the rabbit disappear. Stare at the hat using only your right eye while holding the image at about half an arm's length. Move closer or further until the rabbit vanishes

ANTHROPOMORPHIC PROJECTION

Close your left eye and look at the hat in the figure using only your right eye. Slowly move the page closer to or further from your eye, at a distance somewhere in the region of half an arm's length, while you stare at the hat. At some point you'll notice that the rabbit vanishes, as though by magic. This is because the part of your retina that should be seeing the rabbit is occupied by your blind spot.

As well as having areas that process basic components of images such as angled lines and colours, the brain has areas that process more complex forms that are particularly significant. Here in Figure 22 is a shape that you'll process in such an area.

Figure 22: This image is nothing more than an ellipse and two dots

Yes, it's a human face.

But of course, it isn't a human face at all: it's just an ellipse with a couple of dots on it. The brain overrides this obvious fact, with the consequence that it takes a real effort not to see the image as a face. The brain seems to contain something similar to a standardized face template, and any object or form that exhibits the basic ingredients of a face will have its shape shunted off to the face recognition part of the brain. Notice how the shapes in Figure 23 on the next page aren't automatically interpreted as faces, even though their components are exactly the same as those in Figure 22 apart from their positions.

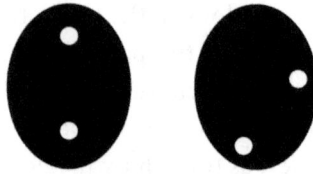

Figure 23: These images are nothing more than ellipses and dots too

When it comes to seeing human faces, the "face recognition software" in our brains is so powerful that not only can we recognise the general shape of faces instantly, but we can also differentiate between millions of different individual real faces when we come across them. This ability is quite amazing, and is extremely useful in the modern world with its teaming millions-too-many people. Its power is quite intriguing however, due to the fact that when this ability was first developed it must have seemed almost like overkill, as in pre-modern times you'd be lucky if you ever had the need to differentiate between a few hundred individual faces at most.*

If the part of the brain that is used for analysing individual faces is damaged it becomes impossible to recognise people from their facial appearance. Sufferers can't recognise their own friends and families, or sometimes even their own reflections. This condition is known as face blindness, or prosopagnosia.

As a result of the mass of face recognition software that it comes bundled with, the brain is rather over-enthusiastic in seeking out faces, so it frequently sees them where there aren't any. In other words, it makes a lot of mistakes.

---

* There seems to be a similar overkill in another of our recognition skills: the ability to hear a tune after a gap of thirty years and to recognise it after only a few notes. What's the point of that then?

ANTHROPOMORPHIC PROJECTION

I realise that "making mistakes" isn't as poetic or romantic a reason for seeing faces everywhere as some readers may wish for. However it's because of its very mundanity and blandness that I suspect that it's probably right. Mundanity generally trumps poeticalness on the principle that if an explanation for anything has an excessively positive or pleasing feel to it one should be suspicious of it on the grounds that it's got the dubious whiff of wishful thinking about it.

The Plus Side of False Positives

The type of mistake that the brain makes when it sees a face where there isn't one is called the generation of a false positive. A false positive occurs when you think that you've made a positive identification of something, but you were mistaken.

Generating false positives is a different type of mistake to the type that you make as a result of carelessness, such as tripping over your shoelaces or forgetting your partner's birthday. False positives are often a necessary consequence of the need to provide a safety margin when making quick identifications.

Here's a typical example of the generation of a false positive, taken from the world of modern domestic gadgetry.

You may be familiar with the movement-activated porch lights that people sometimes install outside their houses. The light should only turn itself on when a person approaches the door, but if the sensor is too sensitive the circuitry will click into action whenever anything that moves, such as a hedgehog, wanders into the range of the device. This over-sensitivity to movement creates the false positive – the light clicking on for a hedgehog. But generally speaking it's better for the light to turn on at these unnecessary times than to not turn on when it is needed. Over-sensitivity is preferable to under-sensitivity.

WHERE ARE WE?

Why do we need to be over-sensitive to human faces, and to therefore generate false positives of them everywhere we go?

Imagine this scenario. You're a prehistoric hunter-gatherer, foraging for berries in a forest. Unbeknownst to you, there's another human lurking nearby, peering at you through a gap in the foliage. For humans, as with many other species of animal, a major source of danger is aggression from members of the same species, with the aggression usually related to issues of territory or reproduction. (The idea that most species other than humans live in harmony with other members of their own species is a romantic myth.)

As a result it's very important to be able to pick out the form of a human face from amongst the chaos of shapes and shadows in a typical forest setting. You never know when an enemy, or at least a rival, may be lurking nearby. Making a positive identification of a lurking person is *so* important that it's necessary for us to be over-sensitive to shapes that resemble the human face and to thus see faces where they aren't – just to be on the safe side. A false positive, or a false alarm, is better than being caught unawares by an enemy. (And an enemy was, unfortunately for our prehistoric ancestors, almost anyone who wasn't in the same kin group or tribe.)

We also tend to see the shapes of animals when we look around us, because animals are possibly the second most important things that we need to recognise, after people. I recently saw a broken branch from a tree floating in a large pond and could have sworn that it was a crocodile (right down to its eyes and mouth), which surprised me enormously because such creatures are extremely rare in the parks of north London.

I think you'll agree though that it's generally safer to mistake a broken branch for a crocodile than to mistake a crocodile for a broken branch.

Similarly, I expect that it's better to mistake an ironing board that's leaning against my kitchen wall for a giant cockroach than it is to mistake a giant cockroach for an ironing board.

So it is that we see human faces and animal forms all around us – in the clouds, in the trees, in the rocks and in everyday household appliances.

Projecting Outwards

As I outlined earlier, once we've recognised a hint of the human or the animal in an inanimate object such as a floating log or a kitchen tap it's easy to invest the object with a degree of consciousness. As I also mentioned earlier, once you've given things like clouds and cliffs consciousness it's then a small step to giving almost everything else on Earth consciousness too, eventually allowing the *whole of nature* to possess the quality.

And why stop there? While we're busy attributing consciousness to just about everything that we can see in the natural world is it any wonder that when we ponder on what may be hidden *behind* the natural world we invest that with consciousness as well, simply by extending the tendency?

As a result we imagine presences that are imbued with human-like personality and consciousness at work *beyond* the physical world. Due to the fact that they are hidden they are often referred to as being *metaphysical* in their nature (or beyond the physical).

These metaphysical presences can easily be thought of as being quite powerful, given their position. In our minds they are thus elevated from the ranks of spirits (which can be our equals but that just happen to reside in trees, rivers and cars rather than in human heads) to the ranks of super-spirits, or *gods*.

Thus it is that we imagine the forces behind nature as being conscious very much in the manner that we are – in other words we imagine them in our own, human, image.

With the monotheistic religions of Judism, Christianity and Islam it can be argued that we've even managed to fashion a single god in our own image and then we've declared that it was actually this god who fashioned us in his image – a wonderful example of the bestowing, or projection, of our own personality traits and preoccupations onto something else.

Almost all of humanity, in all of its disparate forms around the world, has this tendency to see various types of consciousness at work behind the immediate physical world (although not always in such an elevated form as we assume, as I mentioned in the description of spirits earlier, on page 55). The very fact that practically everybody does this may be taken to indicate that there must be something in it, something valid about this tendency and some rightness in the conclusions that it evokes. Surely the universality of it is evidence that it contains some truth – a sort of mass endorsement of its correctness.

While you're thinking about that, I'd like you to try your hand at a simple puzzle that will be relevant to the next point that I want to make (so don't skip it).

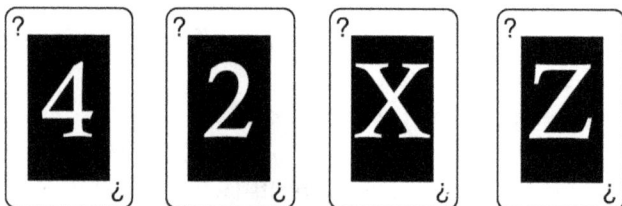

Figure 24: Take four cards...

Above, in Figure 24, are four cards– similar to playing cards.

ANTHROPOMORPHIC PROJECTION

Each card has a number on one side and a letter on the other.

What you have to work out is which *two* cards you would have to turn over in order to verify whether or not the following statement is true.

The statement is "If a card has a 4 on one side, it has a Z on the other."

Easy. Remember your answer, which we'll come back to in a moment. In the meantime, back to the main thrust of this chapter.

From what I said earlier, it could be argued that when pondering the nature of the universe, coming up with the concept of a human-like god or gods as being what's behind it all seems to be the intuitive and obvious answer. "What other answer could there be?" people might ask. "It just seems right". Or they may say "It seems improbable, but nothing like as improbable as the alternatives." It's either god/gods or nothing. What's more, the vast majority of people agree on it.

But because an answer seems intuitive or obvious, or because most people believe it, doesn't necessarily mean that it's right.

Take the answer to the card puzzle that you (hopefully) did just now.

Did you come up with the answer 4 and Z?

About three quarters of people do.

So you're in good company in getting it wrong.

The correct answer is in fact 4 and X.

Here's why.

The statement that you were asked to consider stated that if there is a 4 on one side of a card then there is a Z on the other. It doesn't mention that a Z has to have a 4 on the other side – just that a 4 has to have a Z – the Z can have any number on the reverse.

However, you need to check that the X doesn't have a 4 on the other side. A 4 on one side and an X on the other proves that the statement is false, because a 4 has to have a Z.

This puzzle is known as the Wason card test, devised in 1966 by the cognitive psychologist Peter Wason, an expert on the psychology of human reasoning.

It illustrates a situation where what seems to be the obvious and self-evident answer is in fact wrong.

If you got the answer wrong you were thinking the way that most people think (and if you got it right there's always the chance that you may have done so because you suspected that the puzzle was a trick, so you devoted extra care and attention to the problem. Or of course you might just be very clever).

Just imagine the situation if you decided to determine the correct answer to this puzzle simply by adding up and comparing the different answers that people gave. By shear weight of numbers the usual, wrong, conclusion would be the incontrovertible winner and would be proclaimed as being the correct answer.

There are implications here for subjects beyond card puzzles.

Take the existence of conscious forces at work behind the scenes in the natural world for instance.

To many people the existence of such forces is an obvious, self-evident truth. The fact that most other people agree with this reinforces the assumption that it's true. But as the Wason card test illustrates, just because most people instinctively come to a particular answer doesn't mean that it is necessarily correct.

Just as the puzzle of the Wason card test usually invokes the wrong conclusion, so perhaps the puzzle of what lies behind life, the universe and everything usually invokes the wrong conclusion too. Simply because most people feel that there's a metaphysical force at work there doesn't actually make it so.

Chapter 4

Some Lunacy Concerning the Moon

To explore further the idea that we project consciousness or metaphysical forces outwards onto other objects in nature let's look at an example of an object in our physical world that seems to have an almost undeniable metaphysical or spiritual power.

You can sense it just by looking at the thing.

It's the Moon.

Our satellite has a great effect on us. It seems to be almost a living presence in the sky. This is true no matter what phase of the Moon you look at, but is especially the case with the full Moon. Even I, as a committed rationalist, feel this.

The full Moon seems to have a special energy that affects things down here on Earth: an energy that may even have the power to affect the human brain.

This is the origin of the word lunatic (*luna*: Latin for moon): a person whose mind is so close to being unbalanced that the power of the full Moon is enough to tip it over into insanity.

And of course on the night of the full Moon anyone who is prone to lycanthropy should stay indoors – because they will have turned into a werewolf.

These are effects of the full Moon that supposedly affect humans (of which werewolves are a subcategory), so their veracity may be open to question on the grounds that we humans are very susceptible to suggestion. However, it seems that the full Moon can affect animals too, which are surely neutral when it comes to opinions and influences.

Let's have a look at an example.

WHERE ARE WE?

The effect that the Moon has on animal life may be observed on certain sandy beaches of the tropics, where in the summer months during the nights around the full Moon the sands may be seen to start mysteriously shifting and churning all along the shoreline.

Just beneath the sand's surface finger-length baby turtles are hatching from the clutches of turtle eggs that had been laid and buried there by their mothers. The tiny turtles break through to the surface to be greeted by the great big face of the full Moon. Not the crescent Moon, nor the gibbous Moon – but the full Moon (Of course there'll always be premature baby turtles and overdue baby turtles, which don't get their timing right, but they are very much the exception).

What more proof do you want of the power of the full Moon?

Baby turtles, still curled up in their eggs, buried beneath the sand, are unbiased when it comes to attitudes as to whether or not the full Moon has any remarkable powers – they just do what they do.

Indeed, buried in their eggs under the warm tropical sand the little turtles can't even see the Moon to know that it's full. They don't even know what the Moon is. How much did you know about astronomical bodies before you were born?

The actions of the baby turtles seem to speak louder than any words of the power of the full Moon – the turtles seem to hatch because the full Moon is exerting some strange force over them.

Or could there possibly be a more mundane explanation for why they hatch at the time of the full Moon?

Let's look at it more soberly.

Surely, when it comes to timing, it would be sensible for the little turtles to hatch from their eggs when conditions are at their best for their potential survival in a hostile world.

Night seems like a good time to hatch, because during the day there are a lot of nasty seagulls around looking for a snack that might be scurrying across the beach.

How do the turtles know it's night, buried as they are under the sand?

Do they know it's night because they can feel the full Moon in the sky through some mysterious sense that we can only guess at, or do they simply notice that the sand's got a bit cooler now that the Sun's gone down?

I'll go for the second possibility. If there's a simple, boring explanation, go for it.

But why hatch at the *full* Moon?

Because at the time of the full Moon the tides of the sea are at their highest.

When the mother lays her eggs she lays them above the level of the highest tide (so that they don't get washed away in mid incubation). If the baby turtles hatch at the highest tide they'll have less distance to scamper to get to the sea.

How do the hatchling turtles know that the full Moon is in the sky, creating a very high tide?

The "mystical" explanation may be that they have a mysterious Moon sensing organ that triggers them into action when the full Moon is overhead.

There's a more mundane explanation though.

Mother turtles lay their eggs at around the time of the high tide created by the full Moon – the mother turtles are aware of the state of the tide and can see the Moon in the sky, so there's no mystery as to how they know that there's a full Moon. The incubation period of the eggs is a month, so the eggs hatch at the next full Moon (give or take a night).

It's as simple as that.

This is a much more boring explanation that the one concerning unusual Moon-detecting powers. In fact it's such a disappointingly boring and unremarkable explanation that it seems that it may be right. The more boring an explanation is, the more likely it is to be correct.

(To fine-tune their hatching to coincide as closely as possible with the high tide of the full Moon I would suspect that the fully developed, but unhatched, baby turtles may press into use an ability to detect when the tide's at its highest by feeling the vibrations of the waves crashing quite near to them on the beach. But I'm just guessing. Again mundane, and thus worthy of consideration.)

So it turns out that it's simply the tides that affect the hatching of the turtles, rather than some mysterious lunar power. What's more, it's the *localised* effects of the tide on the beach that are significant, not the tidal effect itself. In other words, the turtles are affected by the state of the sea, not by the state of the Moon (although its light is extremely useful).

The Moon's tidal pull may not directly influence the behaviour of turtles, but perhaps the pull can be the explanation for the Moon's supposed effect on other things.

It's often said, for instance, that because the Moon creates tides in the sea, it must surely also create "tides" in everything else too. Such as in people's brains. And perhaps in women's wombs. This would perhaps explain the supposed monthly mental imbalance of lunatics and the undisputed month-long female menstrual cycle.

This is an interesting speculation that deserves looking into. But first let's have a closer look at how the Moon affects the tides that we know about for sure – the ones in the sea.

It's generally known that the pull of the Moon on the Earth's oceans creates the tides, and that the heights of the tides vary with the phases of the Moon – with some of the highest tides occurring at the time of the full Moon.

However, as well as there being a very high tide at the full Moon there's also a very high tide at the new Moon.*

A high tide at the new Moon? That's a bit strange isn't it – isn't the new Moon the time when there's *no* Moon?

Yet it has the power to affect the waters of the world so much?

No Moon – what am I talking about? Of course there's a Moon. It's simply that it's so close to the Sun that you can't see it. The Moon is obviously always in the sky: it's just that at different times its surface is illuminated differently – that's what its phases are after all.

When, for instance, the Moon appears to us as a crescent (Figure 25), what is actually happening is that the half of the Moon that is illuminated by the Sun is mostly facing away from the Earth, so all we can see is a thin edge of the illuminated half.

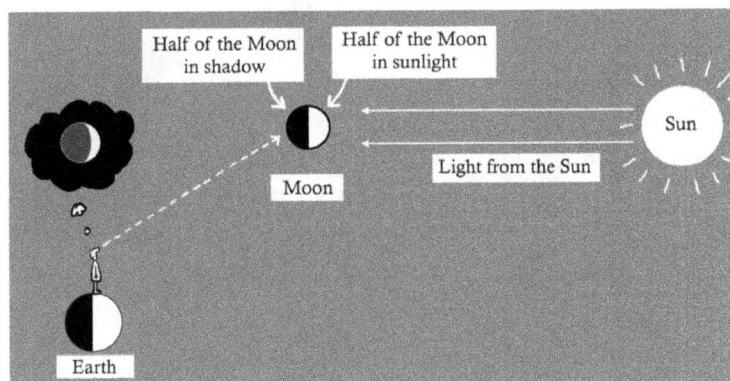

Figure 25: When we see the crescent Moon we are just seeing the edge of the illuminated half of the Moon

---

* The term new Moon is confusingly used to refer to two totally different phases of the Moon: when it's nearest to the Sun (and is thus invisible) and when it's first visible. Here I refer to the phase where it's nearest to the Sun.

As the Moon proceeds in its orbit of the Earth we see different amounts of the part of it that's illuminated by the Sun, as shown in Figure 26.

(If you're thinking that you don't need this schoolbook explanation of the phases of the Moon – because it's common knowledge – my apologies for wasting your time. However, in my experience it's surprising how many people don't know the cause of the phases, regardless of their level of education. Maybe it's the sort of thing that you learn as a child or not at all.)

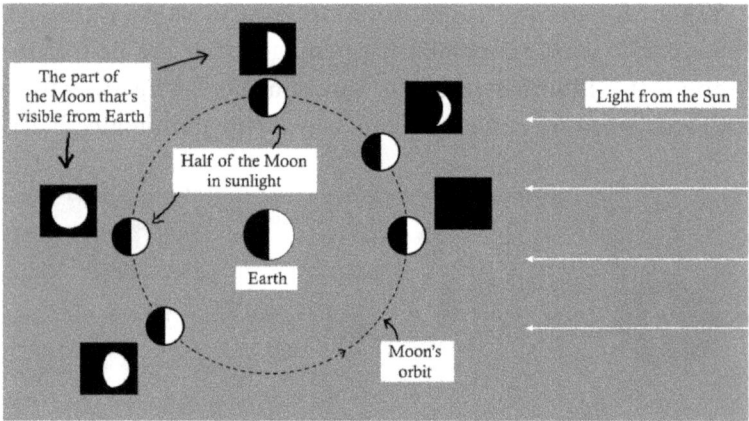

The part of the Moon that's visible from Earth

Half of the Moon in sunlight

Earth

Moon's orbit

Light from the Sun

Figure 26: The different phases of the Moon

What you're looking at when you look at the crescent Moon very definitely isn't just an object that in its entirety is a thin curved strip suspended in the sky – despite appearances. The rest of the Moon's still there, a great big round ball of rock – unilluminated and therefore invisible.

This is all really obvious when you say it, but we don't think like that all the time. When I see the crescent Moon in the sky, in my own mind that narrow, curvy, pointy thing is all there is that exists of the Moon. The fact that there is a huge unnoticed rocky globe nestling between the horns of that crescent doesn't even cross my mind.

It takes some effort to remember that the Moon doesn't actually grow (or shrink) as its phase changes – that the whole phase thing is just an attention-grabbing lighting effect.

I'll come back to this interesting way in which we perceive the Moon later, but for now let's go back to the tides.

While it may be true that surprisingly few people are aware of the underlying cause of the phases of the Moon, I think it can safely be said that most people are aware that the tides are the result of the Moon's effects. But even so, surprisingly few are aware of the actual processes involved.

Here is a quick summary of those processes.

Before we look at the way that the Earth and the Moon (and the Sun) actually interact to create the tides, it's a good idea to imagine what the oceans of the world would be like if the Moon and the Sun weren't there to exert an influence on them. Imagine the Earth suspended alone in space, without the Moon or the Sun in attendance. Not only that, purely for simplicity's sake imagine that the Earth is a perfectly smooth sphere rather than the slightly knobbly object that it really is.

On this simplified version of the Earth the oceans would be of an equal depth all round its surface (Figure 27).

Figure 27: If there were no Sun or Moon the waters on the Earth would be the same depth around the globe

Now let's introduce the Moon, orbiting the Earth. Ignore the Sun for now.

The Moon is quite a massive body, and it's quite close to the Earth, so its gravitational pull on the Earth is far from negligible.

The pull is strong enough to pull the waters on the Earth's surface towards the Moon – which is the effect that we experience as the tides. These effects are shown in Figure 28.

The gravitational attraction of the Moon pulls the oceans of the Earth into a bulge of water on the moonward side of the Earth, as you'd expect.

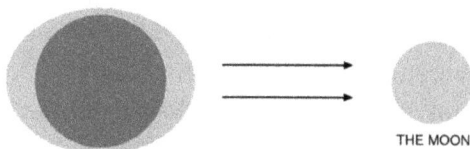

THE MOON

Figure 28: The pull of the Moon affects the depth of the water on the Earth – but why is there a bulge on the "wrong" side of the Earth?

But Figure 28 shows something that's at first sight quite unexpected. The water is not only bulging out on the moonward side of the Earth, it's also bulging out on the other side of the Earth too. Surely that's the wrong side?

It's tempting to think that the water in this opposite bulge must be being "pushed away" from the Moon, because that's what it looks like – which all seems very counterintuitive. However, this isn't what's happening at all.

To understand what's going on you have to bear in mind that the Moon isn't only pulling the water on the Earth's surface towards itself, but is pulling the whole Earth too. The Moon is pulling on the Earth and its oceans together – it isn't simply pulling the water and dragging it round the Earth towards itself as you may have thought. What's more, the pull of the Moon gets weaker with distance, so the side of the Earth that's further from the Moon is pulled less (along with the water on that side). The result is that the whole Earth, including the water on it, is slightly "stretched" towards the Moon. A good way to visualise this is to think of an image of the Earth on a sheet of stretchy material such as rubber (Figure 29). When one edge of the sheet is held stationary and the other is pulled, the perfectly circular image on the sheet stretches into something like an ellipse. This ellipse-like form is what gives us the twin bulges of the tides.

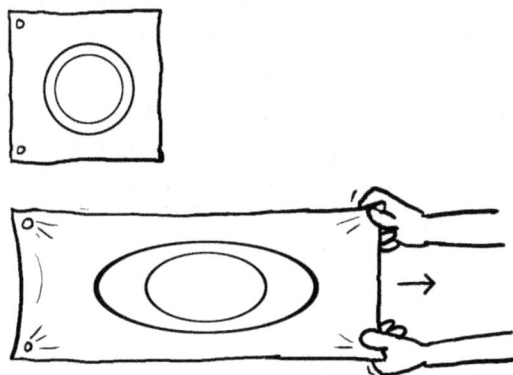

Figure 29: How the twin tidal bulges form due to the pull of the Moon pulling on the whole of the Earth

These twin bulges are the reason why there are two high tides a day rather than just one.

The Moon isn't the only celestial body that influences the Earth's tides however. That would be just *too* simple.

The Sun also pulls on the oceans, in the same way as the Moon. The pull of the Sun is about half as strong as that of the Moon due to the great distance of the Sun. This creates a similar though smaller tidal effect (including its own twin bulges), which is added to that of the Moon to give the resulting tides.

Due to the fact that the Sun and Moon are usually pulling on the Earth from different directions the combined tidal effect of the pair is quite complicated and varies depending on the relative positions of the two bodies in the sky.

For instance, when the Sun and the Moon are more or less at right angles to each other relative to the Earth (Figure 30) their tidal pulls are perpendicular to each other, with the result being that the respective bulges that they create in the oceans are at right angles to each other too. The bulges therefore don't overlap, and indeed cancel each other out to some extent as they have to share the finite amount of water that's in the oceans between them. This creates relatively unspectacular tides, with lower high tides (and higher low tides) than would be caused were only one of the bodies exerting an influence. These tides are known as neap tides.

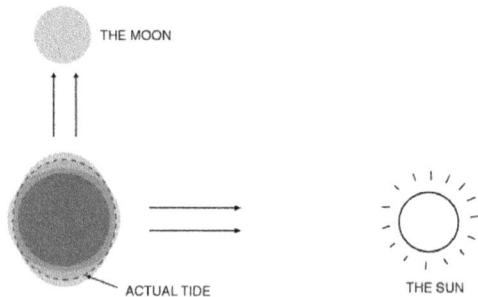

Figure 30: The positions of the Sun and the Moon at a neap tide

In contrast, when the Sun, the Moon and the Earth are lined up, the pulls of the Sun and the Moon combine to create very high tides indeed, known as spring tides (Not named after the season, but after leaping upwards).

Figure 31 shows the configuration of the Earth, Sun and Moon at the time of a full Moon, and the resulting spring tide.

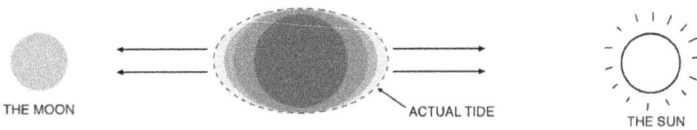

Figure 31: At the time of a full Moon a spring tide is created

You can see that the Sun and the Moon are pulling at the Earth from opposite sides. Although the Sun and the Moon are pulling on the Earth from totally different directions their effects don't cancel out however, due to the fact that the twin bulges that are induced by each body are added together – producing extreme tides. It's a bit like stretching the Earth from opposite directions in a cosmic tug-of-war game.

Now look at Figure 32, which shows the situation at the time of a new Moon.

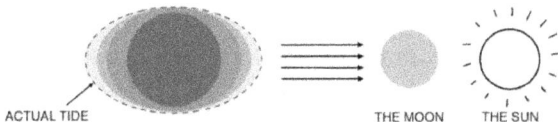

Figure 32: The tidal effect at the new Moon

Here the Sun and Moon are in the same direction in the sky

(meaning that the Moon is therefore invisible to us on Earth), and their forces are pulling together, again creating extreme tides.

So it is that the tides of the new Moon are very much the same as those of the full Moon.

However, ask most people which phase of the Moon creates the most extreme tides and they will almost inevitably say the full Moon – purely because the full Moon imposes its presence on us so that we notice it. Yet, despite appearances, the reclusive new Moon is the showy full Moon's equal. The moral of this is – beware of appearances.

(You may have noticed that this moral is something of a recurring theme in this book.)

That's how the gravitational pulls of the Sun and the Moon work together to create tides in the oceans, so surely it's only reasonable to assume that they must pull on other objects too, creating tidal effects in them as well.

As mentioned earlier, surely they create tides in objects such as human brains.

It's often said that the pull of the Moon affects this organ, creating mood swings (if not full-blown lunacy at the full Moon).

And then there's the womb of course, with its menstrual cycles, which is also said to be affected by the power of the Moon. Even the word menstrual is linked to the Moon – menstrual means monthly, and a month is based to a large extent on the length of the lunar cycle. The word month should really be *moonth*. It's true that menstrual cycles don't all peek at the full Moon itself, but just the fact of being based on the length of a lunar cycle is a pretty good second best.

It may sound reasonable at first sight to think that these things may be linked to the pull of the Moon, but then, think again...

Why are these phenomena only ever associated with the pull of the *full* Moon? Why is the equally powerful pull of the new Moon, which creates equally high tides as we've just seen, totally ignored? The answer may simply be that it's because the new Moon doesn't make its presence or its power known by shining in the sky (You could say that it's hiding its light under a bushel).

This fact – that the effects of the new Moon aren't factored into the theory that the tides affect human physiology – makes the whole theory begin to look a little shaky.

On top of the glaring omission of the new Moon from the theory there are other factors that make it unlikely to be true.

Just because the gravitational pull of the Moon has a noticeable effect on the oceans doesn't mean that the same applies for small objects. The reason that the tides in the oceans are noticeable is that they are the cumulative effect of the Moon's pull on the whole planet and on an awfully large amount of water. The tidal effect on each cubic inch of water is almost immeasurably small. And the same applies to its effect on brains and wombs.

On top of this, the gravitational effects of the Sun and the Moon on small objects are probably totally swamped by the gravitational pull exerted by relatively large objects that are much closer to hand, such as mountains, buildings or buses.

So, the power of the Moon may not be quite what some of us assume it to be, although it is none-the-less there in its ability to move the earth and the oceans as a whole, with the new Moon being in gravitational terms the equal of the full Moon.

The upshot of this is that any Moon worshippers amongst us who celebrate the power of our satellite by going out at night to dance under the light of the full Moon should perhaps be dancing under the new Moon too. However, if they were to do so they would notice one of the major drawbacks of the new Moon: the dancers would keep bumping into each other in the dark. This would certainly bring home to them the one special power that the full Moon definitely has over all of the Moon's other phases (and especially over the new Moon).

Its light.

In our world of artificial lighting the power of the Moon to illuminate the darkness of night frequently goes unappreciated, but in places beyond the reach of man-made light the Moon makes all the difference between a world that's pitch black at night to one where there's enough light to be able to move around. The brightest phase of the Moon, when it's easiest of all to move around, is of course, the full Moon.

Being able to see at night makes it possible to do many things that would otherwise be impossible: things such as hunting or travelling.

It may even be the *light* of the Moon that is the force that determines that the length of women's menstrual cycles are about the same as a complete cycle of the Moon's phases. There is some evidence that in the absence of artificial lighting women ovulate at about the time of the full Moon. It's tempting to imagine prehistoric peoples slipping out of their family groups on moonlit nights in search of sexual liaisons with members of other groups – liaisons which would quite possibly result in pregnancy due to the fact that the women were ovulating at the time. (The urge to seek out members of other groups for procreative activities was probably instinctive, as it would lessen the danger of inbreeding.) Maybe this is one reason why the full Moon is instinctively thought of as being romantic.

So, it seems that the really important thing about the Moon is that it supplies us with some light at night. Meanwhile, the importance of its gravitational pull is probably over-rated and is indeed insignificant in terms of everyday human existence (though not of turtle existence, as turtles need the tides).

The Moon's illumination is the product of simple reflection of light off what is essentially a barren sphere of rock – making it in many ways a very mundane source of light.

Yet because of its light the Moon is elevated by many to the status of a semi-mystical entity in the sky, raining strange and mysterious powers down upon the earth. Despite the Moon's intense normalness, it is raised to a level of the supernatural.

This tendency of ours to attribute mystical properties to perfectly normal things such as the giant sunlit sphere of rock that's orbiting our planet has significant consequences when it comes to the way that we interpret the universe and our place in it. Of which more later…

The ultimate message of this chapter is that just because something looks powerful and significant (such as the full Moon) doesn't mean that it is – and just because something goes unnoticed (such as the new Moon) doesn't mean that it isn't.

A final footnote: it's interesting to compare our attitude to the Moon with our attitude to electric light bulbs. The light from the Moon is in many ways much less astounding than the light that's produced by a light bulb, with its legions of excitable subatomic particles darting around and making it glow. The light bulb does after all emit its own light rather than borrowing it from somewhere else. However, no-one attributes semi-mystical properties to light bulbs the way that they do to the Moon. We've become very blasé about our electric light bulbs, and electricity in general, in recent years.

Chapter 5

Mother Nature's Dubious Parenting Skills

The full Moon isn't the only thing in the natural world that we have a tendency to misinterpret and romanticise.

We do it with the whole of nature itself.

We often have an uncritical propensity towards thinking of nature as good and harmonious – a fact that in recent years has been exploited to the hilt by advertising, where just about every produce under the Sun from shampoo to sausages makes a claim to contain "natural goodness" or "nature's health-giving ingredients".

It's true that some bits of nature, such as "the countryside", can look very nice from a car window or when you're on holiday in a carefully selected part of it, but take away the painstakingly constructed comfort buffer that we create with our modern technological know-how and you find that nature's altogether a different kettle of fish.

Nature is in many ways a harsh and unforgiving thing, best avoided. After all, on a cold winter's evening the freezing draught that's creeping under the door is simply nature trying to get in to remind you of just how unpleasant things can be in the outside world. For a lot of the time you're probably better off indoors with the door firmly closed, and with a draught excluder in place.

If you're feeling generous it can be argued that there is a degree of harmony in nature and in the cosmos that contains it, but only in that they operate by laws rather than by acts of chaotic and anarchic randomness.

The laws that govern the underlying workings of the universe are very scientific. A typical example would be Newton's third law of motion, which states: For every action there is an equal and opposite reaction.

These are the laws that work away quietly behind nature, keeping things functioning without us noticing them. There are other laws however that govern the workings of nature specifically at the level of living things, of plants and animals. This is the level that we normally think of when we think of the "natural world".

Here are just a few of these laws:

1) If you're weak, you die.
2) If there's a chance that you'll make a nice meal, you die.
3) If you're ill, you die.
4) If you're alive, you die.

Such are the laws of harmonious nature.

Imagine these laws being passed by any government. Civil rights campaigners would be down on them like a ton of bricks, quite rightly.

How come there isn't an organisation dedicated to having these laws of nature changed? All we've got are organisations that are dedicated to keeping nature exactly the way it is.

And these brutal laws were all created by nature, which we misguidedly personify as a beneficent female: Mother Nature.

If I were a woman I'd push to get the "Mother" part dropped from that name. (And for the same reason, if I was a mystically inclined woman I think I'd quietly drop the Goddess part from the popular "Earth Goddess" concept.)

MOTHER NATURE'S DUBIOUS PARENTING SKILLS

Mother Nature seems to be such a bad parent that she should be on trial for the abuse of her children. Have you noticed that she eventually kills every last one of them?

Nature is given a female persona because nature is thought of as being nurturing.

There is of course a large amount of nurturing in nature, but it's very tightly targeted by its practitioners, as it generally only occurs between members of the same species, and even then predominantly between blood relatives, so there's actually no way in which nature can be described as nurturing in any form of universal or indiscriminate way.

Whenever there's any nurturing or cooperation evident between members of different species it's almost definitely because there's some form of symbiotic relationship involved. Each party gets something useful out of it, otherwise they wouldn't bother (A typical example of symbiosis is the way that ants actively protect the caterpillars of the common blue butterfly from predators – and are rewarded by nectar secreted by the caterpillars).

In a world full of creatures that only look out for themselves and their blood relatives, it's a strange fact that it can be argued that there's only one species of creature that actually seems to care at all about any other forms of life on the planet whatsoever.

Humans.

You may find this hard to believe, bearing in mind that the received wisdom is that we are some sort of malevolent mutant plague-species that is on the verge of wiping out most of the other life on the planet at any moment.

The tendency that's making us wipe other life out (which we are definitely doing, unfortunately) is a different tendency to the one that makes us care for it. We have the two tendencies, while most creatures only have one of them – the tendency to wipe other life out. We tend to think that we possess more of this particular destructive trait than other creatures simply because of the fact that we put it into action more efficiently.

To get a bit of perspective let's look at the caring capacity of another species of animal: one that we're well positioned to study at close quarters: the domestic cat. You'd never see a cat caring for a bird with a broken wing the way that you'd see a human doing, would you? We all know what a cat would do with a bird with a broken wing. And when it's done it we (or at least the cat apologists amongst us) excuse the cat because such acts are "in its nature".

Imagine what would happen if we used that sort of excuse for all of our own actions.

It would mean that murderers could get away with murder, and rapists with rape, simply on the defence that it was "in their nature" (while ironically there'd be a danger that anyone who professed to being an upstanding citizen couldn't get away with such crimes should they ever commit them, because such acts of violence weren't in *their* nature).

Most creatures have a total lack of concern not only for creatures of different species but even for most members of their own species. You can see this if you watch almost any natural history documentary on television, unless it's been censored to eliminate any unpleasantness.

Take for example a documentary that's set on the African savannah, in which a cheetah is hunting zebra. The cheetah rushes towards a herd of zebra and all of the zebra start galloping around in a state of panic trying to get away from the fleet-footed predator. But once the cheetah's caught an unfortunate zebra what do the other zebra do? They stop running around, and start grazing. They return to the task of eating their meal, the one that was interrupted by the arrival of the cheetah in the first place. They start grazing right there, next to where one of their fellow zebra has been dragged down and is now being torn to pieces by the claws and jaws of a large carnivore. Do they all gang up on the cheetah and drive it away, saving the stricken zebra's life? No. Because if they did so, the cheetah would still be hungry and would soon be back – and this time it could be them. The only thing on the zebra's minds, if anything, is "It wasn't me."

Similarly, you may watch enraptured by a nature documentary featuring the progress of a family of baby owls in a nest. The opening shots of the programme may show a group of four very cute, down-covered nestlings. Mysteriously though, part way through the programme a strange thing may have happened. For some reason there are only three nestlings to be seen, rather than the previous four. Where has the fourth one gone? The fourth one, the runt of the litter, has been eaten by its siblings. Eaten! By its brothers and sisters! Can you imagine the outrage if that happened in a human family?

It sounds as though I may have something against nature, judging by the tone of this section, but I haven't.

I actually think that nature's rather wonderful.

It's just that I don't think that nature's very nice. Except, as I said, through a car window.

I think that we have a misguided tendency to view nature as good and us as (unnaturally) bad. This, I believe, is a gross misinterpretation and distortion of things, and is probably the result of guilt that we've acquired due to the fact that we now bestride the earth as an all-consuming and all-conquering colossus.

Our success is our burden.

But it's not our fault that we're so successful. It's just "in our nature". It's in our brains. Like the cat with the injured bird, we simply can't help ourselves.

(However, the time has now come where we indeed have to go against our nature and change our ways, before we cause any more damage.)

We're successful because we have a problem. This problem is that we just can't stop doing things, no matter how hard we try. For instance, part of me wants to just sit around watching the grass grow, but I can't. I'm compelled to write this book instead!

Part of *you* probably wants to just sit around watching the grass grow too. Then why don't you just do it instead of reading this book?

Why is it in our nature to be this way – to be incapable of stopping doing things?

The possible reason is explored later, notably in Chapter 17, and Chapter 18: however before we look into that particular issue, let's look a little more closely at our attitudes concerning the small matter of our relationship with the rest of the universe.

Chapter 6

Size is Everything?

I suggested towards the end of the previous chapter that we dominate this planet to such an extent that as a result we feel guilt about the way that all of nature seems to be suffering at our hands. As indeed we should. We rule our planet unchallenged (although it's possible that avian flu may make a bid to knock us off our perch in the near future). Here on our planet we're very much in control (or out of control, depending on your viewpoint).

However, it's a different story once you look upwards from the earth and peer outwards into the depths of space.

In cosmic terms we're insignificant specks of dust in the incomprehensibly mind-numbing vastness of the universe. Our lives are less than the blink of a gnat's eye in the staggering immensity of eternity.

We're as nothing in the great, overwhelming, infinite scheme of things.

How many times have you heard such things being said? In fact you've probably said them yourself more than once.

If we, the creatures that dominate our planet so completely, feel so insignificant in cosmic terms, then imagine what other life-forms would feel like if they were capable of such thoughts. It's probably just as well that they aren't.

Perhaps we'd be better off if we didn't think about it either. The trouble is that we do – we just can't help it. It's lodged in our brains, damn them.

Our brains are fickle things however, and in different

87

situations they are prone to think about such matters as size and scale in completely different ways.

Here's an example taken from personal experience.

I recently painted my kitchen, and it took me ages.

I usually think of my kitchen as being tiny and cramped, but while painting it, its space seemed to become miraculously larger as the enormity of the painting job that I had undertaken slowly revealed itself. It would take me days. I ended up getting a man in. True, my kitchen is quite small, especially when compared to the enormity of the universe, but for that brief moment in time it seemed huge. In fact for a few days my kitchen *became* the universe. I was so totally immersed in it that I stopped thinking about oceans and mountains and rivers and stars and galaxies – the only concept that I could hold in my brain was "thixotropic emulsion". (To complicate my feelings about the size of my kitchen further, I was using white paint. As you probably know, using light colours on walls has the effect of making rooms seem larger, while dark colours make them seem smaller. Consequently the room actually seemed to expand in size as a direct result of the lightness of the paint that I was applying.)

Hang on though. Is my kitchen large, or tiny? It can't be both.

Well actually, in some ways it can be.

It's all a matter of how it's affecting my life at the time.

Size is relative.

I've got a woman friend who tells me that her nose is too big. Apparently it's too big by about three millimetres.

That's interesting I told her, because your nose is a lot smaller than my kitchen, which, apart from when I'm engaged in painting it, seems somewhat on the small side to me. And on the scale of the universe, I consoled her, your nose hardly exists – get things into perspective.

SIZE IS EVERYTHING?

This got me thinking (while I was sitting over a coffee in my nice new kitchen).

Three millimetres on a nose is a big issue, but three millimetres on my kitchen would be nothing. Even three centimetres on my kitchen, which is *ten times as much*, would be nothing. Thirty centimetres may be useful though, as then I could fit a nice new coffee machine on my worktop.

There we have a significant point I think. It's not necessarily the size itself that matters, but its relevance.

Three millimetres on the size of a nose holds more significance than three centimetres on a kitchen. And, jumping up a few rungs on the ladder of significances, those three centimetres on a kitchen hold more significance than three million light years on the size of a universe. Would you have noticed if the universe had suddenly expanded by three million light years yesterday lunchtime? I think not. (In fact, I believe that it did.)

When it comes to whether or not size matters, relevance is everything.

In fact, when it comes to weighing up the significance of almost any quality of anything, the thing's direct relevance to you personally is of paramount importance.

Take this example.

Let's look at something dramatic: something that you can hardly miss.

Explosions.

Say for instance you're in your kitchen, and the coffee machine explodes, because you forgot to put any water into it.

Okay, it's a very small explosion, and the only damage that's done is that it creates a burn mark on the kitchen wall. But it's very significant to you. Especially if you've just had the kitchen decorated.

Now, imagine that at about the same moment that your coffee machine goes up in smoke a gas leak elsewhere in your town destroys a local clothes shop. No casualties, thank heaven, and it was a shop that only sold clothing items for a gender and age group that you don't belong to, so you never used it – but it affects you none-the-less, as your feeling of security and wellbeing would be a little precarious when you walked past the wrecked store for the next few days. You couldn't help thinking that if all of the gas mains in town were that dodgy then maybe a shop that you frequented yourself – perhaps the one that you purchase coffee from – would be next to go.

At the same moment that your coffee machine and the clothing shop in town explodes, a lorry loaded with diesel explodes at the other end of the country. It kills the driver and a hitch-hiker he'd picked up. It's on the national news. You feel a brief pang of sadness because the hitch-hiker was, by pure chance, a student at the same college that you'd attended. You obviously feel sorry for the lorry driver too, but he doesn't lodge in your consciousness in quite the same way as the hitch-hiker because he was foreign.

At the same moment that these three simultaneous events occur, a ferry in a third world country (the name of which escapes you) explodes due to an engine malfunction. It kills most of the passengers, of whom there were many. It's on the news, but you are in the kitchen looking with dismay at the remains of your broken coffee maker, and though you hear the coverage on the TV in the other room, you ignore it.

By chance, at exactly the same moment a planet in a distant solar system is vaporized when its star exploded into a nova, snuffing out the peaceable civilisation that existed there. The nova makes it onto the pages of popular science journals, but only because the star involved was briefly visible to the naked eye here on earth. No-one even knew that the star had a planet orbiting it in the first place.

Simultaneously, a galaxy on the far edge of the universe explodes as the result of some scientific principle of which we are at present blissfully unaware. The galaxy was beyond the range of our most powerful telescopes, but its disappearance signalled the end of hundreds of thousands of planets hosting civilizations far more advanced than ours could ever hope to be in a million eternities.

Which one of these explosions is the most devastating to you?

The coffee machine in your kitchen of course.

This is not you being selfish. This is just how things are.

Events that affect you are more important to you than events that don't.

These events follow a simple law.

The closer things are to you the more effect they have on you.

This law applies to many phenomena in the physical world, not only to things that have psychological effects such as explosions. It applies, for instance, to such phenomena as the effect of gravity or the illumination created by a light bulb, both of which get weaker with distance.

The general dropping off of the importance and the effect of things the further they are from you is good news when it comes to the issue of the ludicrously huge size of the universe. It means that things that happen close to you, such as in your house, are of riveting interest, while the degree of personal interest that you can muster in the goings-on further afield, such as in the next street, is significantly lower. As for anything that's going on in the street after that, your interest is lower still, and so on, until by the time we've got as far away as, say, the orbit of Pluto, you couldn't care less about what's going on at all.

For some people of course the orbit of Pluto is pushing it, as they don't give a damn about anything that's happening further away than, say, their refrigerator.

The consequence of this is that though the universe stretches almost endlessly beyond the orbit of Pluto, so what?

It doesn't really matter. We won't be going there. After all, walking as far as the TV set to change channels when the remote control's been mislaid seems like a huge inconvenience to most of us.

So next time someone tells you "The universe is millions and millions of light years across – doesn't that make you feel *really* insignificant?" you can reply "Well, due to the way that the significance of phenomena diminishes with distance – actually, no. And by the way, you've grossly underestimated the size of the universe."

Or, at the risk of sounding even more smug and self-satisfied, you could point out that the whole huge universe/insignificant person dichotomy is possibly only an issue because we make it into one.

Because people don't like feeling dwarfed by things. It's bad for their self-esteem.

It's an ego thing.

Maybe if people worked on reducing the size of their egos a little they'd find that the size of the universe mysteriously stopped being a concern.

Maybe the universe isn't too big after all – maybe it's egos that are too big.

The next time that you find yourself feeling uneasy because the universe seems so mind-bogglingly vast, try looking at things in the following way instead, as a little experiment.

Imagine how you'd feel if it turned out that the universe wasn't huge at all. Imagine if it was actually really quite small.

Just think how you'd react if scientists discovered that

everything which is more than a few thousand metres above the ground was in reality some weird sort of optical illusion, and that beyond that point everything was in fact nothingness. Everything stopped just above the air corridors that you use when you fly off on your holidays. (All space probes and manned space flights that have seemingly progressed beyond this level were in fact part of a government conspiracy to hide this incredible truth. This includes the Moon landings, which you may have been suspicious about already.)

Could you cope with a universe that small? That parochial? That claustrophobic?

Me neither.

If the universe was that tiny your life would be noticeably significant in the whole scheme of things. You'd be elevated into being quite an important person. Personally I can't handle that much significance. It's scary.

I want my impact on the universe to be a bit more inconsequential than would be possible in such a confined space.

I want to be insignificant enough to be able to have a lie-in some weekends and not feel too guilty about it. To be able to do something slightly immoral, like watching a bit of daytime television when I should be doing household chores, without feeling that I've set the entire cosmos on a course towards decadent disintegration.

I want to be just a tiny bit meaningless. What a weight off my shoulders.

I like to think that the bigger the universe, the smaller one's problems.

When it comes down to it, whether the universe is huge or minute, our feelings about its size may tell us more about ourselves than they do about the universe.

Chapter 7

Worlds Within Worlds

Instead of looking out at the universe and pondering on its stupendous size let's turn around and look inwards for a moment.

Let's look really closely at something. Let's look really, *really* closely. What shall we look at? Anything will do. Something convenient. Your hand perhaps. When you look really closely at your hand what do you see?

You see that it's composed of lots of tiny, tiny atoms.

Okay, you don't actually see that it's composed of atoms, because they really are very tiny indeed, but you know that your hand is made of atoms, so just use your imagination and pretend that you can see them now.

Because you're a carbon based life-form you can see a lot of tiny carbon atoms. Here's a carbon atom in Figure 33.

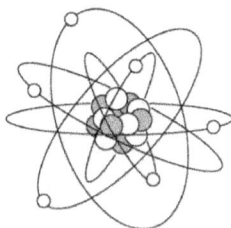

Figure 33: A carbon atom

These carbon atoms have got the looks of typical atoms: a central core composed of protons and neutrons with a fleet of electrons circling in orbits of different heights. Because they're carbon atoms most of them, apart from a few wayward isotopes, have six protons and six neutrons forming the central core, with six electrons in orbit. (There's more about the structure of atoms in Chapter 8.)

You may have noticed that the layout and appearance of these atoms is uncannily similar to that of our solar system, with its central sun and orbiting planets (Figure 34). The chief difference seems to be that the planets in the solar system orbit in a more or less flat plane like a plate while the electrons in the atom whiz round at all sorts of angles creating a spherical shell of orbits round the central nucleus.

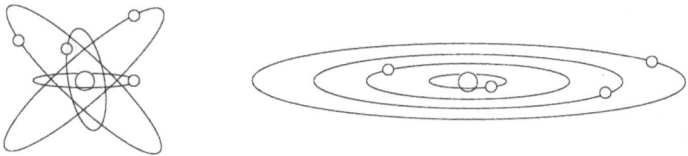

Figure 34: A typical atom and a typical solar system compared

When comparing the solar system and the atom this similarity in structure, and the accompanying dissimilarity in size, invites a particularly entertaining concept to pop into people's heads.

Maybe, like me, you've indulged in the fantasy that atoms are not just similar to miniature solar systems, but actually *are* miniature solar systems, with the electrons as planets and the nuclei as the suns. Perhaps like me you've fantasised that these electrons/micro-planets are inhabited by vanishingly tiny life-forms. It's not much of a leap to then imagine that everything on these micro-worlds are themselves made of unbelievably small atoms of their own – and that these atoms are actually tiny solar systems themselves. And so on and so on, like Russian dolls, forever and ever.

Similarly, you may have fantasised that our solar system, with its planets orbiting the Sun, is in fact nothing more than a giant atom itself – perhaps part of a chair leg or cheese grater in a gargantuan larger universe.

It's a very attractive idea, but it suffers from two major drawbacks.

The first of these is simply the fact that it's a very attractive idea, which should therefore set alarm bells ringing. Attractive ideas should be treated cautiously because of their seductive powers.

The second drawback is that the notion is suspiciously based on the concept of a cosmos that functions on all levels in the same way that it functions at the level at which we happen to find ourselves.

You need to be very careful about using observations of things at our everyday level as a basis for concepts of how things function at other levels.

Here's an everyday example of why.

I remember from my schooldays a teacher telling the class "According to the laws of aerodynamics, a bumble bee can't fly." A big round body and tiny wings – there's not a hope of it getting off the ground.*

You've probably seen bumble bees flying around, despite the

---

* This myth supposedly came about in the 1930s in Germany, when an aeronautical engineer did a quick calculation over dinner while chatting to a biologist. He used the aerodynamics of fixed-wing aircraft as his starting point, which was a mistake. He'd probably had a few glasses of wine too, which would be another mistake. He realised his error later, but by then it was too late because the story was too good to ignore and "had wings".

laws of aerodynamics. So how do they manage it?

One of the reasons that a bee can fly is because although it's big and round in insect terms, it's actually quite small, as you can verify if you possess a ruler. At bumble bee size the world is a totally different place to the world that we inhabit. Not only are other insects scarily huge, but the very air itself is different. To a creature the size of a bumble bee the air is not the insubstantial medium that we think of it as – it's closer to being like a liquid. This is a very buoyant medium, so a bumble bee has little trouble floating around in it, even with those tiny wings. Think of the bee as swimming rather than flying (Our arms are no good for making us fly, no matter how much we flap them, but they work very well to help us to swim).

In similar vein, you may have seen small spiders floating on the breeze attached to a single strand of silk. They float easily. Scaled up however, the whole dynamic breaks down. It would be the equivalent of you holding one end of a hundred yard long length of rope and expecting to float away as a result.

Of course, while we have a tendency to think of the air as insubstantial, we frequently experience it as otherwise, such as every time the wind blows. If you've ever tried to ride a bike very fast you'll be aware of the mounting air resistance as you speed up. Racing cyclists sometimes go to the extent of shaving their legs to combat this air resistance (Conversely, perhaps bumble bees are as furry as they are in order to exploit air resistance as a way of increasing buoyancy. This theory has just occurred to me as I write this, so there's a strong possibility that it's nonsense).

So there you are: this simple example of similar objects at different sizes – small bee, large person – shows that at different sizes things are very different, so you can't simply scale things up or down and expect them to work in very much the same manner.

Consequentially, this brings into question the advisability of our tendency to think of things such as atoms and solar systems in terms of hierarchical systems of similarly functioning, though differently sized, structures.

Our tendency to create scaled hierarchies doesn't simply apply to physical objects such as atoms and solar systems though – it applies to other, more abstract phenomena too.

We invoke the same Russian doll model when contemplating our own nature as sentient entities in the universe.

We see ourselves as conscious beings that are capable of modifying the world around us in various creative ways (or destructive ones, depending on your outlook and personality profile). As a result of our tendency to think in terms of hierarchies of similar phenomena we can hardly help but to imagine greater, grander versions of ourselves, further up the hierarchy that are doing very much the same thing that we do but on a more epic scale.

This inclination, coupled with our propensity for projecting human qualities or "spirit" onto things with abandon, is a contributing factor in our proclivity for creating gods. In some cultures the god at the top of their hierarchy is so powerful that there is only room for one of them.

If you agree with the notion that you should be suspicious of stacked hierarchies of similar concepts, on the grounds that the properties that are possessed by the objects in the hierarchies aren't necessarily transferable between scales (as in the non-aerodynamic bee), then this notion that there may be a grander version of ourselves out there controlling things could be in need of a little re-evaluating.

Our tendency to perceive many aspects of the functioning of the natural world in terms of such hierarchies probably stems to some extent from our innate psychological make-up and our nature as social animals. Human societies are organised hierarchically, as are those of most social animals, with a dominant member of the group at the top – often, for better or worse, an alpha male. So it's not surprising that we extend this hierarchy outwards and upwards, and thus place a supreme dominant being at the top of everything – often, for better or worse, an alpha male.

More on this particular alpha male later.

It's interesting to speculate as to whether or not a highly sentient creature that somehow lived a totally solitary life and that had no concept of society would come up with such a concept of hierarchies. Imagine perhaps a particularly intelligent creature that lived alone on a desert island (of the type in the cartoon cliché). What sort of model would this creature formulate when pondering the underlying nature of the universe? Would it, amongst other things, conceive of a higher version of itself as somehow being at work behind it all? Possibly not – or at least not in a way that we'd understand.

Chapter 8

Nothing Matters

As described in the previous chapter, we have a tendency to see the physical world in terms of hierarchical, similar structures that extend all the way down to atoms, which we sometimes envision as being like mini solar systems.

To disabuse ourselves of this vision let's look a little more closely at these atoms, to see what they are really made of.

By the time you reach the end of this chapter you'll have discovered that atoms are more bizarre than we can possibly imagine; that they exist in a place where what seems to be solid becomes insubstantial – a place that straddles the borderline between the existent and the nonexistent.

You may rightly be intrigued by this idea that the "stuff" that atoms are made of is bizarre, incomprehensible and mind-boggling – that atoms are weird. However, bear in mind that atoms are the building blocks of everything in the universe. So if atoms have these qualities, so have all of the things that are made of atoms. Any terms that we can apply to atoms, such as "existing on the borderline between the existent and the nonexistent" must also apply to everything else – because after all, everything is nothing more than a large collection of atoms.

This applies to things in the everyday world that we inhabit. And it applies to us.

For all of its seeming robustness, our physical world of mountains and oceans and tables and chairs is in reality a disconcertingly insubstantial place balancing on the edge of existence.

WHERE ARE WE?

We don't notice this fact because we're right in the midst of it, and we take our world for granted because we see it every day – but that doesn't mean that it's not amongst the most bizarre things imaginable.

To see just how bizarre, let's look deep into the atom.

The idea of atoms has been around since at least the times of the ancient Greeks. They postulated that if a large amount of any substance was repeatedly subdivided an amount would eventually be reached that was so small that it couldn't be divided again. This piece of the substance, incapable of further division, was the smallest possible piece of that substance that could exist. The name of this tiniest speck of substance, an *atom*, was derived from the Greek term for uncuttable (*a-tom*: the *a* means not, as used as a prefix in other negative words such as asymmetrical and atonal; and the *tom* comes from the verb *to cut*, which is most familiar nowadays as a suffix to medical surgery that involve cutting, such as tonsille*ctomy* or appende*ctomy*).

All matter is made up of atoms, with the atoms of each element being different to those of the other elements, which is what makes gold different to carbon, carbon different to hydrogen and so on.

For several thousand years the idea of atoms being the smallest, uncuttable level of matter worked extremely well.

However, things started to get more complicated as experiments started to be made into the phenomenon of electricity during the Victorian period.

In 1897 Joseph John Thomson, the son of a Manchester bookseller, was the first person to discover a particle smaller than the "uncuttable" atom. While experimenting with cathode ray tubes he discovered the almost weightless subatomic particle that carries a negative electrical charge – named the *electron* due to its relationship with electricity. (If you think that cathode ray tubes are old-fashioned contraptions that were only good for outmoded television sets and now-uncool computer monitors, remember that we wouldn't have discovered the electron without them. They were in some ways the Victorian equivalent of the Large Hadron Collider). Thomson won the Nobel Prize for his discovery.

Thomson proposed that the electrons were distributed within the atom in what is sometimes described as "plum pudding" manner, with the negatively charged electrons distributed randomly inside a positively charged cloud (thus making the whole atom electrically neutral).

The discovery of the electron was followed in 1911 by the discovery of the atomic core, or nucleus, by New Zealander Ernest Rutherford. He determined that the nucleus contained positively charged particles, which he christened *protons*. These particles are much heavier than the almost weightless electrons – around 1,800 times heavier in fact.

Rutherford postulated that the atomic core also contained particles with no electrical charge at all. Some years later, in 1932, his theory was proved correct when the *neutron* was discovered by Sir James Chadwick at the Cavendish Laboratory in Cambridge University. Yet another Nobel Prize. The neutron was very very slightly heavier than the positively charged proton.

So it was that by the mid 1930s atoms were seen as being made up of three fundamental particles – protons, neutrons and electrons – rather than as being the single, indivisible, uncuttable entities that they had been conceived as previously.

The atoms of different elements had different numbers of these fundamental particles, which was why each element had different properties. Figure 35 shows a typical atom: that of helium.[*]

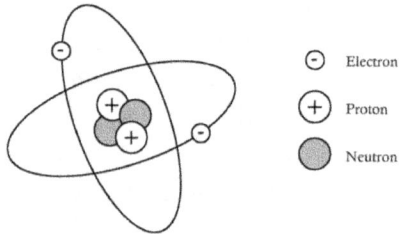

Figure 35: An atom of helium

There are a hundred or so different elements (92 natural ones, rising to 112 when you include man-made ones produced in nuclear physics laboratories under special conditions). It's a nice idea that this large, rather unwieldy number of elements are all composed of the same very small number of basic particles, as this simplifies things no end. It's a good principle in general to assume that complicated things are made up of simpler things.

Three basic subatomic particles is simpler than a hundred or so basic elements, I think you'll agree, but there's something slightly odd about there being *three* subatomic particles.

Things could be simpler. *Two* subatomic particles would be simpler for instance, with one of them being positively charged and the other negatively charged. There's a nice symmetry to that.

This simplicity could be achieved if the neutrally charged neutron turned out to be nothing more than a proton and an

---

[*] The only element that isn't a combination of protons, neutrons and electrons is hydrogen, the lightest element, which is composed of a single proton and electron, with no neutrons.

electron stuck together.

That's nice and simple.

Now, what if those two subatomic particles, the positive and the negative one, were simply the *same* particle, but in different configurations (such as different ways up)? Looking at the particle one way up you would see a positive particle, while looking at it the other way up you'd see a negative one.

That would give just *one* subatomic particle.

You can't get much simpler than that. It sounds right.

There seems to be something odd going on though: one way up the particle has a different mass to the other way up. How can *one* particle have *two* different masses? This seeming paradox may possibly be explained by the following analogy.

Imagine that the single subatomic particle is cone shaped, as shown in Figure 36. (Remember, this is an analogy purely for visualisation purposes – I'm not implying that such a particle actually is cone shaped.)

Imagine that the cone is resting on a soft and giving surface (such as rubber).

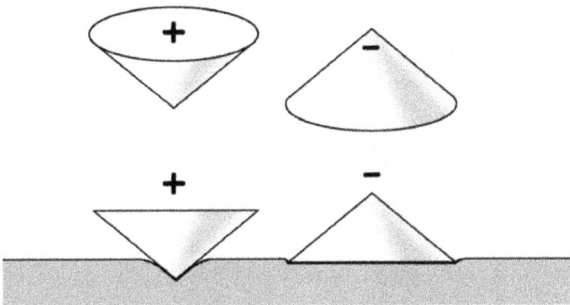

Figure 36: The analogy of a cone to explain the different manifestations of mass. The cone makes a deeper impression one way up than the other

Depending on which way up the cone is orientated it manifests itself as either a positively charged heavy particle or a negatively charged light particle.

One way up the cone stands on its point (exhibiting its positive charge), while the other way up it rests on its base (when it exhibits its negative charge). When resting on its base the cone makes a relatively shallow impression in the surface on which it rests, due to the large area that's in contact with the surface (in a similar manner to that of a snow shoe on snow). In contrast, when standing on its point the cone sinks deep into the surface, as its entire force is concentrated on a small area (in a similar manner to that of a high-heeled shoe on snow).

The depth of the impression in the surface is the thing that we experience as mass. Thus the same object can exhibit different masses depending on its orientation.

That's quite neat as far as it goes, but there's a problem.

This way of looking at subatomic particles would be fine if there were only three fundamental particles, protons, neutrons and electrons, as was once thought. But it turns out that there are more. Many more. By the end of the 1930s other, more elusive, subatomic particles were being discovered as a result of improved technology.

These particles were harder to detect than the proton, neutron and electron for a variety of reasons.

For instance, one of these subatomic particles, the *neutrino*, is very much like the electron in that it is almost weightless, but it differs in that it has no electrical charge. The combination of weightlessness and lack of charge means that neutrinos don't interact much with other particles, making them extremely tricky indeed to detect. As a consequence they remained undiscovered until 1959. Although they are extremely elusive they are surprisingly common. In the time it takes you to read this sentence untold billions of them will have flowed through your body, while numbers of them beyond all imagination will have passed through the entire earth completely unhindered and unnoticed.

By the 1960s the number of subatomic particles that had been discovered was in danger of becoming ridiculous. So much for simplicity. Most of these particles were only observable in special conditions such as in the atom-smashing apparatus in nuclear physics laboratories and didn't seem to be stable components of the atom in the way that the proton, neutron and electron were. They frequently existed for only a fraction of a second before disappearing in a puff of energy, but they were there all the same.

All of these subatomic particles vary wildly in how heavy they are. For instance the proton is 1,836 times heavier than an electron, while another particle, the *pion*, is 273 times heavier, and another, the *muon*, is 207 times heavier.

Although their masses vary so greatly all of the particles have a restricted choice of electric charge: either plus or minus one, or no charge at all. Charges of plus or minus one are essentially the same charge in opposite directions, so in some ways they can be thought of as being the same as each other – so in reality the particles either have the same charge or no charge.

This implies that charge is something *very* basic, because of the fact that when it exists it seems to only exist at one value. Mass however isn't quite so basic– as its value varies far too much from particle to particle for that to be the case.

This problem of the large number of disparate masses, or the *mass of masses mystery*, may be explainable by using an analogy that's not too dissimilar to the one I used a page or two ago, in which a single object (a cone) exhibited different weights in different configurations.

WHERE ARE WE?

This time compare the subatomic particles with the Moon rather than with a cone.

The Moon is an object that looks different at different phases, even though it is just one object that simply seems to be different depending on the direction of the light that's illuminating it. If you were to imagine the Moon to be a giant fundamental particle the mass of which was for some reason dependant solely on how much of it was visible, the thin crescent Moon would exhibit a very low mass while the full Moon would be very massive. The new Moon, when the Moon is invisible, would have no mass at all. The same Moon would exhibit a different mass at each phase: one subatomic particle would seem to be many.

Appealing as this metaphor is, it turns out to be unnecessary (at this stage – but I'll come back to something similar later), as it's now generally assumed that the reason there are such a large number of different fundamental subatomic particles is because these particles aren't actually fundamental at all, but are made up of a deeper level of even more fundamental particles.

These even-more-fundamental sub-subatomic particles were given the name *quarks* when their existence was first postulated in the 1960s.

It was proposed that protons and neutrons were composed of two types of quark, these quarks being essentially the same except for their electrical charges. They were named *up* quarks and *down* quarks – names chosen simply to infer difference rather than any intrinsic up-ness or down-ness. The up quarks had a positive charge, while the down quarks had a negative charge – however, the up quarks' positive charge was twice the strength of the down quarks' negative one.

The proton and the neutron are each composed of three quarks (Figure 37). The neutron is composed of one up quark and two down quarks (with the result that, because positive up quarks have twice the charge of negative down ones, the combined charges neutralize each other). The proton is composed of two up quarks and one down quark, giving it an overall positive charge.*

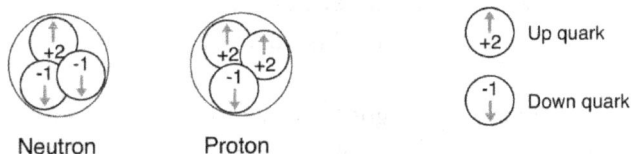

Neutron   Proton

Figure 37: The quarks that make up the proton and the neutron, with their relative electrical charges

By the way, the component parts of the atom aren't tightly packed billiard balls as shown in these (and most other) diagrams of atoms. The individual components are tiny, if indeed they can be said to have any size at all, but they define a volume because they take up a certain amount of "personal space". You could try imagining them by thinking of the way that when you wave a torch around on a dark night you see an after-image of where the torch's light traces out a shape: the shape isn't solid, but it defines a region in space. The

---

* In my figure I've given the quarks charges of +2 and -1: these numbers are ratios rather than units. It's actually conventional to assign the quarks charges of +2/3 and -1/3, so that the arithmetic adds up to a proton with a positive charge that's conveniently +1. In other words, by convention the charges are based on the proton's charge being the unit, rather than the quarks' charges being the unit. For the purposes of this explanation I've given the quarks whole number charges to make the arithmetic simpler (but I'm also a bit suspicious of conferring fractional values onto a property of a "fundamental" particle).

components are only shown as being large balls because if they were represented more realistically there'd be nothing to show. Not only that, the scale of these diagrams is completely unrepresentative of the true scales involved: in Figure 35 for instance (a representation of a helium atom), at the scale at which the atom's nucleus is represented the electrons would actually be whizzing around several miles away. To say that there's a lot of empty space inside an atom would be an understatement.

So, let's see where we've got to now in our quest to find the simplest, most fundamental level of matter.

An atom is essentially composed of electrons, protons and neutrons, while a whole menagerie of other subatomic particles exist in supporting roles. The protons and neutrons are composed of two types of quark. The electron is so small and simple that it's assumed to be indivisible, a bit like a quark itself – the quarks however are about 600 times heavier than the electron, with the electron having three times the charge of the negative quark.

Things don't seem to be getting that much simpler, do they?

In fact, things seem to actually be getting a touch more complicated.

And they get even more complicated still. It turns out that in order to account for all of the different types of subatomic particles other than protons and neutrons there aren't two types of quark needed, but six.

Added to this, it transpires that there are also six types of electron-like particle – almost weightless subatomic particles that are thought to be fundamental in their own right, a little like quarks.

That's twelve types of fundamental particle.

It gets worse still.

Each type of subatomic particle, from protons and electrons to quarks, has a twin that's opposite in all of its characteristics (of which opposite charge is only one). For instance the negatively charged electron has a positively charged twin, the positron, and each of the quarks has a corresponding doppelganger, called an antiquark (from which such particles as antiprotons and antineutrons are made). These "equal though opposite" particles are known as antimatter.*

So, the twelve fundamental particles – electrons, quarks etc – have suddenly broadened to twenty-four. Surely that's too many particles to be fundamental? We're getting back to the earlier, confusing level where atoms seemed to be the smallest particles – even though there were a hundred or so different ones.

There are (at least) two possible answers to the question of why there seem to be so many different "fundamental" particles.

One is that there aren't that many, and that the ones that there are simply exhibit different properties in different circum-stances, as described in the analogies of the cone and the phases of the Moon a few pages ago.

The other possibility is that the fundamental particles aren't fundamental at all. They are constructed of something that's even more fundamental.

What could that "something" be?

Well, whatever it is, to use the word "particles" is probably stretching it a bit.

The word particle implies something that has some semblance of solidity. Solid things are objects like bricks and

---

* The prefix *anti* in antimatter doesn't mean that antimatter is some sort of *opposite* of matter, whatever that might mean. Antimatter is as real as ordinary matter - it's just that it does such things as spin the opposite way round. The only thing that's truly negative about it is that when it comes into contact with normal matter they cancel each other out.

billiard balls. The tiniest object that can meaningfully be labelled solid is probably the atom. But when you get smaller than an atom everything becomes a bit fuzzy and the use of words like particle becomes rather imprecise and misleading, even though the things are usually depicted as being rather billiard-ball-like. Instead, think of something closer to that torch that I mentioned a few pages ago, tracing out a region in space as it's waved around.

Just as the light from the torch is a form of energy, think of the component parts of atoms as tiny bundles of energy too (Exactly what "energy" is is open to debate needless to say, but at least it's a suitably nebulous term for whatever's going on at the subatomic level). The fact that the components of an atom are actually composed of energy is why they have electric charge – electric charge being one of the ways that energy manifests itself.

If subatomic particles are actually nothing more than energy this means that as a result solid objects can be thought of as quite literally being made up of nothing more than energy too.

The main difference between the energy as we experience it when we touch a live electric wire and the energy in solid matter is that in solid matter the energy has a stable configuration, tied up within its atoms. So when you sit in a chair the energy in the atoms of the chair stops you falling through it, while when you sit in an electric chair the consequences don't bear thinking about.

We're so used to the idea of the energy of electricity that we tend to forget that we don't really know what it actually is, only what it does. You have to go back to the nineteenth century, when the humble electric light bulb was a cutting-edge invention, in order to relive the feeling of wonder that the phenomenon of electricity evoked.

Think of the solidity of matter as being the result of the

electric forces acting within each atom – that each atom is in essence nothing more than a stable force field that stops other atoms entering the particular volume of space that it occupies (a little like mini versions of the force fields or deflector screens that are generated by spacecraft in many science fiction stories – the main difference being that while science fiction force fields are used to stop photon torpedoes or other advanced and improbable weaponry from reaching a spaceship, atomic force fields are more commonly associated with stopping coffee cups falling through table tops, at least in philosophical discussions).

So, if atoms are made up of bundles of energy that are in a configuration that forms a stable entity, what form does the energy take at a truly fundamental level?

The currently favoured theory is that at the most fundamental level everything is composed of vibrating strands of energy called *strings*.

The idea that the stuff of the universe is composed of vibrating strings gives the impression that even at this fundamental level the "stuff" is "solid" in some way: the idea of strings sounds very much like the idea of particles after all. However, the string involved is only one-dimensional, with no thickness, like an infinitely thin line (although they have other dimensions "wrapped up" inside them, for mathematical reasons).

These strings are thought of as vibrating at different frequencies, with each frequency making the string manifest itself as a different subatomic particle – a little like the way that the strings on musical instruments give rise to different notes or that different wavelengths of light give rise to different colours.

String theory isn't the only game in town however. Other theories propose that everything is composed of point-like entities rather than extended string-like ones, while others invoke sheets or membranes of some fundamental "medium".

Points, strings, sheets: take your pick.

Whether string theory is correct or not, the idea that the fundamental "stuff of existence" is essentially something that vibrates does possess a quality that seems to be essential for a theory of the fundamental nature of everything: the essential stuff of existence must be *very* simple, yet be able to manifest itself in more complex ways. In other words, if the "stuff" is a vibration, then the same sort of vibration can give rise to all of the different manifestations of matter and energy, simply by vibrating at different rates.

Let's by-pass the issue of whether the fundamental nature of the stuff of the universe is closer to strings, membranes or whatever, and instead just concentrate on the concept that it is a *disturbance* of some kind, or an irregularity of some sort, in the empty nothingness of the "primordial void".

Here we start running into serious conceptual difficulties, as this primordial void or expanse of nothingness is a tricky thing to get your head round, to say the least.

How to imagine nothingness?

Of course it's impossible, partly because our brains just aren't wired to conceive of such a thing (for everyday purposes it's a pretty pointless and needless exercise after all), but also because nothingness simply isn't like anything. Mainly because it isn't anything.

It's probably best to not even try to imagine it, and to just accept that it's there, if "there" is a word that can be used in this situation. However, if we do want to have a go at imagining it we have to resort to slightly unreliable and inadequate metaphors.

A suitable metaphor for nothingness may be to think of it as being like a flat, perfectly still surface of water extending endlessly, with the flatness of the water representing the total featurelessness of nothingness. To differentiate between this profound ultimate nothingness and other more day-to-day nothingnesses let's call it Nothingness – with a capital N. In fact let's call this endless flat expanse the Sea of Nothingness. In this infinite, shoreless Sea of Nothingness any disturbances in the form of ripples on the surface could be likened to the vibrations that give rise to "stuff".

These particular ripples or vibrations aren't to be confused with the vibrating strings of string theory. The vibrations I'm describing here are metaphorical vibrations or ripples in a metaphorical medium – the Sea of Nothingness. (If anything, think of these metaphorical vibrations as *giving rise* to the vibrations of the strings in string theory – imagine that the strings of string theory are floating on the surface of the Sea of Nothingness and that the undulations in the sea are causing the undulations of the strings – because the strings are riding the sea's undulations.)

The idea that everything in the universe, all matter and energy, is the manifestation of ripples in Nothingness, and that these ripples are the simplest "things" that exist, is quite appealing because of one important factor. A ripple, in essence, is a form of wave that has only *one* fundamental characteristic or property: it goes up and down. If you're thinking that this up-and-down-ness gives the wave *two* characteristics rather than one, think of the crest and the trough of the wave as being inseparable parts of the same single characteristic – that a single wave automatically has both parts in very much the same way that a single coin automatically has a heads and a tails, and in fact can't exist without having both.

The ripple's possession of only one characteristic is important because whatever it is that exists at the most fundamental level, it can only have *one* property. This is because, working on the assumption that only one property can arise at a time, having *two* properties makes something more complex than absolute fundamentality allows.

Grafted onto this one property are other characteristics such as its wavelength and amplitude as secondary features.

Not only is the simplicity of the concept of a wave-like disturbance being the fundamental phenomenon that manifests itself as matter and energy appealing, but the concept has yet another appealing feature.

Look at the wave in Figure 38. This represents a ripple on the surface of the Sea of Nothingness (Notice the flat, featureless nothingness extending endlessly on either side of the ripple).

Figure 38: A ripple in the Sea of Nothingness

As you can see, the wave goes up and down, as waves do: it has a crest and a trough.

Imagine the crest of the wave as being "positive" energy, and the trough of the wave as being "negative" energy, as depicted in the graph in Figure 39.

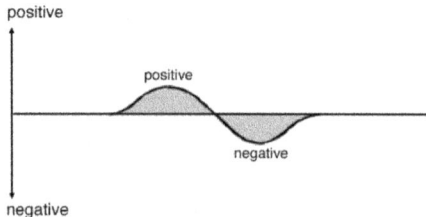

Figure 39: The positive and negative energy in a ripple in the Sea of Nothingness

You can see that the positive energy and the negative energy (the shaded areas in the figure) are the same, but are in opposite directions. This means that when the energy of the crest and the energy of the trough are added together to give the wave's total energy they add up to *nothing*.

This is very pleasing philosophically, as it means that although the wave exists, the sum of its parts is zero, so in some ways its existence adds up to nothing.

Because this ripple is a disturbance in Nothingness, it can be said that Nothingness actually becomes Something – and that because the up and down parts of the ripple cancel out energy-wise and don't add anything to the overall status of Nothingness, you can still say that Nothingness nevertheless contains nothing.

Because the ripple straddles either side of the flat line in the graph – the line that represents Nothingness – the universe can be thought of as hanging on either side of Nothingness.

I expect that you've been asking yourself "These ripples in Nothingness are all very well, but what caused them?"

Here we run slap-bang into the infinite regression problem – what made the thing that made the thing?

Bear in mind that my ripples in Nothingness aren't real ripples, they are *metaphorical* ripples. And metaphors, after all, are by their nature imprecise comparisons of the things that they are standing in for – if they weren't imprecise they'd actually be exactly the same as the thing they represented, and thus wouldn't be metaphors at all. Due to this imprecision you could say that if metaphors were elastic bands you could stretch any metaphor until it snapped.

The metaphor of ripples is just a way of visualising something that is impossible to comprehend. The ripples in the Sea of Nothingness are, by definition, the most basic disturbance in the uniform, all pervasive state of Nothingness that underlies everything. The phenomenon that these metaphorical ripples are standing in for is not caused by anything (at least in any way that we can meaningfully understand). They are just something in the nature of Nothingness (Again, whatever that means).

In fact, if anything, they are the thing that's at the beginning of the infinitely regressive chain of events that I just mentioned. They are the thing that caused the thing.

The idea of ripples in a (metaphorical) Sea of Nothingness may be seized upon by those amongst us who are of a religious inclination, who may then say "Ah-ha, yes. The ripples are caused by God dipping his fingers in the Sea of Nothingness!"

This, unfortunately (or fortunately, depending on your outlook), isn't possible, as the ripples are the *simplest* thing that there can be, by definition. This means that they can't be caused by something that's *more* complex than they are themselves, such as an all-knowing entity that happens to have fingers. Even metaphorical fingers.

Talking about complexity, there's one final point that has to be mentioned about these metaphorical ripples. I've been stating that they are the simplest thing in existence: that there is nothing simpler than they are. However, if you look at the shape of the ripple you can see that it itself is not totally simple: it starts to rise up gradually, then rises steeply for a while before flattening off and then dropping down again. That's quite a lot of things to be going on for something that there's nothing simpler than. In "reality" the ripple would be a single blip, with no initial gradual appearance and final decay – it would in fact be more like a digital pulse that's just "there" rather than an analogue wave that rises and decays.

So there you have it. Despite its incredible complexity the universe is little more than the result of disturbances or ripples in the void. And despite the universe's "content-rich" appearance the sum total of its contents (the peaks and troughs of the ripples in the void) adds up to nothing.

You could indeed say that because the crests and the troughs of the ripples cancel out when added together, and they thus in combination add up to nothing, the end result of the ripples is less than the sum of their parts. While of course, just looking at the universe around us shows that at the same time the end result of all of these ripples is definitely greater than the sum of their parts.*

The universe is both everything and nothing. It just sounds right (to me, at least).

Nothing becomes Something. But at the same time it all still adds up to nothing, and thus it remains Nothing. You could actually say that the universe is composed of Nothing. That "Nothing exists". As in "Something exists".

This rather disconcerting fact that the universe and all of the matter within it is made out of nothing at all could at first sight seem to imply that the universe is totally meaningless. You can't get more meaningless than nothing, after all.

However, the fact that matter is nothing doesn't in any way imply that nothing matters.

In fact, because the universe is made of Nothing (the capitalised Nothing that exists in the Sea of Nothingness), it can very much be said that *Nothing matters.*

If only so that people like me can mess about playing with

---

* I keep talking about ripples in the plural here. In fact it's just as conceivable, or even more so, that there is just one ripple at the beginning of all things. This one ripple could then give rise to secondary "events" such as "currents" or "eddies", or it may simply start to ripple in ever more complex ways itself, creating the illusion of many ripples as it snakes around.

words in this rather silly and irritating way.

I'd better move on.

But before I do so, here are a couple of footnotes to this chapter, held back until now simply so that they didn't interrupt the flow of the chapter as a whole.

You may be wondering how anything as complicated as a universe can manifest itself out of something as simple as ripples. A ripple, after all, has only two components – an up part and a down part.

It's not as far-fetched as it first sounds. Bear in mind, for instance, that the entire contents of a computer, ranging from the calculations that it performs, through to the photos and videos that it displays and the music that it plays, is composed entirely of different sequences of only *two* states: *on* and *off* – or as it is expressed digitally, of zeros and ones. This two digit "language" is known as *binary code* and is the underlying principle of all digital technology.

It's not only computers that have a very basic code underlying their ultimate complexity. Life itself has such a code too. The genetic code that is carried by the DNA that is the building-block of all living things is essentially created by a sequence of only *four* separate chemicals, adenine, thymine, cytosine and guanine (known as A, T, C and G for short), spread along the DNA double helix molecule (Figure 40). One side of the helix is from the mother and the other side from the father: the sides fuse together like a long zip, with the A molecules on one side linking with the T molecules on the other, and the C molecules with the G molecules. The order in which these chemical bonds occur along the molecule determines the genetic characteristics of their possessor. Very simple – but just look at the results in the mirror!

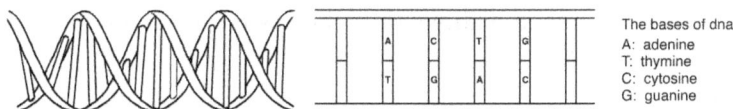

The bases of dna
A: adenine
T: thymine
C: cytosine
G: guanine

Figure 40: The structure of DNA, in which the chemical "rungs" from the two sides only join together in very limited combinations (A to T and C to G)

Illustrated next is a nice graphic example of how easy it is to generate complexity from very simple beginnings.

To start, take a couple of black dots (Figure 41). Move them so that they overlap slightly. Then make the regions where the black of the dots overlap "cancel out", leaving white.

Figure 41: Take two dots, make them overlap, and make the overlapping parts cancel out

Not a particularly complicated outcome, you may quite rightly be thinking. But now, instead of using a couple of single dots, do the same thing with two simple grids of dots such as the one shown in Figure 42.

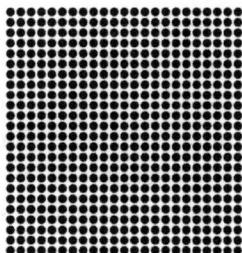

Figure 42: Take two grids such as this one

Place the grids one above the other, with one at an angle, as here in Figure 43.

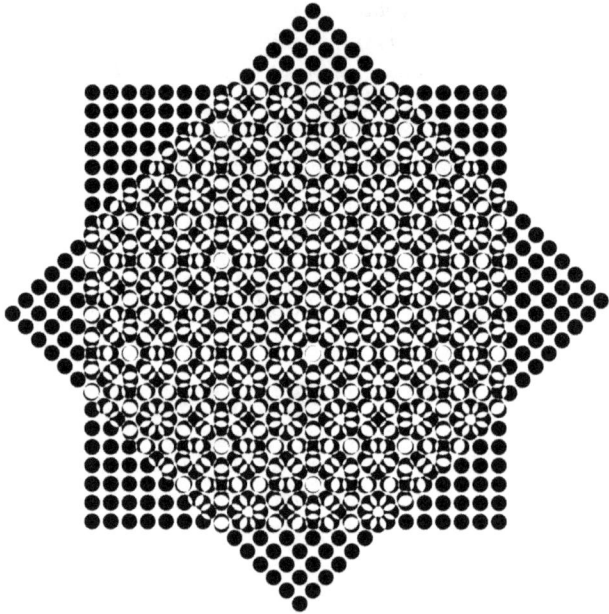

Figure 43: The grids superimposed, with the overlapping black areas cancelled out

Just look at all of those flowers! Or are they snowflakes? Or mini-eruptions of some sort? All simply the result of overlapping areas of black cancelling each other out on very basic grids of dots. It couldn't be much simpler.

You can see an animated version of this phenomenon, where the grids rotate relative to each other in spectacular fashion at www.chrismadden.co.uk/complexity.html.

Another point that I mentioned earlier in this chapter was the enigma concerning the fact that the electrical charges of subatomic particles are always either plus or minus one (or zero), while their masses vary incredibly. A model that accommodates this relationship between charge and mass can be built into the metaphor of vibrating waves, such as those in the Sea of Nothingness.

Imagining that a subatomic particle is not an actual particle at all but is the manifestation of a wave, the electrical charge of the particle may be thought of as a manifestation of the amplitude, or height, of the wave (Figure 44). If all waves had the same amplitude for some fundamental reason, then all electrical charges would be the same (though positive or negative depending on whether they went up or down).

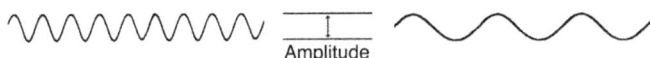

Figure 44: Waves of different frequency but the same amplitude

Meanwhile, the mass of the particle may be thought of as a manifestation of the frequency, or wavelength, of the wave. The wavelength may be capable of varying greatly, hence the large variety of masses that subatomic particles manifest.

If you have trouble with the idea of a wave's frequency somehow manifesting itself as something that's as "solid" as mass, look at it this way. Think of the mass of an object not in the way that we normally experience it – as something that has the feel of kilograms or pounds about it – but as the magnitude of the *effect* or *impression* that the object has on its surroundings. A massive or heavy object has a greater effect than a light one.

Figure 45 shows an analogy that demonstrates what I mean.

Figure 45: Shades of impressionability

The figure shows a number of circles of varying shades. As you can see, the impact that each circle has on the page is different, depending on its shade. If the shade of the circles were to manifest themselves as *weight* rather than *tone*, the black circle on the left would be the heaviest, as this circle has the greatest effect on the page. The two gray circles would weigh less, with the lighter gray circle being the lighter in weight.

What you probably didn't notice when you looked at the series of circles in Figure 45 is that at the right hand end of the row there's a circle that's almost white. This fourth circle is for all intents and purposes invisible, and thus it has no effect on the page at all. If its tone were translated into mass, this circle would be practically weightless. It's the metaphorical equivalent of one of the almost massless subatomic particles such as an electron or a neutrino.

So in this analogy the black circle represents a particle that is analogous to a wave that has a frequency or wavelength that makes a great impression, while the white circle represents one that makes practically no impression at all. Yet, despite the difference in their impacts, the only real difference between the different circles is the frequency of the waves that form their contents.

NOTHING MATTERS

Finally, one last note on the subject of nothingness.

If you find the notion of "nothing" being "something" a bit of a tricky concept to hold in your head, you're not alone. Neither can I. Our brains just aren't meant to work with such concepts (As I mentioned earlier, why would they need to?).

In a similar way, only one and a half thousand years ago people didn't have the concept of the number that denotes nothing – zero.

This number is something that we now take for granted, but back then the concept of giving "the absence of a quantity of something" a numerical value just seemed bizarre. If your friend had five oranges, while you had no oranges, and you had to write down how many oranges you each had, you'd be able to write 5 for your friend but you'd be at a total loss to know how to express your own quantity. It wasn't until around 500AD, in India, that our current understanding of the concept of the number zero began to be developed.

Today we think nothing of it.

Chapter 9

If it's Mind-Boggling it Probably Doesn't Matter Anyway

The idea that the physical universe is composed of nothing more than ripples or blips in nothingness is somewhat disconcerting, and may indeed create a few ripples or blips in your brain as you try to reconcile yourself with the concept.

To try to regain some sort of composure let's stop looking inwards to the fundamental nature of matter, and try looking outwards instead, as we did earlier in the book. Let's look up into the sky: at the countless stars, the untold millions of galaxies, the mind-spinning expanses of space. Let's look far into the blackness of the cosmos and peer into the infinite.

Or then again, let's not. It's just far too unsettling.

Whenever we think about the extremes of reality, either by looking inwards or outwards, we can't help but feel discomfited. Interestingly though, we tend to feel most discomfited when we're looking outwards.

This is probably partly to do with the simple fact that we feel intimidated by things that are larger than we are. Personally I feel intimidated and insignificant when I look at a large hill, so there's little hope when I gaze at the ever-retreating immensity of the cosmos beyond it.

Another reason that we feel more troubled by the outward scale of the universe rather than the inward scale may be that when we look outwards we can actually *see* the scale of the universe as we stare into the vast night sky going outwards forever. When we look inwards we can only see as far as something that's as small as a speck of dust, which is actually quite large and which is at a reassuring proximity to us.

You may be relieved to hear that when you look at the vastness of the night sky with the unaided eye you're not actually staring infinity in the face and seeing space recede forever – it just seems that way. You can see lots of stars in the sky, it's true, but they are all unimpressively close in cosmic terms. Most objects beyond our own galaxy are just too far away to be seen with the naked eye at all. Of the galaxies without number that are out there you can only see one or two of them, and that's only if you know where to look.* These galaxies are M31 (in the constellation of Andromeda) and M33 (in Triangulum). Considering the majesty of what these galaxies are you'd think that they'd have been given impressive names rather than mere catalogue numbers: the M stands for Charles Messier, the 18th century French astronomer who catalogued all of the "fuzzy" objects in the sky so that people didn't mistake them for comets, and they are simply numbers 31 and 33 on his list. M31 is just over 2.5 million light years away while M33 is about 3 million light years away, making them the most distant objects that you can (just) see without a telescope.

A light year is the distance that light travels in one year. It sounds like a measurement of time, but it's a measurement of distance.

This principle of using time to measure distances is the same one that we use when we measure distances on roads in terms of the time that a journey will take: if you're travelling in a car at 60 miles per hour and your destination is 120 miles away you may

---

* Not including the Magellanic Clouds, which are small satellite galaxies of our own galaxy. They are visible only from the southern hemisphere.

say that it's two hours away. More accurately you'd actually say that it was two *car* hours away. If you walked the same distance (at 4 mph) you'd find it more convenient to say that the destination was a distance of 30 *pedestrian* hours away. Light travels at about 186,000 miles per second (300,000 km per second), so a distance of 120 miles can also be expressed as 0.00065 light seconds (1/1,500 of a light second). As you can see, measuring local distances in terms of the speed of light is impractical.

With the furthest galaxy that we can see with the naked eye being three million light years away, and the furthest one that we can see by using the latest technological gadgetry being close to 14 billion light years away (and with more distant ones being noticed all the time), it turns out that we only see a rather parochial corner of the cosmos when we stare at the night sky with the naked eye. I'm not sure whether this fact is reassuring or disconcerting.

How far away are the various "local" celestial objects that we can see in our parochial corner?

The Sun is about 8.5 light minutes away, while the nearest star beyond our solar system, Proxima Centauri, is just over 4 light years distant. These sound quite close.

But look at it this way.

If you were in the car that I mentioned a moment ago, travelling at 60mph, and the car was somehow capable of space travel, a journey to the Sun would take about 175 years, barring the usual hold ups in the vicinity of Venus (In other words, the distance is 175 car years). To reach the Sun would take seven human generations – which means that if you set off in your car while leaving an infant daughter or son behind on earth, by the time the car reached the Sun you may be a great great great great great great grandparent.

WHERE ARE WE?

If you felt the urge to travel further afield, say to Proxima Centauri (the nearest star), the journey would take longer, obviously. It would take about 50 million years. In other words, by the time the car arrived at the star the status of your grandparenthood would have about two million greats in front of it (which would add an extra 6,000 pages or so to this book if were I foolish enough to write them down in full).

A journey to the nearby galaxies, M31 or M33, would take longer still – over three trillion years. Out of the question really. By car at any rate.

So, our small, local corner of the universe is unimaginably large. And the rest of the universe is unimaginably larger than that.

Possibly infinite.

And it may be only one of an infinite number of universes. All of which are infinite.

The whole thing can play havoc with your composure. We just can't take it all in.

There's a very good reason for this. Our brains developed in a world where our main concerns were such things as hunting woolly mammoths and running away from sabre-toothed tigers. Back then, a whole day's travelling might take you about twenty miles (approximately 32.1868 kilometres) if the terrain was good. Twenty miles was a long, long way back then.

In fact it was such a long way that it was very hard to actually conceive of the physical distance itself. It would be much easier to think of it as "a day's travelling distance". (Notice that this "incomprehensible" physical distance of twenty miles is being expressed in terms of the time that it takes to travel it – very similar to the way we measure cosmic "incomprehensible" distances by using the time that it takes for light to travel the distance.)

It's the same to this very day – we still find twenty miles, or even a single mile, hard to comprehend when we actually think about it. This is because people don't perceive these distances directly. Unlike very small distances. Compare trying to comprehend *one mile* with trying to comprehend *one yard* (or a kilometre with a metre).

All of our direct distance judgements tend to be limited to distances that we can actually see, and even then they're most accurate when the distances involved are less than the height of a human. How wide is the room that you're sitting in right now? You can't tell for sure, can you? Without getting out a tape measure. See what I mean. And how far is this text from your eye? You may be able to make a reasonable guess at that one.

The further a distance is, the harder it is to judge it, because it's less significant. You simply don't need to be able to judge long distances, or even medium ones. This is because of the rule mentioned in Chapter 6 (Size is Everything?) when referring to explosions, that the further away something is the less important it is. The corollary to this is that the further away something is, the less important the actual distance is itself, and the less important it is to be able to measure it.

Let's look at the significance of this factor of diminishing importance with increasing distance in terms of something concrete – such as, say, sabre-toothed tigers.

Imagine at the dawn of humanity, a group of stone-age people are out hunting and gathering.

If the group were aware that there was a sabre-toothed tiger that lived some distance away, say a couple of hours' walk over a mountain pass, they'd want to know vaguely which direction it was in so that they could avoid getting too close by mistake, but that would be all, as the tiger obviously wasn't in any way a threat. If they knew that there was a tiger that lived quite close by, and that there was a likelihood of an encounter if they weren't careful, they'd want to know quite precisely which bend in the river marked the edge of its territory, and they'd make a point of not going beyond that bend. If they knew that they were inside a tiger's territory they'd want to know *exactly* which tree the tiger always lay beneath. If, heaven forfend, a tiger were to creep up unnoticed behind a bush and pounce on someone, that person would suddenly be acutely aware of the exact position of the tiger – and especially of its claws and teeth. All of a sudden an inch is the difference between life and death.

So, it turns out that it's very important to be able to judge distances accurately if they're very close to you, with the degree of accuracy getting more and more important the nearer things get. If a tiger's teeth are a few hundred yards away from you, you need to know more or less where they are – if they're inches away from you, you need to know exactly where they are. If they're twenty miles away, who cares?

So we can't accurately conceive of twenty miles, because we don't need to be able to judge such distances. A sabre-toothed tiger that's twenty miles away is an irrelevent sabre-toothed tiger: it may as well be on the Moon.

And there-in lies the reason why you find the scale of the universe ungraspable.

If we can't comprehend twenty miles what chance have we got with billions upon billions of light years?

The universe is a size that we can't conceive of because we don't need to. We find its size is mind-boggling because it's useless information.

There's good news in this realisation.

It's that anything we find mind-boggling is probably something we don't really need to know about in the first place. It turns out that mind-bogglingness isn't a sign that something's overwhelming, it's a sign that it doesn't really matter.

The cosmos is mind-blowingly enormous – that's heartening – it means that we can ignore most of it.

Mind-bogglingness is so reassuring.

Chapter 10

Never Mind the Size – Feel the Complexity

So, it seems that the reason that we can't truly (or even partly) comprehend the size of the universe is that for normal everyday purposes we don't have to. Grasping the scale of the universe is impossible because it's greater than the distance you'd expect to have to walk to find your lunch.

As a result the universe seems impressively and awe-inspiringly huge.

But size can be deceptive.

Notice that the word "huge" that I used there was preceded by the descriptive terms "impressively" and "awe-inspiringly".

This is because although we're not particularly proficient at judging sizes accurately we are certainly obsessed with using size as a yardstick for gauging the significance of things. Essentially, the bigger something is, the more important it is. You very rarely hear of anything being described as pathetically huge.

In our normal everyday world, especially in the past when everything was simpler, there was some justification for this approach, which is probably why our brains think that way.

In stone-age times the biggest sabre-toothed tiger was the most dangerous (unless it was twenty miles away of course), while the biggest woolly mammoth would feed more people.

The consequences of our attitude to size can be seen all around us at a day-to-day level. For instance, on a summer's afternoon in the garden, imagine that you're sitting relaxing with a glass of wine or fruit juice. You notice that a very small fly, perhaps a couple of millimetres long, and of indeterminate species, has rather annoyingly drowned itself in the drink. What do you do? If you're like most people, you'll fish the fly out with a finger and you'll then continue to drink your drink. However, if a large fly were to drown in your drink, what would you do? You'd throw the drink away. Is the small fly really less disease-laden than the large one? It's just as likely to have flown in straight from the same unmentionable object that's festering under the hedge.

To prehistoric people size mattered on the personal side too. The biggest man in a nomadic group was probably the strongest and was therefore most likely to be the leader of his group. Things were much more straightforward and unsophisticated back then. A small man in the group might have been the cleverest and wisest, but so what? In those days the big guy could win any argument just by caving the little guy's head in with his fist.

The world is different now of course, and intelligence is generally more useful than physical size, but we still have that fossilized imprint in our heads that big is better, messing everything up for the short guys.

The attitude that big is better isn't just a human obsession. It's relatively ubiquitous in the whole of the animal kingdom. In the world of insects there are species where the males measure up the size of potential rivals by standing head to head and checking who's got the longest antennae. Needless to say the one with the longer ones wins and the short-antennaed insect scurries away (usually without a blow being exchanged).

In the world of mammals similar things happen. Take the Irish elk, *megaloceros giganteus* (which is Latin for gigantic bighorn – these Latin names are rarely as fancy as they sound), shown in Figure 46. This was a form of giant deer that's now extinct, in which the males had unfeasibly large antlers, probably largely for the purpose of impressing the females (The antlers stuck out sideways, for maximum visual effect, and thus were probably as much ornaments for display as armaments for fighting – although their visual effect could aid rival males in the task of sizing each other up too, a little like those insects with their antennae).

Figure 46: The Irish elk with its gigantic antlers, compared to a human

The extinction of the elk used to be attributed to the fact that it was endowed with these overwhelmingly cumbersome appendages, and that the beast had therefore ceased to be able to function properly. It was thought that it probably fell victim to such silly misfortunes as becoming trapped in the middle of forests because it couldn't walk between the trees.

If you ever see an Irish elk skeleton in a museum you'll observe that the total span of the antlers is truly awesome (in fact they are so wide that it's hard to guess their span without taking a tape measure to them), and you'll think that the idea that the elk's extinction was due to these inappropriately proportioned protrusions seems entirely appropriate – it is in fact the theory that will pop into your head almost entirely unbidden when you gaze upon the creature.

Not only does the theory look right, but you really want it to *be* right too. The idea that a species could be undone by its acquisition of a feature that's a combination of ostentatious ornamentation and grossly excessive armamentation seems so much like poetic justice, and to so much parallel our own dubious grip on the priorities of life, that it's almost irresistible.

But it's wrong.

The Irish elk died out for the same reasons that most things die out, due to such causes as changes in the environment (resulting in diminished food supply and so on).

The "hoist on its own petard" theory of the elk's extinction falls neatly into the category of theories that you have to be suspicious of because of their appeal.

Even if you weren't swayed by the desire to think that the elks were the victims of their own arms race, it would still seem reasonable to assume that the huge antlers were at least a contributing factor in the elk's downfall. Jumping to this conclusion is similar to reaching the wrong conclusion in the Wason card test (on page 64). It's a good example of a case in which what seems to be the obvious answer is in fact wrong – a recurrent theme of this book.

Let's explore the subject of size further by moving away from its significance in the natural world and by having a look at it in the world of our own making – specifically in the world of electronic machines. A world in which size most definitely isn't everything.

Here, in Figure 47, are drawings of computers from different ages: an ancient one, from around 1960, and a new one, from 2009. Which one do you suppose is the better computer? Which one can do more and faster computing? Which one is the more intricate in terms of its electronics? Which one is the more *complicated*?

Figure 47: An old computer and a new computer: which one is the more powerful?

Yes, the answer's obvious: it's the little one.

The drawing above shows the difference in physical size between the two computers reasonably accurately. In contrast, in Figure 48 below I've drawn the same computers in a different way. Instead of drawing them in terms of their physical dimensions I've made their sizes reflect their relative complexity. The more modern computer is thousands of times more powerful and complicated than the older computer, so I've drawn it thousands of times bigger. (Please don't check the drawing for accuracy of scale though – it's purely illustrative.)

*Figure 48: The two computers from the previous figure
scaled by complexity rather than physical size*

Below, in Figure 49, I've used the same representational principle to compare a modern laptop computer with a pre-electronic mechanical typewriter. Physically they are about the same size, as shown in the top half of the illustration, but in terms of internal complexity they are separated by many orders of magnitude.

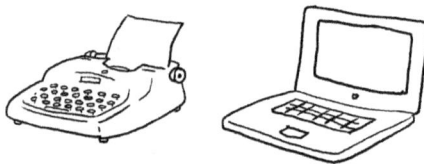

COMPARISON OF PHYSICAL SIZE

TYPEWRITER

COMPARISON OF COMPLEXITY

*Figure 49: A mechanical typewriter and a laptop
computer compared by size and complexity*

Now let's be a bit bolder and attempt to use the same technique to create a model that somehow represents the complexity not of typewriters or computers, but of the whole universe.

The complexity of the universe is essentially the sum of the complexities of all of the objects within it, so let's have a look at a few of these objects to see what we've let ourselves in for.

What do you see when you look up at the rest of the universe on a dark night?

Usually clouds if you reside in the part of the world where I live, but just occasionally, stars. Millions of them.

The universe is full of stars.

Stars: massive balls of incandescent gas heated to incredible temperatures by the energy of hydrogen atoms fusing together under the force of the stars' own gravity, creating heavier atoms in the process.

Stars are very impressive it's true, but in that last paragraph I've actually managed to describe what they are and how they function in just one sentence (I've simplified things a little of course).

There's not actually much complexity in a star when you really get down to it.

What's more, there may be untold millions of stars in the universe, but they're all doing more or less the same thing. Millions of stars all doing the same thing doesn't make those millions of stars acting together millions of times more complex. If anything it makes them more boring.

I wouldn't want to belittle the nature of stars, but you have to guard against being seduced by their seeming incredibleness. Bear in mind that just because the temperatures within stars are amazingly high doesn't make the temperatures within stars amazing in themselves – they are only incredible to us on earth because such temperatures are unusual here (and are in general inadvisable).

One more thing. Just a few paragraphs ago I said "The universe is full of stars."

That needs slightly amending. The universe is actually full of empty space, with stars popping up as ridiculously infrequent pinpoints of matter in the almost endless void. I think that it's safe to say that this endless void isn't complex (even if it turns out to be full of clouds of invisible "dark matter") and that it contributes very little to the complexity of the universe.

In fact, amazingly, there's more complexity in the short distance between your head and the words that you are reading now than there is in the space between the Earth and Proxima Centauri, the closest star to our solar system. And that's an understatement. For one thing, you've just breathed out a lung-full of viruses and bacteria, and I'm prepared to wager that there aren't many of them floating around in interstellar space.

Having done my best to deflate the importance of stars, let's move on now and look at the galaxies that contain the stars. It has to be said that galaxies look incredibly spectacular, with their swirling spiral arms spinning in space. But the underlying mechanism that generates those spirals is relatively straight-forward: in fact it's no more complex than the mechanism that makes bath water spiral down the plug-hole. Indeed the two phenomena are quite comparable (right down to the fact that in both cases the material in the spiral rotates around a black hole at the centre).

This has an interesting implication. It means that if you were to create images of a galaxy and of water going down your bath plug-hole based not on their physical size but scaled by complexity (as with the computers and typewriters above) the spiralling water in your bathtub would be the same size as a whole galaxy, at least as far as the physics behind the spiralling effect goes. Here is the result, in Figure 50.

Again, I'm oversimplifying here, for effect – but you get the idea.

Figure 50: The spiral effect of water going down the plug-hole in a bath compared to the spiral arms of a galaxy. Spot the difference

It seems as though the universe, which is essentially made up of stars and galaxies swirling around, expanding, contracting, collapsing and so on, is actually quite a simple place, contrary to what you'd think from a cursory inspection.

However, there's one thing that's floating in this vast sea of cosmic uniformity that's very, very interesting indeed. What's more, despite the fact that the universe is untold billions of light years across, you don't have to look very far to find this thing.

It's right here on Earth.

What are the chances of that!

This thing is *life*.

Life is the single most complicated phenomenon in the entire universe, by a long chalk (as far as we know).

Incredibly, the life on our planet is so varied that the

complexity of the surface of the earth is greater than that of the rest of the entire universe put together.

(Of course there could easily be life elsewhere in the universe, which would instantly confuse matters, but to keep things simple and to keep the effect dramatic, I'll only deal with the universe "as we know it". The existence of life elsewhere wouldn't significantly alter the gist of my argument anyway.)

To better appreciate the incredible complexity of life on earth let's look at a typical representative of the phenomenon. Let's look at a mouse.

A mouse is made up of chemicals that are so complicated that they don't exist anywhere else in the known universe beyond earth. These chemicals are arranged into structures that are themselves immensely complicated – legs, eyes, ears, mouth, stomach, heart, liver, lungs, tail, fur and so on. These complicated structures made out of complicated chemicals are performing incredibly complicated tasks, such as running around and eating cheese – although we often don't give them a second thought because we're so familiar with them (unlike the processes that go on inside stars for instance, which as a result we think of as being incredibly exotic).

A mouse's brain is composed of about 16 million neurons. Neurons are cells that process information. They transmit information to each other by using pathways or connections known as synapses. On average there are about 8,000 synapses per neuron. That results in approximately 136 billion (that's 136,000,000,000) synapses in total. In the brain of a mouse.

This all makes a mouse a creature of awesome complexity.

Now let's look at a galaxy by way of comparison.

Galaxies tend to contain somewhere between 10 million and a trillion stars. Our own galaxy, the Milky Way, which is actually larger than the average galaxy, has an estimated 200-400 billion stars in it. Stars are relatively simple structures, as I mentioned, collapsing in on themselves and producing a lot of heat and light in the process. That's about it.

The number of synaptic connections in a mouse's brain is up there with the number of stars in an average galaxy. If I were to include an illustration in this book comparing the complexity of a mouse with that of a galaxy the mouse would be much bigger than the whole galaxy. In fact you can easily argue that a single mouse is much more complex than a whole *cluster* of galaxies.

Bear this in mind next time you catch one in a trap.

A mouse is indeed a very impressively complex thing compared to a galaxy. In fact, we know of few things in the universe that are more complex than a mouse. We do know of some things that are though – and all of them are different life-forms living right here on our planet.

And what's the most complex life-form that's living on our incredibly complex planet?

We are.

We humans.

Where a mouse has 16 million neurons in its brain it's estimated that we have a staggering 100 billion. That's about 6,000 times more.

Not only are we more complex than mice in terms of the physical makeup of our brains, but the consequences of what we do with our brains generates further complexity still: by devising languages, composing music, building things, destroying things.

If a single mouse is more complex than a whole cluster of galaxies, just try to think how complex a single human is.

It's actually been calculated that, incredibly, the possible number of brain states, or permutations of possible activity in the human brain, is greater than the number of elementary particles in the known universe.*

Just let that sink into your unbelievably complex brain for a second before you move on. (And stop thinking "That can't be true!" I don't actually know quite what that statistic means to be honest, so I can't comment on it – but even if it's wildly inaccurate the general principle of the sheer stupendousness of the human brain is nicely expressed by it.)

Next time that you're feeling like an insignificant speck of dust in the vastness of space call to mind the fact that you yourself are more complex than the whole of the known universe that extends beyond the earth's atmosphere.

A single human brain is as complex as the rest of the cosmos – and there are six billion humans on earth, each thinking different thoughts and doing different things (up to a point). That means that the collective complexity of the human population of our planet is possibly greater than that of several million universes.

If you add together all of the life-forms on earth the complexity of our tiny planet would put the combined forces of who knows how many universes in the shade.

As a result of this, if we were to make models of the universe and the earth scaled to complexity rather than to size we end up not with a huge universe alongside an earth that's the size of a grain of sand, as is usually envisaged, but with an unbelievably immense earth compared to the rest of the universe which is the size of the grain of sand. Everything flips round.

This way of measuring things based on their complexity is not simply a mathematical diversion or meaningless but interesting exercise. It's as valid a method of measuring things as is to take a ruler to them.

---

* V. S. Ramachandran. *Phantoms in the Brain*, p 8. Fourth Estate.

NEVER MIND THE SIZE – FEEL THE COMPLEXITY

(Physical) size isn't everything.

I know that earlier I said that our insignificance in the vastness of things could be thought of as a bit of a comfort. Now I'm saying that we're the biggest thing that there is, by a very very long way. You may also like to draw comfort from this fact too.

That may sound contradictory: drawing comfort from both the fact that we're insignificant and that we're hugely significant. But personally I think that it's very healthy to hold seemingly contradictory views. It shows that you're a complex person (if you want to feel even more complex than you obviously already are, with your brain that's bigger than the universe).

You can then choose whichever status you prefer – insignificant or significant – to suit the mood that you're in at any particular moment.

If you feel the need to throw off responsibility, maybe because you've had a hard day at the office, adopt the "The universe is vast and we're tiny specks of dust" stance. On the other hand, if you need to feel more important, perhaps because you've had a hard day at the office, opt for the "We are the biggest thing in all of creation" approach.

Whatever's right for you at the time.

As you read this you may be feeling a little unsettled because you're not too keen on the idea that, measured in terms of complexity, people are the biggest thing in the known universe.

Your objection to this concept may be along the lines that it elevates the significance of we humans to what you think is a totally unacceptable level. You may be worried that if we start thinking in that way we may become too big for our boots (as if we weren't already). You may think that the whole thing smacks of supremacism on a megalomaniacal scale.

If, as a result, we indeed ended up as a species of obnoxious supremacists it would be unpalatable in the extreme. However, the inverse view of our place in the universe – that we're tiny insignificant dots – is also fraught with danger in itself. Amongst other things, it breeds insecurity. This insecurity may in turn foster aggressive overcompensation as manifested in psychological states such as the Napoleon complex. (Named after the theory that Napoleon was driven to conquer half of the known world as overcompensation for his allegedly short stature. The fact that Napoleon's height is not known precisely and may indeed have been the average height for his time is conveniently ignored. Perhaps Napoleon's real complex was that he was so average.)

Feeling that we're insignificant has another down side. It encourages us to think that because we are small and inconsequential then whatever we do to our planet is inconsequential too, allowing us to delude ourselves as to our actual significance – a sort of inversion of the Napoleon complex in fact.

If, having weighed up these considerations, you're still feeling unsettled by the whole idea of having a brain bigger than the universe, don't fret.

I have personally conducted a psychological test, selflessly using myself as the guinea pig. In the test I had a shot at wandering round thinking that my brain was bigger than the cosmos, to see how it felt, and to my surprise it didn't actually make an iota of difference. I kept forgetting the fact. Even if it *is* a fact it seems to be something that we're not psychologically equipped to hold in our heads – possibly because, amongst other things, we're all painfully aware that our brain is only a heartbeat away from being nothing more than a three pound lump of inert mush.

Part II

What Are We

?

Introduction

While you're busy staring at the vastness of the night sky, marvelling at how big the universe is and how much bigger your brain is in comparison, you'll almost inevitably find yourself asking "What's it all about? Why am I alive? What's the purpose of existence? What's the meaning of life?"

Common questions indeed.

Questions to which I have no answers.

The truth is that at our present level of knowledge it's impossible to know what the meaning of life may be, if indeed it has one at all. It's just too difficult a question to answer: so much so that pursuing it almost seems like a pointless and doomed exercise.

Or perhaps it's just too meaningless a question to answer. Which would definitely make pursuing it a pointless and doomed exercise.

However, there is a different question that we certainly can ask – one with which we might make some headway. It's a question that I first mentioned at the very beginning of this book: "Why do we want to know what the meaning of life is anyway?"

After all, you can't expect to find an answer until you know why you're asking the question in the first place (as I also mentioned at the beginning of the book).

Well, needless to say, I don't know why you're asking the question in the first place either, but here's a theory. This theory has the advantage of being very simple, which is always a good sign.

INTRODUCTION

We ask because we're innately, chronically dissatisfied.

That's basically all that there is to it. A one line answer.

The usual reasons that are put forward to explain our urge to quest, to probe and to ask questions are our high intelligence and inherent sense of curiosity, but personally I think that's an inadequate response (In fact I could say, rather appropriately, that I'm rather dissatisfied with it).

We need to ask where *those* two traits, our high intelligence and inherent curiosity, came from to begin with. The theory that I'll elaborate on in the following pages is that they developed primarily as a result of our aforementioned innate feeling of dissatisfaction.

Intelligence and curiosity aren't fundamental mental traits – they are built on a foundation of more basic qualities. Think of intelligence and curiosity as being a bit like the protons and neutrons in an atom – they are composed of something more fundamental. With protons and neutrons it's quarks (or whatever): here I'll explain how intelligence and curiosity are perhaps founded on "quarks" of dissatisfaction.

I'll delve into this topic soon, but before it's possible to talk about our feelings of dissatisfaction and where they come from it's a good idea to have an understanding of where *any* of our feelings or emotions come from.

Emotions can be defined essentially as mental states that emerge from an awareness of what's going on in the world around us.

Okay – but then you have to ask, what is this thing that I've just referred to as *awareness*? (Do you detect a strong current of regression here? If you do, you're absolutely correct.)

Let's look much more closely at what awareness might be.

We tend to think of awareness as being a form of mental state or cognitive process itself (such as when you say such things as "I'm aware that I'm thinking about this issue at the moment") but at it's most basic level awareness is simply an ability to respond to a stimulus in the environment by automatically reacting to it, with no mental input involved in the process whatsoever. This is the level of awareness that is possessed by life-forms that are totally lacking in mental faculties, such as, say, a blob of slime mould. Even the possession of mental faculties, however, doesn't necessarily turn awareness into a cognitive process, as we shall see soon.

Chapter 11

Awareness Spotting

Awareness is a property that's possessed by different living things to different extents. This fact can be observed simply by going for a nature ramble around your neighbourhood and looking at a few life-forms that you come across, where you'll see the state manifested to hugely differing degrees.

On your walk you may see a sunflower for instance, and notice that it turns its head to face the Sun (As do many types of flower, so quite why sunflowers were given the name and the reputation I'm not sure. Size I suppose). This shows that the sunflower is aware of the position of the Sun in the sky. But this is a particularly basic form of awareness, almost a sort of pseudo-awareness if you like: the plant is simply turning because of biochemical changes in its structure caused by the Sun shining on it. It's somewhat analogous to the way that a weather vane turns to point into the wind – and you'd never suggest for a moment that a weather vane was actually "aware" of the direction of the wind (I hope).

Sunflowers and other plants, being rooted to one spot, possess a rather limited repertoire of movements, and thus need to possess relatively limited amounts of awareness of what's going on around them.

Life-forms such as animals and birds – ones that are not anchored to the ground but that move around – tend to exhibit much more awareness. They need this awareness so that they can avoid bumping into things and so that they can chase food (as they can't simply sit in one spot absorbing energy from sunlight in the way that plants do). Equally, they may need to possess a degree of awareness so that they can escape when they themselves are being chased by other mobile life-forms that are seeking food.

However, in the more simple varieties of mobile life-form the level of awareness is still manifestly basic.

On your neighbourhood nature ramble you should be able to find examples of such simple mobile life-forms in a local pond, in the shape of the single-celled organisms with which it will hopefully be teaming (unless it's polluted).

These protozoans don't seem to be aware of much, although they are capable of movement. They probably propel themselves around in their aquatic environment simply by reacting to changes in their immediate surroundings. They would do this, for instance, in order to stay in a layer of water that's at the right temperature for them to survive in. Their awareness may simply be at the level that allows them to push themselves off in the appropriate direction whenever they detect something like an undesirable temperature change approaching, somewhat like animated thermostats.

There's more about this particular level of awareness later, in Chapter 13, but because unicellular pond life is quite tricky to observe (due to it being so small and living in a rather wet and smelly environment), let's move on for now and have a look at a more convenient life-form that's somewhat higher up the awareness scale. Let's look at houseflies.

You can't deny that houseflies are aware.

A housefly is very good at dodging a rolled up newspaper that's bearing down on it for instance, so it seems to be aware of the existence of newspapers and of the threat that they pose.

However, this reaction to the descending journal is very

much at the knee-jerk level. The fly doesn't in any way think, "Newspaper alert – take evasive action!" The departure of the fly from the surface on which it was settled is simply an automatic response triggered by the glimpsing of a disturbance out of the corner of its compound eye.

A fly may escape a hostile newspaper because of this automatic reaction, but this doesn't mean that the fly is aware of all dangers, as can be deduced from the following drama that can be observed on the insides of windows around the world.

You may have observed a housefly spending many hours banging its head on a closed window in a futile attempt to drill its way through it. This isn't actually the drama that I have in mind, but is often the prelude to it. (The fact that the fly gets nowhere by the action of banging against the window may indeed be evidence that the fly has rather limited awareness, due to the pointlessness of the activity, but let's be generous and put this behaviour down to the fact that a fly isn't mentally equipped to deal with new-fangled things such as glass that don't exist in the natural world, so that as a result the fly just doesn't know what to do when it comes across it.)

The drama to which I refer is the one in which the head-banging fly on the windowpane blunders into a spider's web that's slung across part of the window. Having stumbled into the web the fly will buzz around frantically in a desperate and determined bid to break free of the web's sticky strands of silk. And sometimes it'll succeed, escaping the approaching eight-legged jaws of death by a whisker. What does the fly do next? Fly off in the opposite direction to get as far away as possible from the site of its near-death experience? No. More often than not it wanders straight back into the web within seconds, and the whole drama starts over again.

The fly doesn't seem to realise that the web is a trap – all it seems to notice is that when it's in the web its movement is impaired. Thus the fly is doomed to repeat its mistake of blundering into spiders' webs for all eternity. Or until it's eaten.

The fly's awareness doesn't extend as far as traps, and indeed seems to be restricted to a very few key subjects, of which the whereabouts of its next meal and the whereabouts of its next mate seem to be high on the list. So (other than an awareness of fast moving newspapers) a fly's awareness seems to be very much on the positive things in life – food and sex. Lucky fly.

A fly's awareness of food and its motivation to eat it is probably based on the fact that the food smells and tastes really nice (The food's possibly emitting the irresistible aroma of putrefying flesh). The fly is motivated by the sensory stimulus rather than by having specific thoughts of a dietary nature – in very much the same way that people are with chocolate (Of course the fly probably "feels hungry" as well, whatever that manifests itself as in fly physiology, but it's its senses that direct it towards eating its chosen foodstuff – ensuring that it doesn't find itself trying to eat, say, grains of sand or stone in preference to the rotting innards of a dead hedgehog).

The fly's lack of awareness of the true nature of spiders' webs hasn't stopped houseflies being incredibly successful creatures however, surviving as they have done for millions of years. They have probably been so successful because their lack of awareness of spiders' webs is more than compensated for by their awareness of the whereabouts of their next meal and their next mate – enough flies manage to mate and produce offspring before they get trapped in spiders' webs to ensure the survival of the species.

Let's move on from flies and look further up the hierarchy of species to try to find something that has a more advanced sense of awareness than that possessed by the average *musca domestica*.

AWARENESS SPOTTING

Let's look at birds.

Birds definitely seem to be much more aware than the run of the mill housefly I think you'll agree. But even birds can seem to do things in rather automatic, unconsidered ways a lot of the time. Why, for instance, do birds that are sitting in the top of trees in my local park fly away when I walk underneath? Haven't they noticed that humans are slow, lumbering creatures that are practically glued to the ground? Why do these birds expend all of that energy on flight – for nothing?

They seem to be simply aware of a disturbance on the ground, so they've just flown away in default mode, without having bothered to think things through.

Birds probably fly off in this automatic mode because, as some people may say, "It works for them." For birds, caution is the watchword: it's held them in good stead since they evolved from the dinosaurs.

Birds don't seem to bother wrestling with the difficult concept of "Should I fly off or should I stay?" They generally seem to be untroubled by the notion of alternatives (As a human you may well know how stressful the awareness of too many alternatives can be. More on this later. Much more).

Let's continue our ramble and try to find a creature that seems to have some sort of grasp of alternatives, that doesn't just do things in automatic mode – that seems to be closer to what we'd really call aware in a considered/cognitive sort of way.

And there's such a creature in that tree over there!

A chimpanzee!

You can tell that a chimpanzee has quite a highly developed awareness of the world around it because it can use a stick to knock inaccessible fruit off a branch.

Tool use! Very important.

Tool use very probably indicates that a chimp has enough

awareness of the world around it to allow it to think in terms of *consequences.*

I'm not crediting the chimp with too much power of logical deduction here though. When the chimpanzee invented "the stick" it probably didn't actually look at a bunch of fruit that was out of reach and then by a leap of imagination conceive of the idea of using a wooden arm extension to reach it. The whole business was probably purely empirical, with the chimp simply noticing that sometimes when it waved a stick around the consequence was falling fruit (the stick having been accidentally "manufactured" in the first place as the consequence of breaking a branch off a tree when it was being grasped while climbing). The chimp didn't deduce that this would work as a way of obtaining fruit: it just found that it did so by chance. It didn't *imagine* what would happen – it just noted the effect once it had.

As a result of this lack of imagination the chimp seems to be capable of only conceiving of the world very much *as it is*, not as it might be. Because the chimp lacks imagination it can't conceive of things being different. Critically, it can't conceive of things being *better.* This sounds like a bit of a drawback, but in fact it means that the chimp is perfectly happy with its stick invention, basic as it may be. It does the job. It gets the fruit.

The ancestors of today's chimps came up with the idea of using sticks as tools, but further chimp generations never bothered to develop the concept of tools to the point where a chimp could construct a rocket and travel to the Moon.

Why was it that when the ancestors of we humans invented tools we didn't call it a day with the invention of the stick, but we just kept right on going, in a scarily relentless manner, to the point where we've now invented so many things that we're on the verge of destroying the planet with them? (To be truthful, once we'd invented the stick, the spear and the axe we had a break from inventing things for an extremely long period of time. The reason for this invention interlude is unknown. However, once it was over we certainly made up for lost time.)

To answer the question of why we just kept on inventing things we need to look deeper into the nature of awareness.

In this chapter I've described a few examples of different degrees of awareness as possessed by various life-forms – the biomechanical rotation of the sunflower as it follows the Sun, the knee-jerk reaction of a fly to an approaching newspaper, the automatic flight of a bird in response to a passing pedestrian, and the more considered use of a stick by a chimp. These examples show various levels at which awareness manifests itself – but where did *any* of these levels of awareness come from in the first place?

I realise that I haven't explained what awareness actually *is* yet.

To try to find out we need to go right back to the very, very beginning of life on earth.

Chapter 12

The Nature of Evolution

Life-forms developed the capability of being aware of the world around them in exactly the same way that they developed any other feature, such as legs and eyes (if they were animals) or leaves and roots (if they were plants) – by the process of evolution.

Evolution is the dynamic by which gradual changes occur in a species over a period of time to the benefit of the survival of the species. No feature of a species, whether physical or mental, can simply pop into existence out of nowhere, fully formed and ready for action.

The way that evolution operates is sometimes grossly misunderstood, so just to make sure that we're talking the same language here's a very quick run down of how it works (It's a surprisingly simple process).

Firstly, let's get one common misconception out of the way. There's a widespread belief that evolution is some sort of deliberate, almost conscious, process or force moving towards a predetermined goal – that birds for instance knowingly developed wings because they fancied doing a spot of flying.

This isn't the case.

You'd be forgiven for thinking that it *was* the case by the fact that whenever the process of evolution is talked about, even by experts, it's very common for verbs of choice or deliberation to be used, as in phrases such as "Evolution chooses the characteristics that are to be passed on to the next generation."

This doesn't mean that evolution purposefully makes a choice by conscious reflection, in the way that you and I make choices. It's a much more inert use of the verb *to choose* – think of it more like the way that we say that a river chooses its route to the sea. Rivers obviously have no say whatsoever in deciding their courses – the flow of their water is simply channelled down the steepest available gradients of the landscape. Indeed it may be a good idea to ditch the concept of choice when it comes to evolution, and to borrow from the river metaphor instead – to say that evolution is *channelled* along the route that it takes (dependant on the ecological "landscape" that's around it at the time).

Here's how this channelling takes place.

When a creature has offspring, those offspring all vary very slightly in quite random ways, such as by being slightly different colours, different sizes and so on. Some of these offspring, purely by chance, will be better suited for survival in their particular environment. For instance, by being a different colour they may blend in with their surroundings better and thus be less likely to be seen, and then eaten, by a predator. These offspring will thus be more likely to survive and have their own offspring – which will on average have inherited the same fortunate variation that improved the survival chances of the parent. Thus the trait will be passed on to further generations.

This process by which such random advantageous characteristics are passed on from generation to generation is known as *natural selection*.

(Charles Darwin, who coined the phrase natural selection, was actually slightly unhappy with the term, as he felt that some people may think that it implied deliberate, conscious selection rather than the purely automatic process that he intended. How right he was.)

THE NATURE OF EVOLUTION

Let's look at a few examples of the process in action to get a better idea of how it works.

Imagine an animal that lives in a very cool, though not freezing cold, sub-Arctic climate. Say a type of fox.

The climate's pretty nippy, but the fox has fur, so it survives quite comfortably.

Gradually, over a very long period of time (quite a few fox generations) the climate changes as the earth moves into one of its periodic ice ages. The fox's world gets noticeably colder and harsher.

Amazingly, as the climate gradually cools, successive generations of fox are seen to sport longer and thicker fur that helps to keep them warm. The foxes' coats get longer almost in step with the cooling climate. This looks very much as though the foxes have decided to grow more fur to suit the new conditions.

But it isn't so.

Here's what really happens.

Whenever a fox has a litter of cubs each cub will inevitably be physically slightly different from the others. Some will be larger, some smaller, some stronger, some weaker, some darker, some lighter, some more furry, some less furry, and so on.

Imagine that a pair of foxes has a litter of three cubs: one that's more furry than its parents, one with the same amount of fur as its parents, and one with less fur than its parents. On average, that's exactly the fur-length distribution that you'd get in a typical sample of three fox cubs.

These three cubs are born into a world that's slightly colder than the one that their parents were born into. The cub that has less fur than its parents finds the conditions too harsh, and dies of hypothermia. The other two cubs survive. However the cub that has the same amount of fur as its parents finds the going tough in the cold, so it grows up to be a less than perfectly healthy specimen within foxdom. The third cub – the one with the most fur – survives quite well because it is adequately insulated from the cold. This cub grows and thrives. It mates with another fox that has thrived (which quite probably also had slightly more fur than its parents). The resulting cubs produced by this coupling will have similar traits to their parents – though as usual with minor variations, including a variation in the density of their fur. Imagine that this pair had a litter of three cubs, just as described for the parents above: one that's more furry than its parents, one with the same amount of fur as its parents, and one with less fur than its parents.

If these cubs were born into a world that was continuing to cool down the cub that would be most likely to survive would be the one with the thickest fur. This cub is slightly more furry than its parents, and is noticeably more furry than its grandparents. So it is, that if the furriest offspring of each generation are the ones that survive, the whole species becomes more furry in small steps.

It's important to realise that the survival of any individual fox is purely the luck of whether or not its characteristics mesh well with the prevailing conditions. I have just described the scenario in which the fox cub with the thickest fur survived as the climate cooled: however if exactly the same three cubs had been born at a time when the climate was *warming up* instead, the fox cub with the *least* fur would have been the most likely one to have survived (as its more thickly furred siblings would have found their own stifling coats a hindrance, just as you yourself find a thick coat a burden on a hot day).

In the example above the reason that the foxes evolved to have a different thickness of fur was a change in the climate. Climatic challenges such as this are however just one of the pressures on creatures that results in their changing or evolving. Another pressure is the threat posed by other creatures that want to make a meal of them.

The advisability of avoiding being eaten was the pressure that, amongst other things, made some creatures develop colouring and patterns that serve to make them merge into their backgrounds, effectively camouflaging them (as I mentioned briefly above). Figure 51 shows a moth that merges with the bark of a tree so well that you can hardly notice it (I know this photo is reproduced in shades of gray, but believe me, the effect is practically the same in the colour version, which is essentially the same but in shades of brown).

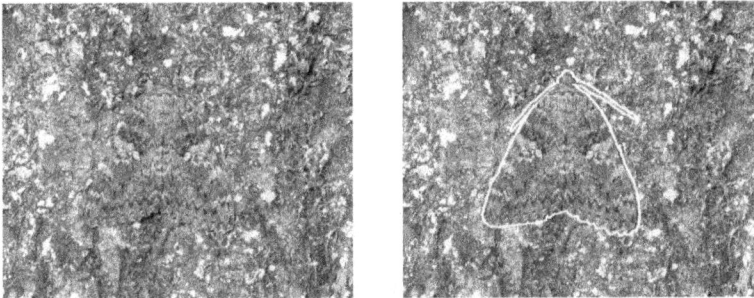

Figure 51: Left: a moth camouflaged on a tree trunk.
Right: The moth outlined

How is it possible for such an incredible congruity of colouring to come about?

Figure 52 on the following page shows a representation of two moths resting on the bark of a tree. The moths are both the same colour and are slightly lighter than the bark, allowing you to see them. The moths aren't particularly well camouflaged, but fortunately they survive long enough to mate and lay eggs, which eventually turn into more moths.

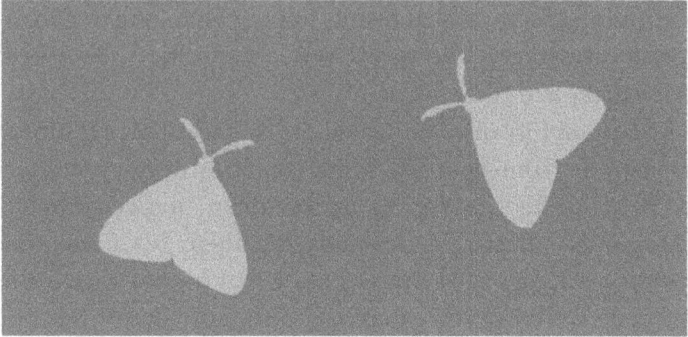

Figure 52: A representation of two moths on a tree trunk

As with almost all of nature, each of these resulting sibling moths is physically slightly different due to genetic variations. Some are larger, some are smaller, some have longer antennae, some have shorter antennae and so on. Some of them are slightly different colours. Of the parent moths' many offspring let's pick three that are different colours, as shown in Figure 53, and look at them more closely.

Figure 53: Three sibling moths on the tree trunk. Each moth is a slightly different colour

The centre moth of the chosen three is exactly the same colour as the parent moths, while one is slightly lighter and the other is slightly darker.

These moths spend most of their time resting on the bark of trees that are the same as the one that their parents rested on, with bark of the same colour. Because each of the moths is a slightly different colour some are easier to see on the tree bark than others.

Unfortunately, the easier it is for a moth to be seen, the more likely it is to be eaten by a passing predator that's on the lookout for a meal. If a moth is eaten by a predator before it manages to breed its characteristics aren't passed on to the next generation of moths. In the figure above it's a fair bet that the moth on the left, the lightest one, would be the most likely to be seen, as it is noticeably lighter than the background on which it sits, and is therefore the most likely to be picked off by a predator. The middle moth (which is the same colour as its parents) is also quite light, and thus has more than a passing chance of becoming a predator's meal at some point, but it might make it to mating age if it's lucky (as its parents were).

The right hand, darkest moth from the trio is more likely to go undetected by predators because it's closer in colour to the tree bark, and thus it's got a much greater chance of surviving long enough to breed.

The offspring of this darker moth will tend to inherit the moth's characteristics, so they will tend to be slightly darker than the average of the parent's generation. Figure 54 shows a small representative sample of the offspring of this moth, all sitting on the bark of the same tree. You may notice that on average they are closer in colour to the tree bark than the moths that featured in Figure 53 above, because their parent was closer to the colour of the tree bark. But they nevertheless vary in colour. Some of the offspring are lighter than the parent, others are the same colour as the parent and others are darker.

Figure 54: Some of the offspring of the darkest moth from the previous figure

As in the previous figure, one of the offspring in this figure is less likely to be eaten by predators than the others.

Imagine that you are a predator that eats moths (perhaps a bird of some kind, or a small child) – which one of the moths in this figure do you think you'd be least likely to notice (and thus least likely to eat)?

It's not too difficult to decide: the moth that you'd be least likely to eat, and which thus would be the most likely to survive and have offspring, is – yes – the *middle* one.

You may now be asking "What does he mean, the middle one? There is no middle one."

But that's where you're wrong: there is indeed a middle one, as you can see if you look at Figure 55 on the next page.

This is the same figure as the previous one, except that it's had the colour of the tree bark removed.

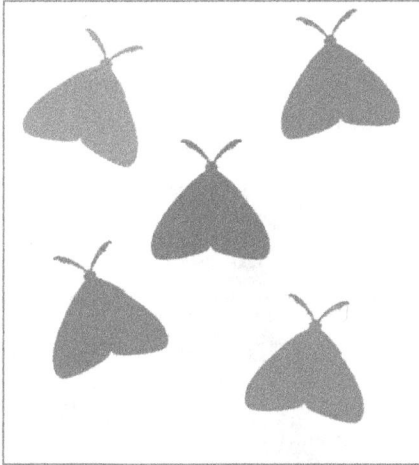

Figure 55: The moths from Figure 54, with the tree bark removed

The reason you didn't realise that there was a middle moth was because it is *exactly* the same colour as the tree bark on which it's resting. You overlooked it for the same reason that a predator would have overlooked it too.

Because of the fact that this moth is much less likely to be eaten by a predator than its siblings it's much more likely to survive and to breed, producing offspring that are likely to be a similar colour to itself (though, as always, not all identical).

A sample of the offspring of this moth are shown in Figure 56. As you can see, although the average colour is the same as that of the parent (the centre, invisible offspring), some are lighter and some are darker. As in the previous examples, the lighter moths are visible against the tree bark and are thus likely to be predated. But now the darker offspring are darker than the tree bark, and are thus also visible – and are therefore likely to be predated too. Once the moths' colour matches that of the tree bark it's no longer an advantage to be darker than your siblings: a state of equilibrium is arrived at, where variation in either direction is a handicap. As a result the moth species stablises at the colour of the tree bark.

Figure 56: When the average colour of the moths is the same as that of the tree trunk it's no longer an advantage to be darker. (Notice the tree-coloured moth in the centre.)

So it is that the characteristic of camouflage that the moths exhibit is arrived at purely as a result of normal variations in colouring between offspring.

This is a nice example of natural selection at work because in one way the moth that is most likely to survive to breed another day is specifically the moth that is *not* deliberately selected for anything (In this case not being selected to be a meal for a predator). The reason that the predator doesn't select this moth is exactly the same reason that you didn't select it when I asked you to pick the most likely contender for survival in Figure 54. How could you (or the predator) select something when you didn't know that it was there? (If you did select the middle moth in Figure 54, perhaps because you saw through my ploy, you're cleverer than the average predator.) The same applies to the moth in the centre of Figure 55.

This process of not selecting something because you don't know that it's there will come up again later in the book, in significantly different circumstances.

You can see from this process that the moths don't deliberately choose their colour so that they are camouflaged. In fact it's quite possible to imagine a species of moth in which the moths are blind (perhaps finding their way around by using some sense other than vision, such as echo-location or smell) and that are thus totally unaware of their own colouration – yet they could still evolve perfect visual camouflage in exactly the same way, due to the fact that predators would eat the least well camouflaged specimens.

Although evolution is normally thought of as being a glacially slow process, with small changes in the features of creatures accreting over vast tracts of time, you can actually see the process of natural selection at work with your own eyes if you look in the right places.

An example involving the colour of moths, as described above, was famously observed in the industrial north of England in the mid twentieth century. Before the 1950s there was a lot of air pollution in the region that made the trunks of trees very dark with grime. A species of moth, the peppered moth, lived on these trees. The moths were dark and were very effectively camouflaged, matching the grimy bark on the trees perfectly, making them difficult for birds and other predators to detect.

During the 1950s the air pollution in the area dropped due to changes in industrial practice and the grime on the trees disappeared, making the trees lighter in colour. This made the dark peppered moths stand out against the trees. Within a few years all of the peppered moths that lived on the trees were lighter in colour, perfectly matching the newly pristine bark.

(This example of evolution in action fell into disrepute in 1999, due to a reported inaccuracy in the data collecting method of the research. The research was discredited to the extent that it was even dropped from school textbooks. However the reported flaws in the methodology were gross exaggerations by interested parties, and the accusation of inaccuracy has since been rescinded. The research, which was carried out by Bernard Kettlewell, was indeed valid.)

A few years ago I was reminded of the evolutionary dynamic that was at work with these moths when I observed a similar process at work in my garden pond. While peering into the water I observed part of the same plot being acted out, except that in this case the players were fish.

The pond at one time had five small ornamental carp in it. They were all exactly the same in every way, except that four were golden in colour (large goldfish in fact), while the fifth was almost black.

A few months after the fish had been introduced to the pond I realised that one of the goldfish was missing: a heron or other bird had perhaps taken it as a meal.

Within weeks there was not a single fish to be seen in the pond. The bird that had taken the first fish had probably been back for the rest.

I thought no more on the matter until many months later, when one particularly sunny and warm day I sat by the pond side and relaxed by gazing down at the now fish-free water.

Suddenly, a movement in the rather dark water caught my eye, and to my surprise I saw the black fish swimming just below the water's surface.

This dark fish had survived for months, avoiding detection by predatory birds (and by me). It had remained unnoticed while its showy golden relatives had been plucked from the water one by one, betrayed by the glint of light on their bright scales.

If there had been a male and a female dark fish in my pond, along with male and female gold fish – allowing breeding to take place – the pond would eventually have become stocked with nothing but dark fish, with no golden ones at all.

(Brightly coloured goldfish do not exist in the wild, because they would instantly become meals for predators. They are the result of selective breeding by man, in unnatural environments. Normal wild carp have a tendency to have a few golden scales amongst their usual duller ones, and it was as a result of people deliberately choosing to breed from the fish that had the most golden scales that goldfish arose. The process could be termed evolution by unnatural selection.)

I hope that's quashed any ideas about the deliberateness of the process of evolution.

There's another aspect of evolution that's frequently misunderstood too. This particular misunderstanding revolves around the phrase "the survival of the fittest" – a phrase coined by the nineteenth century philosopher Herbert Spencer. This phrase is often misinterpreted as meaning "survival of the strongest", while in fact it more accurately means "survival of the most appropriate", as the word "fittest" in this context means "most fitting". You just have to look at the cases of the moth and the fish above to see this point perfectly illustrated: the members of the species that survived did so because of a quality that was nothing to do with physical strength at all – colour variation.

In fact it's easy to imagine scenarios in which supposedly "superior" physical qualities such as greater strength or size can actually be a handicap.

Imagine, for instance, two penguins walking across very thin ice. One penguin is big and strong, while the other is smaller and altogether weedier. Which penguin is most likely to make the ice break under its weight, thus falling through into the sea below and ending up in the jaws of a leopard seal or killer whale? Yes, the big strong one. In this case survival of the lightest would be an appropriate phrase.

Thus it is that not all creatures are big and strong like lions, but some are small, light and relatively weedy like mice.

So there you are. That's how evolution works, in a very small nutshell.

That explains briefly how evolution can account for the physical features of living things, such as their colour, size and so on. But how can the process of evolution explain the existence of non-physical qualities such as the one that we're concerned with now – awareness?

Here, in the next chapter, is a possible route.

Chapter 13

One Dawn after Another

The Dawn of Awareness

As I mentioned earlier, awareness is similar to other features of living things (such as legs, arms, leaves, wings, roots or teeth) in that it evolves in stages over time, becoming more complex with the passing generations.

As I also mentioned earlier, different life-forms exhibit different degrees of the quality – such as the sunflower with its basic awareness of the position of Sun and the chimpanzee with its more sophisticated awareness of the usefulness of sticks. And then of course there's us, with our ridiculously highly developed sense of awareness.

All forms of life sit at their own specific points along a scale of awareness levels, starting at zero awareness (for a blob of inert chemicals), passing upwards through intermediate levels for protozoa, sunflowers, houseflies, birds, chimpanzees and so on, and ending, for our purposes here, with us (The spectrum of awareness levels may well extend into invisible zones that are beyond our comprehension, analogous to the way that the visible spectrum does, but by definition we can't actually be *aware* of those zones).

To study this spectrum of degrees of awareness, let's start by considering how the very *lowest* level of awareness may have come into existence to begin with – the foundation on which the whole edifice of awareness is built.

Let's go back three or four billion years, to a time when life on Earth was just starting to develop.

Exactly how life came into being is shrouded in mystery, as you'd probably expect, but that hasn't stopped people coming up with numerous theories on the matter.

A common thread in the more sensible of the theories is that life started in water.

The theories often go like this.

In the time immediately before life started there was possibly a bringing together of complex chemicals (such as amino acids) in certain localised bodies of water, forming concentrations of these chemicals in relatively small areas. This was the natural consequence of normal physical processes – for instance seawater may have gathered in shallow coastal regions and evaporated, creating abnormally high concentrations of chemicals in the water that remained in small rock pools. These concentrations of complex chemicals were then in a propitious position for being acted upon and altered (and thus made more complex still) by a source of energy such as sunlight, or possibly lightning.*

It's possible that as a result of their chemical makeup these concentrations of complex chemicals may have formed into small roundish masses or globules. It's then quite possible that the outer surfaces of these globules became more solid than their interiors (due to some normal chemical processes, analogous to the way that a crust forms on cooling lava or the film of ice forms on freezing water). As a result the globules would have formed membrane-like shells, holding the contents

---

* A more recent theory is that life may have started deep in the oceans in the regions round hydrothermal vents - fissures in the ocean floor that emit chemical-rich water that's been heated deep within the earth. These fissures were only discovered towards the end of the twentieth century.

of the globule in a secure package. These globules were the precursors to the living cell.

Over time, and aided by the heat in the water around them, the trapped chemicals within the membranes of these cell-like globules would have reacted with each other to produce the antecedents of the proteins and nucleic acids that are found in modern cells. They would also have begun to interact in a way that caused the individual globules to split into two (or more) separate globules.

The fact that these globules could split into more globules meant, in other words, that they were *self-replicating*. This ability to self-replicate is one of the most fundamental and important features of living things. The globules fulfilled the most basic criterion of being alive. They had become primitive living cells.

The chemical composition within the cells was intimately locked onto the structure of the longest nucleic acid molecule within the cell. In these early cells this molecule was probably RNA (ribonucleic acid), which is related to the DNA (deoxyribonucleic acid) that is found in all living cells today.

Whenever one of these cells split into separate cells each new cell was almost identical – but not quite. The imperfection of the split meant that the nucleic acid in each cell, and thus the whole chemical makeup of each cell, was very slightly different.

This difference between the cells – this imperfection – meant that different cells would react ever so slightly differently to their surroundings, as I'll illustrate in a moment. This, in turn, meant that the cells could, through successive splitting, develop more complexity, resulting in more complex life-forms.

You may have noticed that in the description that I've just given, the origins of life are brought about by nothing more than an amalgamation of appropriate chemicals and a heat source such as the Sun. There was no special "spark" or "life force" that was somehow brought into being at one significant instant, or that was mysteriously injected into the chemicals involved. The only thing that happened was that clusters of complex chemicals split and formed other, slightly different and more complex clusters of chemicals. Quite boring really.

A crucial element in the development of these simple cells on their extremely long haul to become complex life-forms was the emergence of the capability to react to the environment that was around them.

Let's see how that may have come about.

(The exact scenario painted here is necessarily speculative, as no-one knows much about the conditions of early life on Earth. However, that isn't a great handicap, as the description here should be treated simply as a model, used mainly to illustrate the general dynamics and interrelationships of the processes that may have occurred. They can easily be transferred to a different setting or stage.)

Imagine a pool of water containing some of the single-celled living organisms just described – the earliest and most primitive of life-forms – life-forms that are indeed only just on the right side of the definition of what it is to be alive. These cells are all the result of the splitting, over time, of a single common ancestor. As a result they are all very similar to each other apart from the minor inevitable variations that are the result of the inherent inaccuracies of the splitting process.

For the single-celled organisms to be able to survive in the pool, the water in which they float needs to be warm. This is because the living cells need energy that they can absorb in order to split or replicate. However the water mustn't be *too* warm or the chemicals within the cells will become too jumbled up to react in this way. For similar reasons, the water mustn't be too cool either. The water must therefore be within a very particular temperature range.

Here in Figure 57 are the single-celled organisms in the pool of water (I've made the organisms look quite large purely so that they can be seen easily in the illustration).

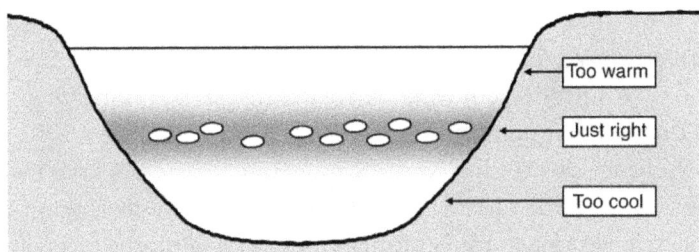

Figure 57: Single-celled organisms floating in a layer of water that's at the correct temperature for their survival

Imagine that the water in the pool is heated by the Sun. The Sun heats the water at the surface more than the deeper water, so the water gets progressively cooler with depth. This change of temperature is known as a temperature gradient.

Our single-celled organisms have to be at just the right temperature in order to survive – if they are too warm or too cold their chemicals will be adversely affected and they will not be able to maintain their integrity – in other words, they will die.

Between the top of the pond, which is too hot, and the bottom of the pond, which is too cold, is a layer of water that's at just the right temperature for the organisms to survive. You can see all of the cells floating in the layer (which I've shaded gray).

It's tempting to imagine that the cells sensed that the water in this layer was at just the correct temperature for their survival and that they therefore chose to float in that particular layer.

However, that's not the case.

These are *very* primitive single-celled organisms remember, and they have absolutely no senses whatsoever with which to notice the world around them. As a result they wouldn't have the ability to detect the temperature of the water.

The organisms do not know – in any possible sense of the word "know" – what the water's temperature is. Indeed they do not know that they are floating in water to begin with. They do not know *anything*.

So how did they come to be suspended in the water that's at just the right temperature?

Before we answer that specific question we need to know why they are suspended in the water at all, rather than floating on the surface or sinking to the bottom, which is what most things do.

The cells are suspended in the water because they happen to have the correct degree of *buoyancy* to make them do so.

What exactly is buoyancy?

Archimedes, mentioned earlier, gave us the answer. When an object is placed in water it tends to float or sink. If the density of the object is less than that of water it floats (An object that's less dense than water is one that weighs less than an equal volume of water – so for instance, if a two inch cube of a material weighs less than a two inch cube of water the material will float). If the object's density is greater than that of water it sinks.

If an object is *exactly* the same density as that of water it will neither float nor sink, but will remain suspended in the water at whatever depth it happen to be at. This state of equilibrium is known as neutral buoyancy. (Humans are almost at neutral buoyancy in water, especially salt water, which is why we hover between floating and sinking when we're swimming.)

The cells in our pool are at neutral buoyancy, so as a result they are suspended, neither rising up to the surface nor sinking down to the bottom.

How come they just happen to be of a density that affords them neutral buoyancy?

Pure chance?

Not really.

Due to natural random variations on replication, cells would be created at a variety of densities, and thus with different buoyancies. The less dense cells would float upwards to the surface of the water, while the more dense cells would drift downwards to the bottom. In both cases the cells would find themselves in water that was of the wrong temperature for them to function properly, and they would effectively "die" (I'm using the term die in a very loose sense here, due to the fact that, as I've emphasized, the cells only just scrape through the most basic definition of being alive to begin with. It's probably more accurate to say that they enter a state of inertness).

As a result, only cells that happened to have the correct density to achieve neutral buoyancy would survive.

I mentioned that objects that are the same density as a liquid, and thus are at neutral buoyancy, can remain suspended at whatever level in the liquid they happen to find themselves.* However, the cells in the previous illustration, Figure 57, are all at the *same* level in the liquid. How can this be?

This is because although the neutrally buoyant cells can be suspended at any level within the water those that are at levels that are outside the "just right" layer will be either too warm or too cold for their chemical contents to replicate themselves (Figure 58). As a result the cells in the too warm and too cool zones will not multiply and will probably have their chemicals

---

* If the density of the liquid changes significantly with depth for some reason the objects will remain suspended at specific depths, however this doesn't affect the general dynamic described in my example.

jiggled around so that they will die (or become inert if you prefer).

The only cells that can replicate are the ones that happen to be in the just right zone.

(The dynamic involved is a little like the one I described earlier involving moths, where only those moths that happened to be the same colour as the tree bark survived. In the moths' case the agent that killed the unsuitably coloured moths was a predator, while with the cells the agent that killed the unsuitably buoyant cells was temperature.)

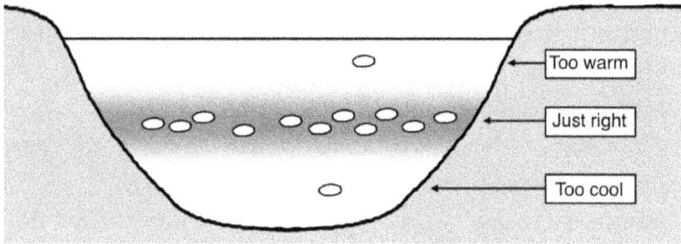

Figure 58: Some cells will be suspended at different levels in the water, but will be at levels at which they will die (or at least become non-functional and non-self-replicating)

So it is that the living cells are found in the layer of water that's at the correct temperature – not because the cells chose the layer but because that's where they just happened to be, in the layer in which they wouldn't die.

When the cells in the just right layer replicate some of the resulting cells would be of different densities, due to random variation, and would drift up towards the surface of the water or down to the bottom, thus exiting the just right zone. These cells would find themselves in water of the wrong temperature and would die.

Cells that remained within the just right zone would survive and would replicate further, with the result being that the just right layer of water would find itself teaming with single-celled organisms, while the rest of the water, being either too warm or too cold, would remain barren and devoid of life, although not devoid of non-functional, non-replicating "corpses".

Thus it is that slight variations in the characteristics of an organism (in this case its buoyancy) may mean either functionality or non-functionality – life or death.

The scenario painted here is fine as far as it goes, with its simple pool of water in which the liquid remains within a stable and acceptable temperature range for the cells to survive. But nothing in nature is static, so the pool in my illustration would not remain stable and acceptable for long.

Forces such as convection currents caused by the Sun heating the water would cause disturbances and would move some of the cells that existed in the habitable zone up or down towards the uninhabitable regions. Some of these cells would inevitably enter the hostile regions and would die.

However, some of the cells that drifted towards the hostile zones may not die – due to fortuitous variations in their makeup caused as an inevitable result of the normal, inherently imperfect replication of the cells.

Imagine the following cell for instance – a particular cell that reacted in a specific way to temperature change.

This particular cell had a slightly different composition to the other cells – a composition that made it react to warmth by partly shrinking or shrivelling up (perhaps by expelling some of the water that was inside it).

When this cell was carried upwards towards the region of warm water (perhaps caught in a convection current that swept it in that direction) it would shrink.

Once it had shrunk the cell would be slightly smaller and denser than it had been previously. This would make it less buoyant, which would stop it rising upwards and would make it drop back deeper into the water – taking it back down into the habitable layer.

As the cell cooled slightly on re-entering the cooler habitable zone it would expand slightly and revert to the state that it was in before it was swept upwards. Its original neutral buoyancy would thus be restored and it would once again reach a state of suspended equilibrium in the water, neither floating upwards nor sinking downwards.

If we'd been on the scene to observe this action we'd have observed the cell drifting upwards towards the danger zone, stopping near the edge and returning to the safety of the habitable zone.

This would look very much as though the cell could sense the unwelcome temperature change as it drifted towards the warm water, and that it had *chosen* to return to the just right zone. But this isn't the case at all. The cell changed direction purely because its size had changed (thus making the cell denser and less buoyant) – and this size change was a simple physical process. The cell was in fact functioning like nothing more than a primitive, organic thermostat.

This property of the cell – of changing size (and thus buoyancy) as the temperature changed – is a definite advantage, making the cell much more likely to survive, and as a result multiply. The cell's offspring would tend to inherit this tendency to change size (and thus buoyancy), subject to the usual minor variations due to the imperfection of replication, and the trait would thus become an integral quality of the new improved, upgraded organism.

It's important to remember that, due to the random variations in offspring that occurs when cells divide, a cell wouldn't necessarily only create offspring that fortuitously *shrank* as they approached the warm water layer (and thus sank back into the "just right" layer), it may also create offspring that *expanded* as they approached the warm water, due to their slightly different internal chemical composition. These cells would thus become *more* buoyant as they floated upwards into the hostile zone and would therefore rise even further into the warm water rather than dropping back to safety. As a result they would perish – making it impossible for them to pass their rather unfortunate characteristic on to future generations.

Such is the way that random characteristics can turn out to be a help or a hindrance, with only the helpful ones surviving to replicate another day. (Again, this is a dynamic that was described earlier, in relation to the thickness of fur on a fox and the colour of a moth: some foxes were unluckily born with thin fur that made them more susceptible to the cold, and some moths were born with lighter colours that made them stand out more on the tree bark.)

Over time, successive generations of the simple single-celled organisms would acquire further characteristics due to the random variations that occurred on replication.

These characteristics would make the cells react to their environments in ever more complex ways. I'll just quickly describe a few of these now. (If you read that sentence and thought "That sounds a bit tedious," fight that feeling, because this is important. It's all about the creation of the blueprints for how we, at our position at the opposite end of the evolutionary scale, still act.)

One of the ways in which the cells may have reacted to their environments in ever more complex ways may have been that they became so sensitive to variations in the temperature of the water around them that they reacted by different amounts when one side of the cell was at a slightly different temperature to the other side (Figure 59).

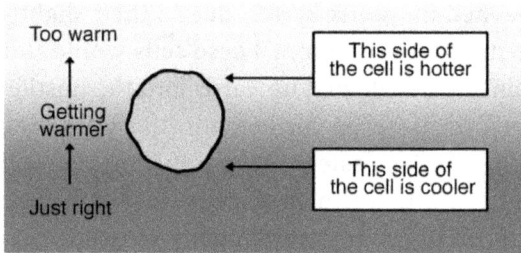

Figure 59: The chemicals in a cell may be sensitive enough to react differently to different temperatures on opposite sides of the cell

The reaction involved could be that the cells changed shape in some way, more on one side than the other (such as by expanding on the warmer side), or maybe the reaction could be that the cells ejected water or chemicals through their surface as they warmed up, with more being ejected from the warmer side than the cooler.

The difference in the extent of the reaction on either side of the cell may have the interesting side effect of making the cell move within the water. This is easiest to imagine in the scenario in which one side of the cell ejects more water or chemicals than the other side. Imagine a cell warming up, and as a consequence water inside it starting to seep through the outer membrane of the cell. More water will seep through the side of the cell that is warmest, and as a result a sort of low grade "jet propulsion" would make the cell drift in the direction opposite to that of the ejected water.

This could have interesting consequences.

It may mean that when a cell was in a region of water at the boundary of its safety zone, where the water was getting too hot on one side, the cell may react to the variation in temperature by moving back into its safety zone.

In this way the organism moves in an advantageous direction. It will have gained the power of what you may call self-propelled movement. But again, as with the movements illustrated previously due to buoyancy changes (in which the cell drifted up or down in the water as its density changed), this motion is instigated purely as a physical reaction to an outside stimulus – the cell is not sensing the temperature of the water around it and then making a choice about moving.

This is made evident, if evidence were needed, by the fact that other cells may just as easily develop a similar method of propulsion but in the *opposite* direction – the direction that's towards the water that's the wrong temperature rather than away from it. As a result, they would perish.

The actual method by which the cell attains movement is not important in itself, the only thing that matters is that it does so. My example of a jet-propelled cell is perhaps rather fanciful, however for the sake of illustration it's somewhat easier to follow than examples involving convoluted changes of cell shape that allow the cells to "ooze" through the water.

Self-propelled movement is definitely an advantage, provided it's in the correct direction, so organisms with this trait would prosper. Self-propelled movement in the wrong direction would mean certain death, so this trait would lead nowhere.

The cells described in the scenarios above definitely react to their environment. This, in the loosest sense of the word, makes them in some way "aware". Their reaction is, however, at the very bottom of the scale of awareness: at the level of automatic reaction at a chemical or mechanical level to outside forces. At this level, although the cells react to their surroundings it can't be said in any meaningful way that they actually *sense* their surroundings.

The Dawn of Repulsion

Notice that in all of the examples that I gave above the organisms involved survive by being capable of staying exclusively within the "just right" temperature zone. They have to be inside this zone to start with (as otherwise they'd be dead), and to stay within the zone they need to be capable of moving *away* from environments that are not conducive to their survival should they start drifting in those directions. They don't survive by having to move *towards* the just right environment (as they are in it already). They in fact exhibit *repulsion* from the danger zones that surround them, which has the happy effect of keeping them safely corralled inside their habitable zone. They specifically don't exhibit *attraction* towards the habitable zone.

Maybe you're thinking "If this organism is exhibiting repulsion from the hostile zone, isn't that the same as exhibiting attraction to the habitable zone? It's simply a different perspective – a different way of looking at it."

Not quite. This is because the phenomena of repulsion and attraction have separate, independent existences. Although they are opposites in meaning they aren't opposites in the sense of being an inseparable pair that must exist together at all times (as is the case with such yoked pairs as top and bottom).

So it was that in this early world of single-celled organisms only repulsion existed. Attraction was nowhere on the horizon. This is important, and will be a recurring theme in this story.

Repulsion sounds as though it has the quality of awareness shackled to it somewhere (as in when I exhibit repulsion whenever I tread on a slug), but again, in the case of these single-celled organisms the awareness that's exhibited is at the most basic level. The sort of repulsion involved here is very much of the mechanical type – analogous to way that the same poles of two magnets repel each other or the way that water and oil repel each other if you mix them. The only difference is that in the case of the cells it's being applied to things that have the ability to replicate, and that are thus, at the most basic of levels, alive.

The Dawn of Attraction

In my description so far the only reactions that have taken place for our single-celled organisms are repulsions – because the organisms involved only needed to avoid entering hostile zones (as they inhabited the just right zone already).

This limited degree of reaction was fine as far as it went, keeping the organisms safely contained in their environmental niche. As long as the environment remained reasonably stable the organisms could exist indefinitely.

But of course things change.

It's at this point that the quality of attraction may have come on the scene, to join its relative (though not its yoked opposite), repulsion.

Here's a description of the sort of route by which this may have happened. (Once again, the scene painted below is not meant to be a description of what actually happened. It is a deliberately oversimplified scenario that is advanced purely to describe the sort of underlying dynamic that may have been in operation – the actual engine that was driving that dynamic could quite possibly have been something totally different, and would inevitably have been more complicated.)

WHAT ARE WE?

Let's return to the layer of just right water that we've been contemplating so far.

Time has passed and the layer would be teaming with life, because the cells in it were thriving in the perfect conditions. The organisms may be moving around a little, using the power of movement that they'd developed, as described previously, that allows them to automatically stay in their comfort zone should they drift towards the edges. The movement of the organisms would result in the water being agitated slightly, sending vibrations out through it.

These vibrations in the water would physically affect the organisms: the vibrations after all are just molecules of water moving, so these molecules of moving water would be hitting the organisms' outer membranes and making these membranes vibrate a little themselves.

You can see in Figure 60 that any organisms that were on the outer edge of the mass of organisms and that were thus closer to the hostile zone would experience fewer vibrations coming from the side that was towards the hostile zone than the other sides, because there would be fewer (or no) organisms in that direction agitating the water, due to the fact that the hostile zone is devoid of organisms (other than dead ones).

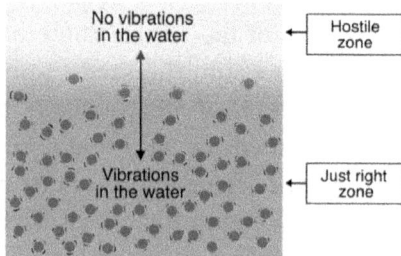

Figure 60: The movement of the organisms in the water set up vibrations in the water

This unequal amount of vibration near the edge of the habitable zone may make an organism that happened to be at that boundary react in a specific way (such as by changing shape) that would make it move *in the direction of* the mass of the vibrations and thus make it move further into the habitable zone. The reaction to this vibration gradient could be very similar to the reaction to the temperature gradient described earlier (Figure 59).

The result of this useful reaction would be that the organism would have by chance acquired another regulatory system that kept it safely in the comfort zone along with its fellow organisms. Remember that the organism is totally unaware of the existence of its fellow organisms, as it's completely devoid of senses and is simply reacting directly and mechanically to the vibrations that are hitting it – but the result is that it moves towards the mass of other organisms.

(Again, some organisms may react to the unequal vibrations on their membranes by moving away from the direction of the source of the vibrations – but these organisms would perish and thus would not pass on this trait to further generations.)

Notice that in this scenario the direction of reaction is *towards* the cause of the reaction (the vibrations), unlike all of the previous examples, which have been *away* from the cause of the reaction (a temperature change). In other words, it's attraction.

One of the important qualities of attraction is that it generally has to work over a distance. With attraction, you frequently have to start with a distance between the attractor and the attracted, with the attracted being impelled to decrease that distance. With repulsion, by contrast, distance may not already exist, with the dynamic being to create it – sometimes as quickly as possible (Think of the repellent force that you experience when you accidentally touch something that's extremely hot).

Notice that the attraction that I'm describing here between the vibrating organisms is a purely physical phenomenon, like everything else I've mentioned so far. It's analogous to the way that an iron nail is attracted to a magnet or that rain is attracted to the ground.

This power of attraction over distance may later have been an important quality in allowing organisms to expand their habitats into more complex and varied environments, allowing them to break out of the narrow confines of their single region of habitable water.

Imagine the following situation.

As I mentioned earlier, the relatively static environment of a stable layer of just right water in a pond is impossible to sustain for long. At the very least, convection currents would inevitably disrupt the equilibrium of the water, making some of the cells in it drift away from the comfort zone. There would probably also be the disruptive effects of occasional inundations of extra water as a result of, for instance, the tidal effects of the Sun and the Moon.

In these slightly more complex and dynamic situations the habitable zone may split into fragments (Figure 61) and an organism may easily find itself in a habitable pocket of water that's isolated from its main area of habitation. This pocket of water would be surrounded by water that's of an unsuitable temperature (being either too warm or too cold).

How could the organism get back to the main area of habitation again, bearing in mind that in order to do so it would have to cross this intervening hostile zone? The organism doesn't actually "want" to get back of course – in fact the organism doesn't care whether it lives or dies, being unaware that it's alive in the first place. However, getting back may have a useful consequence in evolutionary terms.

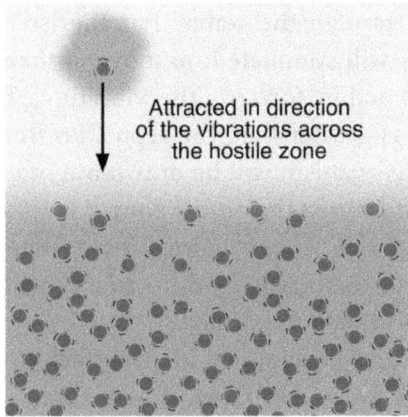

*Figure 61: An organism within a habitable pocket of
water that's been detached from the main body of
habitable water*

If the organism simply reacted directly to its immediate
surroundings it would stay in its isolated pocket. This is because
all of the processes at work within the organism would be
repulsive forces that would ensure that it didn't actually move
out of its mini comfort zone into the more hostile zone that
surrounded it and that separated it from the main body of
habitable water.

In order to "jump" across the hostile zone the organism needs
a mechanism that overrides the processes of repulsion that are
stopping it entering the zone. It needs a mechanism for reacting
to the presence of its original habitable zone over a distance – a
mechanism that provokes a greater reaction than the ones that
would otherwise make it stay put in its isolated comfort zone.

Fortunately, the capability for reacting to vibrations, as
described above, may provide such an ability.

The greater mass of organisms still within the main volume of
the habitable zone will be moving around as usual and sending

vibrations out through the water. For the isolated organism, these vibrations will stimulate it to move in their direction. As long as this attraction towards the vibrations from the main habitable zone is greater than the repulsion from entering the hostile zone the organism will be drawn out of its isolated mini comfort zone and across the hostile zone.

Provided that the organism isn't in the hostile zone long enough for major damage to be done to it, it will thus return to its normal environment unharmed.

This ability to traverse a less than perfect environment is a major advantage for an organism, allowing it to break out of the confines of its immediate, corralled surroundings.

With time, organisms would develop characteristics that allowed some of them to survive for longer periods in the hostile zones, allowing the organisms to occupy a wider range of habitats. As described earlier, these characteristics would be the result of random variations between organisms, and would only become standard features if they were useful. Such characteristics could be a thicker outer membrane or "skin", a greater ability to move, a different colour (allowing them to absorb heat to a greater or lesser degree) and so on. As a result of being able to occupy a wider range of habitats these organisms could find themselves in more complex environments where it would be advantageous to react in even more complex ways. Thus the complexification of life would continue apace.

In all of these examples concerning the manner in which simple organisms interact with their environments I've been careful to try to imply that the organisms simply react to their environment in an automatic way. They aren't truly *aware* of their surroundings in what we think of as a meaningful manner.

How could they be? They possess no senses with which to be aware of their environments, as they have no sense organs.

Or do they?

It's a fuzzy line when it comes to definitions, especially at the basic levels that are being considered here. For instance, I mentioned earlier that the outer membrane of single-celled organisms could vibrate when they were struck by vibrations travelling through water, and that the organism may then react to the vibrations. The whole membrane sounds very much like a full-body, cell-encompassing eardrum to me.

That means that at least on one level the cells can indeed sense vibrations. Whether or not this is a valid use of the term is perhaps open to debate – after all, does a thermometer "sense" temperature changes just because the mercury rises? (But then, thermometers are temperature *sensing* devices.)

Chapter 14

The Evolution of the Senses

As life gradually became more complex, so too did its capability for reacting to its surroundings – with the emergence of what we would regard as fully fledged senses.

I've just described the way that the outer membrane of a single-celled organism could, by reacting to vibrations in water, act as a form of basic vibration detector – or ear – allowing even this incredibly simple organism to develop the capability of being able to "hear".

The same process was at work for other stimuli too. As well as developing the ability to react to vibrations, simple organisms were developing the capability of reacting to light.

How could such an amazing facility arise – how did creatures harness the ability to react to such a mysterious and immaterial thing as electromagnetic waves?

And how, over the eons of evolutionary time, did some creatures eventually expand this ability into the seemingly incredible capability of being able to *see*? How did some of them end up with *eyes*?

The whole process is much simpler than you may think.

The phenomenon of being aware of light seems mystifying to us partly because we tend to think of light as a rather other-worldly, ethereal and insubstantial thing – however, its ability to affect physical objects is reasonably straightforward.

To us light has a sort of magical quality (to the extent that one of the memorable phrases at the beginning of the Bible is "Let there be light"). This is largely because we have eyes that utilize light in such a complex and wonderful way, and as a result we tend to forget that light is just a normal part of the physical universe like everything else.

Now, to understand how creatures react to light, and how they developed eyes in a relatively straightforward manner, follow this description of how you, as a person, experience the energy that reaches you from the Sun.

When you stand in the Sun you experience solar energy in two very different ways – as light and as heat.

In terms of their basic nature, the heat from the Sun is almost exactly the same thing as the light from the Sun – they are both waves of energy in the form of electromagnetic radiation. The only difference between the heat and the light is the wavelength of the radiation (See Figure 4 near the beginning of the book). The light has wavelengths between 400 nanometres (4 billionths of a centimetre) and 700 nanometres. We see the 400nm light as violet and we see the 700nm light as red, with the wavelengths in-between being seen as the other colours. The radiation that has wavelengths longer than red is invisible to us, but we are aware of the presence of some of it because it is what we experience as heat. This radiation is part of the range of wavelengths known as infrared radiation (infrared meaning below red). The Sun emits radiation at many more wavelengths than those of visible light and infrared radiation, but only these ones, along with radio waves, can penetrate the earth's atmosphere and reach us on the ground.

Now, we as humans don't give heat from the Sun the same semi-mystical status that we give to the light that it emits (despite the fact that heat-seeking holidaymakers are often called Sun worshippers). This is because the main way that we detect the heat from the Sun is as a (usually) rather pleasant but vague physical sensation on our skin, while we experience light via all of the complexity of our sense of vision.

Not only does the whole concept of heat seem more mundane than does that of light, but the underlying physical processes that allow us to detect it seem more mundane too.

These are the processes.

When waves of infrared radiation strike atoms, the energy from the waves is transferred to the atoms, making them vibrate. Which makes them hot. That's what heat is: moving atoms. And that's about it. Infrared radiation is generated in the first place by atoms moving rapidly because they are hot – so when that infrared radiation in turn strikes an object and makes the atoms in that object hot in turn the whole process is simply a form of transference of energy.

When we stand in the Sun on a nice day we can tell where the Sun is in the sky even if we've got our eyes covered, purely due to the heat that we feel from it. The infrared radiation from the Sun makes our skin hot – and specifically it makes our skin hot on the side that's facing the Sun, the side that's struck by the infrared radiation. You notice this especially when you keep one side of your body directed towards the Sun for an extended period of time, such as when you're sunbathing.

Our entire skin is like a full-body heat detector. However, and very importantly, the skin isn't a *specialized* heat detector dedicated to only that one function – heat detection is merely one of the roles that it plays, along with, amongst other things, holding our insides in. (There are strong parallels here with the outer membrane of the single-celled organism described earlier – where the membrane kept the contents of the cell in place and was also capable of detecting vibrations in the water and thus of "hearing".)

Now, although your experience of heat when you're out in

the Sun is quite generalized, you've probably noticed that the parts of you that truly "face" the Sun are much more subject to the effects of heat than other parts – for instance your shoulders or the back of your neck are affected more than your elbows. The same applies to the top of your head if you're bald. This is because the infrared radiation from the Sun is hitting these areas full on, while it's hitting your elbows at an angle. Heat that strikes a surface at an angle is spread out over a larger area, and thus its intensity is diluted (Figure 62). This is one reason why the heat from the low winter Sun is weaker than the heat from the overhead summer Sun.

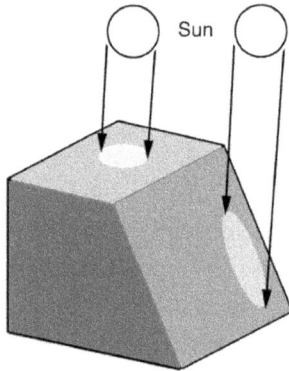

Figure 62: When energy from the Sun strikes a surface at an angle the heat is spread over a larger area than when it strikes full on, resulting in lower temperatures

When any organism is exposed to the Sun the parts of it that directly face the Sun get hotter than the rest of the organism: areas that are at an angle to the Sun are heated up less intensely, while a large proportion of the organism is exposed to no heat from the Sun at all as it's in the shadow created by the organism itself. As a result, different parts of the surface of any organism that's in the Sun are at noticeably different temperatures. If the organism possesses a means of registering those temperature differences it has a way of detecting the direction that the heat is coming from, or in other words, of detecting the direction of the Sun.

Here in Figure 63 is a hypothetical, simple spherical organism. It could be a tiny single-celled organism or it could be a larger though essentially simple multi-cellular organism – perhaps one that for some bizarre reason was the size and shape of a football. It's easy to see that even an organism with such a simple structure may be able to detect the direction of the Sun quite precisely if it has the means to translate the temperature differences on its surface into a useable sensation.

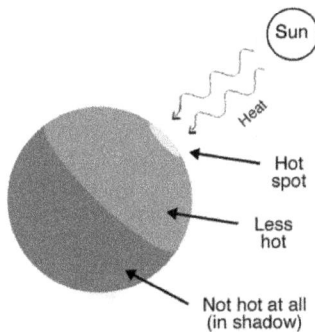

Figure 63: When the Sun strikes a curved surface the area of the surface that's directly facing the Sun is subject to the most intense heat, creating a "hot spot". At the same time, any area that's in shadow is subject to no direct heat at all

Although the simple spherical life-form depicted in Figure 63 is potentially capable of detecting the direction of the Sun, life-forms that are more complex in shape than this have an even greater potential for doing so, as the complications in the shape provide more opportunities for the organism's surface to be exposed to different amounts of heat.

Such organisms don't have to be *that* much more complicated in shape though. Take, for instance, an organism that is spherical but that has a single bump on it. The bump provides a second set of curved surfaces that are presented to the Sun at different angles, thus increasing the organism's sensitivity to the position of the Sun. On top of this the bump also creates a shadow area that would help to reinforce the effect. As a result, any organism with a bump on its surface will be better at detecting the direction of heat than one without bumps (This doesn't only apply to simple organisms such as the hypothetical one described here – it applies to you and me too. A protrusion such as your nose would be a good example of such a bump).

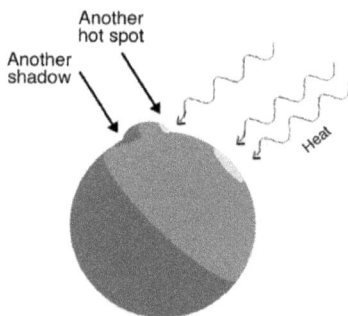

Figure 64: When an organism has a bump on it the organism is more sensitive to the direction of heat

The principle that extra curves on an organism's surface make it more sensitive to the direction of the Sun doesn't only apply to bumps and protrusions – it applies to *dents* as well (Figure 65).

202

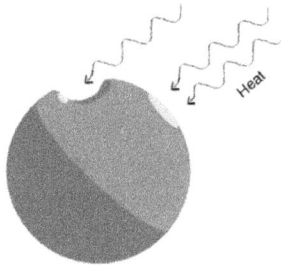

Figure 65: A dent increases sensitivity to the direction of heat in much the same way that a bump does

A low bump or dent would improve the accuracy of detecting the direction of the heat from the Sun, while a more pronounced bump or dent, with a greater curvature, would improve the accuracy further, as the greater the curvature the more localized the effect of heat on the surface, and the greater any shadow area, thus the greater the sensitivity.

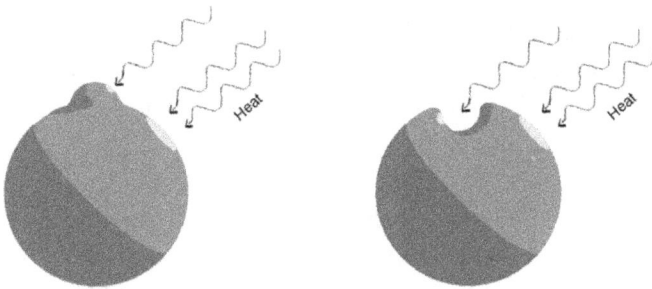

Figure 66: The more pronounced the bump or the dent, the more sensitive it is to the direction of heat

Hopefully that sounds reasonably straightforward, and with any luck you can relate to it due to your own experiences in going out into the Sun (and possibly getting a bit too much of it on your nose or shoulders).

Although I'm talking about living organisms here, it's important to realize that for an object to be affected by heat the object doesn't have to be alive. After all, anything that's exposed to the Sun heats up. The surface of an inert object that's the same shape as the living organisms just described, with all of the attendant bumps and dents, would heat up in exactly the same way, with different parts heating up to different extents. The crucial difference between the way that an inert object and a living one react to heat is in the potential complexity of the reaction, in that the living organism may register the effect as a physiological sensation.

So far I've been talking about the way that an organism is affected by, and is sensitive to, heat – however, the very same principles apply to the way that it is affected by light. This isn't surprising: light is, after all, almost exactly the same thing as radiant heat except that it has a different wavelength.

Whenever light strikes an organism (or indeed anything else for that matter) it agitates the molecules on the surface, in very much the same way that infrared radiation does. The molecules will be agitated even if the organism doesn't "notice" the fact that they are being agitated.

For an organism to become sensitive to the agitation caused by light it needs to evolve a method of registering it as a sensation, very similar to the way that the agitation caused by infrared radiation is registered as the sensation of heat.

Some of the molecules on an organism's surface will happen to react to light in a manner that is relatively easy for the organism to notice, and these molecules will be the ones that are "monitored" for their effect – let's call them light-sensitive molecules.

Bear in mind that these suitably light-sensitive molecules on the surface of the organism are not there *because* they are noticeably affected by light – they just happen to be there, and their reactivity to light is just a random property. There may indeed be similar light-sensitive molecules scattered throughout the whole organism, and indeed throughout the surrounding environment, but the light-related properties of these particular molecules is redundant and is not harnessed.

In primitive organisms these light- sensitive molecules would possibly be distributed randomly and evenly over the surface of the organism (because they are just there). Therefore, when the molecules are affected by light hitting them the resulting "monitored" sensation that they produce could be a vague, rather undefined, sensation that's analogous to the vague, undefined sensation that we experience as heat.

In many situations the ability of an organism to detect light even in this vague manner would give the organism a distinct advantage over its fellow organisms, and it would thrive, thus creating offspring that were also capable of detecting light in this way.

The more accurately an organism could tell which direction the light was coming from, the more of an advantage it would have. I'm still talking about relatively low levels of accuracy here, possibly analogous to the level of accuracy that you yourself have when detecting the direction of an electric heater by using your heat-detecting skin alone (with your eyes closed). This level of accuracy would allow organisms to detect the direction of approach of a possible predator, due to the moving "shadow" that the predator would produce (similar to the way that, using the electric heater analogy, you can detect the presence of a person if they move between you and the heater).

As with an organism's abilities to detect heat, it's more

accurate to detect the direction of light on curved surfaces – and the more curved the surface the greater the accuracy. Organisms that had bumps or pits on their surface would be better at detecting the direction of light and shadows than their smoother surfaced cousins (as in Figures 63 to 66 above), and would thus thrive relative to them.

Let's look more closely for a moment at the organisms that sport pits on their surfaces, ignoring for now those that have bumps.

An organism with a deep pit (as on the right in Figure 66 above) would be able to detect the direction of light much more accurately than would an organism with a shallow pit (Figure 65) – resulting in deep-pitted organisms thriving in comparison to shallow-pitted ones.

Over time and over generations the pits would get deeper and more recessed, as in Figure 67 below, purely because deeper pits make for more acute and directional light detection and are thus more propitious to survival.

Figure 67: A very deep pit creates the most accurate level of directional light detection

Yes, that deep pit in Figure 67 does look suspiciously like an eye, doesn't it?

However, this "eye" is nothing more than a recess in an organism's body: it doesn't, for instance, have a lens.

The recess would differ from the rest of the organism's surface in that it would contain a relatively high concentration of light-sensitive molecules compared to the rest of the surface.

Why would this be? It sounds somewhat fortuitous or contrived to say the least. How could such a seemingly deliberate accumulation of light-sensitive molecules just where they are needed come about?

It's because in nature, as in most things, nothing is uniform, and there would be a natural tendency for the light-sensitive molecules on any organism to be distributed at least *slightly* unevenly over the organism's surface, whether the organism had a recess or not. Over the course of the evolution of the recess, as it got deeper over the generations, those organisms that had more light-sensitive molecules inside the recess (due to pure random distribution) would thrive more than organisms that had fewer, because they would be more sensitive to light: they would fair better and would reproduce more, and thus the tendency for a concentration of light-sensitive molecules in the recess would be reinforced.

Eventually an organism would exist where the recess was so deep and round that it was practically closed over, leaving only a small hole through which the light could enter. This would provide the greatest directional accuracy of all for detecting which direction light (and shadow) was coming from, so creatures with this feature would thrive.

Very usefully, when light passes through a very small hole such as the opening in this recess it doesn't simply fall on the surface behind as a diffuse glow. The restriction caused to the light by the small hole is so great that light from any given direction only hits quite a small area on the inside of the recess, with the cumulative effect being that an actual *image* is mapped out on the surface. This happens without the benefit of a lens, using exactly the same principle that's at work in a pinhole camera. The resulting recess is thus a basic, image-forming eye – fashioned purely by an accretion of minor variations that reinforce each other.

From here it's only a matter of time before the descendants of the organism develop the "circuitry" that could analyse the image that's formed on the inside surface of the recess. Similarly, it's only a matter of time before the "pinhole" at the top of the recess becomes covered by a thin, transparent membrane that would usefully act as protection against contaminants entering the cavity and clogging it up. It would then be only a matter of time before this transparent membrane acquired a variable thickness – and became a lens. The recess changes from being a pinhole camera into a digital camera.

And voila – the eye!

The eye is such a useful and surprisingly simple adaptation that it has developed in different creatures along completely independent pathways. Each path possibly diverged from the same light-sensitive patch of molecules on a very early, shared ancestor, but from that point they followed different routes. One such route was that taken by the insects, with their alien-like compound eyes, while another route was taken by the cephalopods, the family of aquatic creatures that includes the squid. Cephalopod eyes work in a very similar way to our own, even though the route by which they were arrived at was different, as can be deduced by anatomical differences between their eyes and ours (In fact the squid's eye is in some ways superior to ours, as ours have various things such as blood-vessels inconveniently interfering with the path of the light).

You may remember that at the beginning of this description

of the development of the eye I mentioned that an organism would be able to detect the direction of light more effectively if it had light-sensitive molecules that were either in a pit or on a bump. You've probably noticed that I've just described the evolution of the eye from the pit – so what about the organisms that had light sensitive molecules on bumps?

The truth is that although at the very basic level bumps were better than smooth surfaces for detecting the direction of light (in very much the same way that they were better for detecting the direction of heat), they were also, unfortunately, something of a dead end in terms of potential further development. Crucially, there was no way that a bump could develop into a pinhole camera (and then into a camera with a lens). The bump route to true vision was very much a blind alley. As a result no organisms that used bumps for light detecting developed truly functioning eyes from their bumps.

So it is that a few light-sensitive cells could evolve, through simple stages, into an organ as amazingly sophisticated as the eye. Partly as a result of its seemingly extraordinary (though strangely ordinary) evolutionary pathway, the eye has recently developed an interesting extra function that lies beyond its light-sensing capabilities – that of being the perfect model of the process of evolution by natural selection at work, as attested by its inclusion in numerous popular science books and internet sites.

Chapter 15

Feeling its Way Forward

In the previous chapter I described the possible route by which the ability to detect light evolved in organisms, starting with a sprinkling of light-sensitive molecules on an organism's surface and ending with a complex, state of the art image-capturing system.

Once an organism can *see* (even rudimentarily) I think that it can reasonably be argued that it is to some extent *aware*. And once it has developed a highly sophisticated eye it can reasonably be said that it possesses a high degree of awareness – one that's nudging towards the middle to upper end of the scale of awareness levels, a very long distance from the base level occupied by primordial single-celled organisms.

Having said that, although the eye may be a signifier of high awareness, a few paragraphs ago I likened its workings to those of a digital camera, an object that isn't aware in any manner that is comparable to that of living things. All that can be said of a digital camera is that it *reacts* to light, in a mechanistic manner. This observation seems to open the door to the question of whether or not that's all that an eye does too – that vision, with all of its attendant workings of the brain, is nothing more than a sophisticated reaction to the world.

So is awareness ever anything more than just a complex reaction?

Would a highly sophisticated robot, for instance, with cameras as eyes, be aware?

211

WHAT ARE WE?

You could argue that robots and cameras shouldn't be hauled into arguments like this as they have been created by creatures that are most definitely aware, and thus they don't conform to the same rules of development and complexity that life has to. The robot's camera eyes simply ape our sense of vision (which is only possible because an ape constructed them in the first place). But then, should that matter? After all, why should robots have to go through millions of years of evolution? We did the evolving, so they don't have to.

As you can see, it turns out to be quite hard to pin down the exact nature of awareness when you look at it closely – and that on top of this it could be argued that awareness in and of itself isn't necessarily a signifier of life at all.

Perhaps it could actually be argued that the only reason that complex life is aware in a complex (and thus seemingly meaningful) way is purely because everything about complex life is complex.

Fortunately, mechanistic reaction to sensory input isn't the only manner in which most higher living things interact with their surroundings: many of them possess extra levels of reaction that overlay this basic response. A look at these reactions should help us to get out of the definitional quagmire into which we seem to be sinking.

These sophisticated reactions are the forms of response that are manifested as *feelings*.

Some of these feelings are quite abstract and exist in the arena of higher mental processes – feelings such as love and hate, aggression and compassion – the realm of the emotions. I'll touch on some of these types of feeling later, but to begin with we'll take a look at a feeling that's much more basic, physical and visceral in its expression.

We'll start with a stab at pain.

Pain

Why do we feel pain? It's such an unpleasant sensation that you may think that we'd be better off without it.

If you do think that, think again.

To understand the reason why we are burdened with such an unpleasantness let's imagine a world in which it doesn't exist.

It sounds almost too good to be true, but just look at the implications.

Let's look at a hypothetical fish that lives in this mythical pain-free world (Figure 68).

Figure 68: This is a fish that feels no pain

Imagine that this fish is blissfully swimming around in its delightful ocean, when a predator sneaks up behind it (Figure 69, left) and starts gnawing at its tail (right). It's a very small but vicious predator, as you can see.

Figure 69: The fish is attacked by a predator

Due to the larger fish's anatomical makeup, it can't see its own tail, so it can't see the predator.

Before the big fish knows it, the predator has nibbled away all of its tail (Figure 70), leaving the fish seriously handicapped. The fish may only realise that it is tailless when it notices that its swimming abilities are perplexingly impaired

Figure 70: The fish's tail has gone before the fish knows it

If you were the big fish you'd probably be glad to have a method of noticing the fact and you were having your tail gnawed off, so that you could swim off before it became serious.

You'd need alerting to the situation.

A vague tickling sensation in the tail region may make you aware of a problem in that area, but you may be rather slow to respond to such a fuzzy feeling, giving the predator time to get its teeth stuck in. What would be much more useful would be a stimulus that really made you shift – and thus got you out of danger as soon as possible.

Anything that could speed up the reaction to a nibbling predator, or any other bad bodily event, is a useful addition to an organism's danger-avoidance arsenal. Thus it is that the useful "prod" of pain developed.

In higher animals – ones that are capable of learning from their actions – the threat of pain, once experienced, will also act as an effective disincentive or deterrent that stops the creature repeatedly getting into situations that give rise to pain.

Thus organisms that register pain are more likely to survive and reproduce than those that don't. As a result, pain is universal in higher animals. Pain is a good thing.

(Pain unfortunately has to be unpleasant. When organisms were first starting to evolve an ability to register sensations due to predatory attack or similar corporeal violations it's quite likely that for some of the organisms the initial, tentative sensations experienced would have registered as pleasant rather than painful (due to random variation), however, creatures that experienced a pleasing sensation when attacked didn't react in a manner that was conducive to survival, hence the tendency was nipped in the bud.)

Pleasure

It'd be awful if we lived in a world were pain was the only sensation. Fortunately we don't.

What's the opposite of pain?

Pleasure, of course.

But wait. Pleasure and pain are normally yoked together as being equal and opposite sensations – but that doesn't necessarily mean that these sensations developed at exactly the same time, in tandem. Pain is a motivating signal for repulsion, while pleasure is a signal for attraction, and there's really no reason why the two should have developed in parallel. You may recall that earlier I described how attraction shouldn't necessarily be thought of as the opposite of repulsion (where I described how for single-celled organisms the capability for being repelled from entering an inappropriate temperature zone would have preceded the capability for being attracted to a habitable zone, because by definition the organisms would have to be in a habitable zone to begin with) – well, the same goes for pleasure and pain (and for similar reasons). It's quite possible that pain developed before pleasure, as it's more important to be repelled from bad things than to be attracted to good things.

The principle that states that pain preceded pleasure works something like this: you will die if you're not immediately repelled from bad things such as predators that intend to eat you, but you can bide your time waiting for good things to come along. You can stumble around for quite a while looking for something nice to eat for instance (until the pain of hunger kicks in that is, by which time any old food will do).

Pleasure as a spur possibly first developed because in any particular population of creatures of the same species any creature that possessed the trait had a competitive advantage over fellow creatures that lacked it – for instance, a creature that had the positive incentive to eat something because the experience was pleasurable was more likely to get the food than a fellow creature that would eat the food when it just happened to come across it. Pleasure, in other words, may have developed because of internal pressure within a species rather than due to external pressure from predators or suchlike.

Pain is a visceral reaction to an unpleasant stimulus, such as a poke with a sharp stick. Pleasure, however, is something slightly different. Its nature lies somewhere nebulously between the physical and the emotional. Although the simplest of pleasures are highly physical and immediate, many forms of pleasure seem to involve several higher levels of information processing, involving a more highly developed nervous system.

For instance, pleasure is often actively sought, implying that the awareness of the sensation can be stored and can be apprehended over time, while it's quite possible for pain to be experienced only at the moment of its application. Pain therefore can be experienced by creatures that only live "in the moment" and that only possess relatively basic, reactive nervous systems that make their possessors jump when they're prodded.

This seems a bit unfortunate for lower life-forms, as it implies that the most significant sensation they can experience is pain (But then, maybe that was a good spur to make some of them evolve into higher life-forms).

Alertness

Gradually creatures became more complex, becoming equipped with various senses such as sight and hearing, and feelings such as pain (and if they were lucky, pleasure).

As the interactions of these functions became more complicated, creatures would automatically develop ever more intricate "information-processing systems" in tandem (This wouldn't be a *consequence* of the increasing complexity as such – it would be an integral, inseparable part of it). These information-processing systems would be in the form of ever more elaborate nervous systems. In the most advanced cases this would culminate with the development of the acme of organic information-processing systems – the brain.

With the advent of brains, and the concomitant advance of the neural processes within them, there would be the emergence of higher levels of information-processing activity – in the form of *mental states.*

Take the following situation, as just one example of the process in operation: the evolution of the mental state known as *alertness.*

Before the existence of alertness it's quite possible that predators simply sidled up to their prey and took a chunk out of it. Pain may then kick in and prompt the prey to retreat – if it was still capable of doing so – but this would be very much a case of shutting the stable door after the horse had bolted. The prey would have a much better chance of survival if it happened to possess an early warning system that could announce the approach of the predator, so that it could react before rather than after it felt the pang of pain caused by the predator's attack. Thus the mental state that manifests itself as alertness evolved.

The possession of alertness would allow a creature to react to things in a way that over-rode simple physical reaction, and the creature would therefore be more likely to survive than a creature that lacked the facility.

You can see the alert facility at work today simply by looking out of a kitchen window and observing the behaviour of birds. If you watch blue tits or similar birds feeding on nuts put out for them in a garden you'll see that they spend a noticeable amount of time glancing around in a startled manner – almost more time than they actually spend feeding. Then as soon as they glimpse you looking at them through the window, they're off.

The alert-reaction coupling here seems to be quite straightforward. The birds are alerted by a disturbance, and the reaction is to make a hasty departure in the opposite direction.

It's important that the reaction to the alert mechanism needs to have a sensible threshold at which it kicks in – after all, if it was triggered by any old movement then even the rustling of a leaf in the wind would provoke the flight reflex, which would have no point at all. When a stimulus is particularly close to the threshold level certain additional mental processes may be necessary in order to decide whether to react or not – the stirrings of the concept of *alternatives* may be born.

You may think that a blue tit's alert-reflex mechanism is set a little bit on the over-sensitive side judging by how readily they flee the garden at the slightest movement in your kitchen. But then, considering how few blue tits survive for more than a single year, perhaps it isn't.

Alerted (and thus fleeing) prey causes a problem for predators – it makes their meals harder to catch. Predators therefore needed to evolve their own reciprocal alert system that would warn them when there was a potential prey creature in the vicinity, giving the predator a chance to capture its prey before the prey retreated to safety.

The predator's alert system would have to work in a more complicated manner to that of the potential prey creature. While prey species only needed the automatic reaction of fleeing when a disturbance was noticed, for predators a different reaction to movement or disturbance was necessary. No carnivore worthy of the name would flee in the opposite direction whenever it heard a rustle in the undergrowth. In fact in some ways the exact opposite reaction may be much more appropriate – to pounce on the object that was causing the rustling, as it may be food. But what if the rustling turned out to be caused by a bigger predator?

It's quite a complicated business for a predator to react to a rustle. Firstly it has to try to discover what it is that's doing the rustling; then, if it turns out to be potential food it may have to stalk it; then finally it has to strike or pounce – all done as much as possible without the prey being aware of its approaching fate until the last moment.

As a result, carnivores have had to develop more complex and agile mental processes than those possessed by herbivores – in other words, they have to be more intelligent.

Herbivores have to be reasonably intelligent too in certain circumstances. For instance when a herbivore such as a gazelle approaches a water hole it has to hold in its head at some level the fact that the hole is a good place, as it contains thirst-quenching water, and that it's also a potentially bad place, as the water may also attract a gazelle-eating predator such as a lion. But the gazelle doesn't have to be as intelligent as the lion.

The relative intelligences of carnivores and herbivores can easily be compared today by simply observing a few domestic creatures that live side by side with humans. Observe a cat or a dog (carnivores) to see their keen interest in their surroundings (except when they are asleep on the sofa). Then look at a cow or a sheep (herbivores) to see their relative lack of mental agility in action. Admittedly these creatures are not representative of the animal kingdom as a whole, as cats and dogs are intelligent enough to be domesticated, while sheep and cows are perhaps unintelligent enough to be domesticated. (For this whole business of the comparison of the relative intelligence levels of carnivores and herbivores to be valid the creatures involved have to be in the same ecological stratum. I think that it can be safely said that a carnivorous worm isn't as intelligent as a herbivorous donkey.)

So it was that creatures had to become more alert and aware of what was going on in the world around them, either in order to eat or to avoid being eaten. The development of the brain was encouraged by the fact that life eats itself.

It's an intriguing thought, that if all animal life had been vegetarian perhaps we wouldn't be here now thinking about these things.

For herbivores and carnivores the sound of any rustling in the undergrowth in their vicinity prompts relatively straightforward mental reactions. For the herbivore: "That may be a predator – I'd better go." For the carnivore: "That may be food – I'd better have a look." Things are much more complicated for a third category of creatures however – the *omnivores*.

For these creatures the rustle of another creature nearby could signal *either* a predator or a meal.

To run for safety or to stay and eat?

The answer may usually be dictated by the nature of the rustle – if it sounded like a big creature, run: if it sounded like a small creature, stay.

The appropriate response may thus be a relatively straightforward knee-jerk reaction. However, in certain special circumstances the best course of action may not be quite so clear-cut. What if an omnivore hears the rustling of a big animal (meaning that it should run), but the omnivore happens to be extremely hungry at the time (meaning that it should perhaps try its chances at getting a meal)? This predicament can create the need for very complex mental processes – where the concept of alternatives is amplified to new levels of complexity and urgency because the alternatives have to be compared and weighed up against each other – the concept of *choice* is born.

The need to confront this dilemma was possibly a key factor in the rise of humanity, as I will explain later.

Emotions

Following on the heels of the sensations and mental states outlined above, the "true" emotions gradually developed. These emotions are, like pain, pleasure and alertness, prods that make their possessors act in specific useful ways.

Emotions are complex mental processes, requiring a decent sized brain in which to operate.

They are types of mental process that prompt their possessors to act in particular ways that are appropriate to the situation. For instance, it's common for a creature that possesses emotions to have a particular emotional reaction when it comes across an attractive member of the opposite sex (lust), while if it meets an attractive member of the same sex it will often experience a different emotion (envy). You may not like the idea that these emotions are the workings of a decent brain, but there you go.

Many large-brained creatures use emotions to guide their day-to-day actions for them.

Even humans, the most intellectual of animals, use emotions to guide their actions most of the time. Despite what we like to think, people frequently don't intellectualise things at all when they're working out what to do next. They usually (or perhaps always) do things on the basis of what they feel like doing, and then rationalise their actions later.

Sometimes, of course, rationalisation isn't necessary.

If you saw a gigantic dog rushing towards you barking, you wouldn't intellectualise about what to do next – your emotions would kick in and take the decision making right out of your hands. It would just feel right to run like hell.

Which brings me to the scary subject of fear.

Fear

Fear makes those in its grip run away from what are potentially dangerous situations.

As a result it's a top ranking survival emotion.

Few other emotions are up there with fear when it comes to the basic task of keeping their possessors alive.

To illustrate this, let's pick a few other emotions at random for comparison. Let's take envy for instance.

You'd die if you didn't flee from a lion, and what's more, you'd die pretty soon, so it's a good job that fear gets you up and running – but you'd survive if your friend was more successful with the opposite sex than you were, no matter how envious you became. Envy's main use is perhaps to act as a prod to make you become more presentable to potential partners, which isn't a survival issue as far as you're concerned personally, but may make a big difference to the likelihood of the production (and therefore survival) of any offspring.

As a result I think it's safe to say that envy is a secondary emotion when compared to fear, and that fear no doubt evolved long before envy reared its head.

Similarly, the emotion of aggression is secondary to that of fear, and probably developed later, although the two are linked. The reason that aggression is secondary is that in a dangerous situation there's generally a stronger chance of survival by fleeing rather than by fighting – hence the truth of the "fight or flight" adage: "He who runs away will live to fight another day."

So it is that the most important emotions and feelings are those that deal with immediate survival issues rather than with speculative future benefits. If emotions were compared to car components it would be like saying that it's more important for a car to have an accelerator pedal than to have sat-nav.

In some ways fear operates almost as an emotional equivalent of pain, because both are devices that encourage the possessor to avoid immediately disadvantageous situations. Unfortunately, in nature, this is the main category of event that creatures need to react to, with the result being that their lives are significantly coloured by pain and fear (although they may only experience these states occasionally, spending most of their time in a state of relatively neutral complacency until they need a prod).

With all of the negative feelings and emotions that seem to be dominating this section of the book, things don't sound good.

Perhaps we'd better not dwell on them. Let's move on.

What comes next?

Dissatisfaction

Can we find a ray of sunshine that will lessen the bleakness implied by the seemingly inevitable inheritance of pain and fear as primary feelings and emotions?

Not yet, I'm afraid.

This is because creatures not only have to be on constant alert for potential life-threatening danger, for which pain and fear are useful avoidance incentives, but they also have to constantly deal with significant though less urgent problems that come their way.

Very few creatures live in a state in which they don't have to react to incessant low-level adverse pressures simply in order to stay alive: there are almost bound to be demands placed on them purely due to minor day-to-day variations in their immediate surroundings (such as temperature fluctuations, changes in rainfall and so on). On top of this there are pressures due to the constant need to find nutrition which is often in short supply (If a creature fortuitously finds itself in a situation where food is available in seemingly boundless quantities you can bet your bottom dollar that the creature will then thrive and have so many offspring that this situation doesn't prevail for long, due to the inevitable fact that the offspring will quickly eat all of the surplus food).

For most creatures this constant exposure to minor negative situations is a way of life. As a result, for most creatures reacting to slightly bad things is one of their most important and time consuming activities.

Reacting to bad things takes precedence over reacting to good things because bad things tend to be more immediately demanding of attention than are good things. This is along the same lines as the principle that it's more important to be able to feel pain than to feel pleasure (or, as in the case of the primitive single-celled organisms that I introduced earlier, that it's more important to be able to react to water of the wrong temperature than to be able to react to water of the right temperature).

In order to react efficiently to low-level or non-life-threatening bad things it's a good idea to have an emotional prod to help override any innate inertia or tardiness that would otherwise hinder reaction.

This emotion can broadly be described as being the one that we refer to as *dissatisfaction.*

Here's an example of how dissatisfaction works at a simple level.

Imagine a moose, standing in the middle of a clearing in the middle of a forest. In the middle of a blizzard. The moose would feel a strong sense of dissatisfaction about the presence of the raging storm. This feeling of dissatisfaction would prompt the moose to do something rather than just carry on standing there feeling generally miserable.

But what to do?

The answer is to go and find shelter.

In order to be prompted to move to a position of shelter the moose has to be aware that this is a possible action – that there is an alternative to just standing in the middle of the blizzard getting cold and wet.

The feeling of dissatisfaction prompts the realisation that things could be better – that there is at least one situation that could be preferable to the present one. For the moose in the blizzard this situation would be to be under some trees.

When a creature is not in a state of dissatisfaction, what state is it in? One of satisfaction, perhaps?

Unfortunately, I think not.

In the case of my moose in a blizzard, when the blizzard is

blowing the moose may feel miserable and dissatisfied due to the prevailing meteorological conditions (which motivates it to do something about it), but when the weather is just right the moose probably doesn't even notice the weather at all. There's no need to. The moose would just stay put, which is what it ought to do in the circumstances. (If the moose ever did feel pleasure at being in "just right" weather conditions it would probably only be when such weather first arrived after a spell of inclemency – and the feeling may then subside disappointingly quickly.)

When a creature is not in a state of dissatisfaction it is normally in a state of neutral complacency, with no particular urges one way or the other.

Again, this is very like the situation involving the primordial single-celled organisms in their pool of water, described in Chapter 13 (The Dawn of the Dawnings), where being in the "just right" zone prompted no reaction. The only difference is that now we've got added emotions to govern the responses to the situations rather than simple automatic physical reactions.

Bearing in mind that things are very rarely "just right" for any living thing, the default mood of any thinking life-form is probably one of mild dissatisfaction.

A sad thought indeed.

In fact, one that I believe provokes mild dissatisfaction itself.

Humans, you may have noticed, have a *huge* capacity for dissatisfaction. This fact isn't necessarily as bad as it sounds though, because it is this tendency towards dissatisfaction that has been crucial in the development of our species, as I'll describe now.

It's what I like to call *evolution by natural dejection*.

Chapter 16

The Descent of Man (from the Trees)

Why is it that our species, the human race, seems to be somehow different to all of the other creatures on the planet? Let's not beat about the bush, we are different, whether we like it or not. Very, very different. For better or for worse.

Why do we seem to have so much intelligence and curiosity compared to other creatures? Why are you avidly reading this book, while a wildebeest wouldn't even give it a second glance?

Why are we so different from even our very closest animal relatives, the chimpanzees, bonobos and gorillas?

As part of our effort to answer these questions let's look more closely at those chimpanzees, bonobos and gorillas, and see exactly how we're related to them.

Figure 71 on the next page shows our branch of the family tree of all living things: the tree of life. Our branch contains all of the monkeys and other apes: all of the creatures that are in the order known as the primates.

Here's a quick rundown (or climb up) our part of the tree.

The tree grows through time. At the very bottom of the primate branch, over 50 million years ago, is the common ancestor of all of the primates. Each fork of the tree above this point shows where different groups of primates branched off from this primogenitor to follow different evolutionary routes, resulting in different species. The lowest fork shows when primates such as lemurs and tarsiers (collectively known as prosimians, or pre-apes) split off on their own evolutionary branch about 50 million years ago, evolving in a separate direction to the rest of the primates. Similarly, the second branch shows when the monkeys of the New World split off. These American monkeys branched off from the remaining primates on their own evolutionary route quite a long time ago, so they differ in a number of ways from Old World monkeys and the other higher primates – for instance they don't have opposable thumbs (which the Old World monkeys and the great apes have), they are less intelligent, and they have prehensile tails that they can wrap round branches and use as aids to climbing and dangling. The tails of Old World monkeys lack this useful ability, and the great apes don't have tails at all.

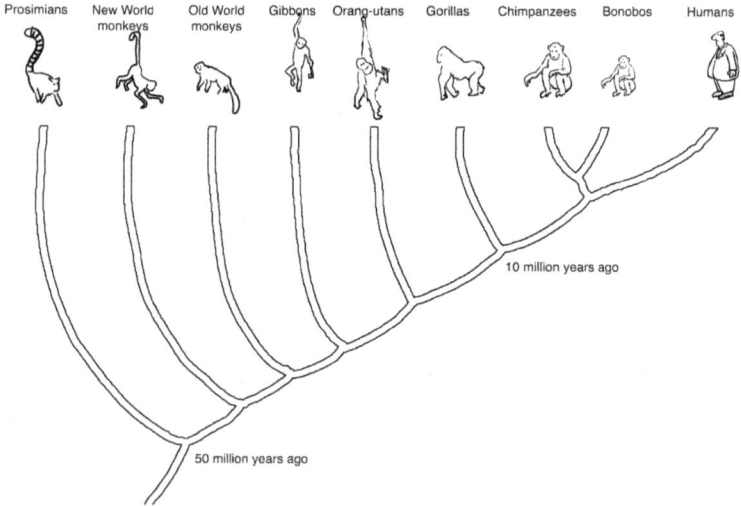

Figure 71: The primate branch of the tree of life

You can see human beings perched on the branch at the far right of the tree, close to our nearest relatives, the chimpanzees, bonobos and gorillas, with the orang-utans a little further away.

This diagram shows all of the creatures perched on the ends of branches of the family tree, and indeed all of the species depicted spend a great deal of their lives perched in the branches of real trees. Except for the humans.

We moved out of the trees about five million years ago.

(Perhaps one of the last vestiges of our arboreally-centred past is manifested in the way that even in the modern world small children feel compelled to climb trees. This activity is suddenly abandoned in later childhood when they decide that it's ludicrously infantile and they adopt more sophisticated pastimes such as standing around on street corners. I wonder if any sociological studies have ever been done to test whether or not the lack of tree-climbing opportunities for modern youth has a detrimental effect on the children's development. It may explain a lot.)

Before I deal with how our ancestors fared when they first left the trees all of those millions of years ago, let's have a look at how our cousins, the chimpanzees and bonobos, are doing right now, today.

Chimps are found in the forests of west and central Africa, living in communities of between about ten and a hundred individuals. In any particular community all of the males will be related, while the adult females will have joined the community by leaving nearby communities that they were born into.

Once chimps have eaten the food they need, and have avoided any ground-lurking predators by climbing to inaccessible spots in their trees, they'll often be found in small groups sitting back and doing nothing very much at all.

Any humans who sat around as much as a chimp does would be strongly disapproved of.

Chimps don't sit back doing nothing all of the time though.

The male members of a community will sometimes suddenly all assemble together on the ground and then walk away from their community in a purposeful line. Their mission is to actively patrol their territory in a gang, and to attack (and sometimes kill) members of other chimp communities that they encounter. Again, if humans acted like that we'd strongly disapprove.

The chimp's closest relatives, the bonobos, act rather differently. These primates are so closely related to the chimpanzees that until recently they were thought to be a subgroup of chimps that just happened to be slightly smaller than the average chimp. They used to be called pigmy chimpanzees as a result. They weren't given the status of being their own species until well into the first half of the twentieth century. They live on the south bank of the River Congo in the Democratic Republic of Congo (Figure 72).

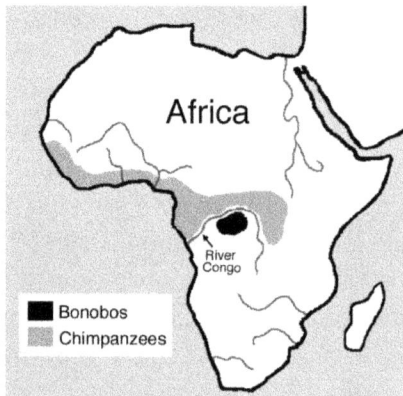

Figure 72: The regions of Africa where the chimpanzee and the bonobo are found

In recent years studies of the bonobos have found that although they look very much like small chimps they don't act very much like them.

Specifically, they don't indulge in attacks on other groups of their own species that live nearby. Generally they actually avoid contact with neighbouring groups, but when they do by chance bump into each other they indulge in a bit of mutual grooming rather than fighting.

They also don't exhibit much aggression within their own group, unlike the chimps. Indeed the bonobos are famous for the fact that they channel most of their energy into promiscuous sexual activity at the slightest excuse. They are a species for which the expression "Make love, not war" could have been invented. They generally seem to be too good to be true (apart from possibly being somewhat over-sexed) and are in great danger of being over-romanticised by sentimental westerners in search of the perfect primate.

Why is there such a difference in behaviour between the chimps and the bonobos? After all, they are very close relatives, and if you look on the map you'll see that they are very close neighbours too.

Looking at the map will also give you a clue as to why they are different. Significantly, although they are neighbours, the bonobos live on the south side of a very large river, the River Congo, while the chimps live on the north side. The theory goes that, as luck would have it, the bonobos live on the side of the river where food is extremely plentiful, so there's little competition for it. As a result there's just no need to fight. Meanwhile, the less fortunate chimps on the north bank of the river live in far from ideal circumstances, with significant competition for food and territory: hence their need to be more aggressive in defending what they've got.

Quite why the hard-pressed chimps don't cross the river and move into bonobo territory I'm not sure. Maybe the river really is *very* wide indeed. Or maybe the theory's wrong.

(It'd be tempting to say that the bonobos have an almost perfect existence. Unfortunately this is no longer true. In recent years human incursion into their territories has significantly reduced the number of bonobo groups, and unless something is done about it very soon they will become extinct.)

That's a quick run-down of what the chimps and the bonobos are doing at the moment. I think that it's safe to say that they're living in ways that are very similar to the ways that their and our common ancestors did millions of years ago, at the time immediately before humans set off to climb their own separate branch of the evolutionary tree.

Since the days of those common ancestors we humans have moved on. We aren't living in the trees any more – in fact we're now busily engaged in chopping them down rather than climbing them. That's progress for you.

Why have we progressed so far, while our ape cousins still live in the trees?

The answer is generally assumed to lie in the fact that we, alone amongst the primates, left the trees in the first place, about five million years ago, never to return to them.

But why did we move away from the trees? It seems like a strange thing to do, as the branches of trees were, amongst other things, a safe haven from the predators that generally roamed around on the ground. Why didn't we just stay up there in the branches, out of harms way?

Did we jump out of the branches, or were we pushed?

It's quite likely that we were pushed – after all, what's the point of spending millions of years becoming highly adapted to life in the trees only to go and abandon them for a life on the ground?

It's a common conception that when our ancestors left the

trees they wandered straight out into the open grasslands of the African savannah. However, there's evidence that they may have actually lived for a considerable period of time on the ground within the forests themselves before venturing out onto the plains. This is deduced from the fact that the remains of forest animals have been found accompanying early hominid skeletons. It's not surprising that our tree-dwelling ancestors may have spent considerable amounts of time on the ground – after all, most modern apes such as chimps and gorillas spend a certain amount of time there themselves. It's quite possible that our ancestors simply spent more time on the ground than other apes, thus becoming reasonably proficient at living there.

The reason that we eventually abandoned the trees for good however is unknown.

One possible reason for our abandonment of the arboreal lifestyle is that in the region where our ancestors lived there was a sudden decrease in the number of trees, possibly due to a period of climate change.*

It's also possible that we were elbowed out of the trees by some of our close relatives, perhaps the antecedents of the chimpanzees and bonobos, who may have been more adept in the climbing department and/or been more aggressive than we were, so they just muscled us out by monopolizing the best trees. (Because our ancestors had started to spend more time on *terra firma* than the rest of the apes they may have lost some tree climbing skill or may have just become accustomed to being on the ground – making elbowing them out a relatively easy task.)

---

* Periods of climate change have occurred throughout history, resulting in repeated changes in the environment. This fact is sometimes used in arguments against the claim that the current episode of global warming is man-made, or in order to try to diminish its significance. Such arguments are, I feel, at best misguided, at worst criminally misleading.

Pressure from chimpanzee and bonobo ancestors would be especially significant in a world of ever decreasing tree availability, due to the increased competition for trees. But our ancestors may have been elbowed out even if there were no shortage of trees. If our ancestors and the chimp/bonobo ancestors lived in geographically distinct regions (perhaps separated by a wide river as in the case of the modern day chimps and bonobos) all that would be needed would be for chimp/bonobo ancestors to gain a foothold in the geographical area that sustained our ancestors, allowing them to spread due to their superior skills or greater aggression, forcing our ancestors out.

This scenario of a more adept/more aggressive species forcing another species out of a habitat is a dynamic that has been repeated over and over again since the dawn of life. It still goes on today, often facilitated by the agency of human activity.

It is how, in Britain, Ireland and parts of Italy, the grey squirrel – a rodent introduced from America – has forced the native red squirrel to the margins of the woodlands and (especially in Britain) to the margins of existence. Similarly, as I write this very paragraph there is a ladybird sitting on the wall of my room here in London: it is a harlequin ladybird, a species unknown in Britain until recently, but one which is currently in the process of pushing the less aggressive native two spot ladybird out of its habitat. In a few years time the two spot may be a rarity in Britain.

Most species that are forced to the periphery of their natural habitat can't adapt and either survive in depleted numbers on the margins or become extinct. Fortunately for us, when our ancestors jumped or were pushed out of the trees they found that they were just about capable of surviving, due to their relatively versatile anatomy and psychological makeup that had evolved during their time in the branches. (To understand how difficult it is for most species to adapt to a new environment, try imagining how some species would have coped if they had been forced in the opposite direction to the one that we took – off the grassland and into the branches of the trees. How would a zebra cope in the treetops for instance?)

Despite all this talk of our ancestors being forced out of the trees due to aggressive relatives or depletion of forests, it is vaguely possible that they simply left the trees of their own volition. It's possible that something in their psychological makeup made them particularly restless and dissatisfied, and made them want to go and explore pastures new. We still do that today. That's why we're busy planning trips to Mars at this very moment. Mars may be the new savannah.

Whatever the reason that we left the trees and moved out into the plains, our ancestors ended up on the open grassland while the ancestors of the chimps and bonobos remained in the place that they were perfectly adapted to – the trees.

And they've been sitting in those trees ever since.

Lucky chimps and bonobos.

And poor us.

Chapter 17

The Ascent of Man (to the Top of the Tree)

Imagine what it must have been like. You're a tree dweller, very proficient at swinging through the branches, and suddenly you find yourself out on the savannah, forced there possibly by environmental changes or by your disruptive neighbours, or both. There's less fruit to eat there, and most of the animals can run faster than you can, because they've evolved to live in that open environment and generally have four long legs rather you're your paltry two. Even the rodents, with legs that are just an inch or two long can run faster than you can.

Let's face it: you're a complete misfit.

Fortunately, because our ancestors seem to have spent a certain amount of time on the forest floor before their enforced and extended stay on the ground, the open country wasn't a totally alien place to them, so they could muddle along, which gave them a sporting chance. But life was still hard.

On the ground any creatures that might make a nice meal for us could run faster than we could (even the rodents). Possibly more importantly, any creature that wanted to make a meal *of* us could also run faster than we could – and in the open savannah we couldn't just climb into a tree to get out of harms way (There are trees on the savannah, but they are more thinly spread than would be convenient).

Fortunately there weren't enough predators around to eat all of our ancestors in one go. This was because in the wild the number of carnivores is always relatively low compared to the number of herbivores, at a ratio of about 100 to 1. If the carnivores were numerous enough to eat all of the herbivores they'd soon run out of food, and would die out themselves.

Our ancestors may have had pathetic locomotive skills on the ground in comparison to those of the other creatures there, but they did have one quality that worked in their favour – they were omnivorous. Most medium to large sized ground dwellers were polarized into either the vegetarian or meat-only camps, but we could eat almost anything. This meant that, very usefully, we could survive by eating from a larger menu than was available to most similarly sized creatures. Choosing from this menu had its problems though, meaning that we had to act slightly differently to other creatures while making our choices.

Take this scenario. A small group of our ancestors are walking across a typical patch of savannah, with its open areas of tall grass and scattered trees. Suddenly, there's the rustling of a largish animal that's hidden from sight behind a bush. How should our ancestors, as omnivores, react to this rustling, and in what ways might their reactions differ from those of other creatures?

Any herbivore – a gazelle for instance – that heard such a rustling would assume that it may be a predator and would head off in the opposite direction, just to be on the safe side. There'd be no point in hanging around. Doing so was potentially dangerous.

Equally, any carnivore that heard a rustling would assume that it may possibly be caused by a creature that was a potential meal, and thus it may stealthily approach the source of the noise rather than flee from it. If the carnivore discovered that the rustling was caused by another carnivore it would probably decide to turn around and look for a meal elsewhere (as carnivores tend to steer clear of one another rather than making meals of each other).

For our omnivorous ancestors it was different. When they heard a rustling the noise could be either a predator or it could be something to eat. They had two choices – either run away and be safe (but hungry), or stay and possibly have a meal (or be eaten). Tricky.

These two conflicting choices, governed by different emotions and different parts of the brain, made life confusing. Rather than simply acting on impulse, on the basis of very straightforward rules, as most creatures do, our ancestors had to work out the correct response to two distinct and opposing drives – they had to be aware of the balance of risk and reward when deciding whether to flee or stay. A whole new area of mental activity needed to gradually develop.

This dilemma, whether to run or stay, applies to all omnivores to some extent. But for our ancestors it was far more pressing than for most. Most medium-sized omnivores eat creatures that are much smaller and lower down the food chain than they are themselves, because they are cowards. Thus an omnivorous warthog will eat a carnivorous lizard. As a result these omnivores could avoid the flee or feast dilemma as long as there is enough potential food around. If they heard something large rustling, they'd sensibly retreat, while if they heard something small, they'd eat.

This didn't apply to our ancestors however. As misfits in an alien environment they had to eat creatures that were frequently much greater in size and strength than was generally advisable.

Thus the awareness that the world held alternatives (the rustling in the bushes may be either predator or prey) developed to a much greater extent in our ancestors than it did in other creatures, and with this the greater awareness that you could, or indeed had to, make choices about which action to take – to run or to stay.

Due to the importance of knowing what type of creature (predator or prey) was doing the rustling in the bushes even though the cause was hidden, it was especially necessary to develop the ability to *wonder* what the cause of the rustling was. This marked a leap in the degree of curiosity that our ancestors possessed. As a result our ancestors developed a highly tuned ability to think about things that were hidden, and an awareness that it was useful to know more about a situation than was immediately obvious.

Not only would wondering about what was hidden heighten our ancestors' curiosity, but the act of trying to envision what was hidden may have been a huge boost to the development of *imagination.*

Under the pressure of the complexities of the new and hostile world that they found themselves in, our ancestors gradually became cleverer and cleverer.

This doesn't mean that they deliberately "thought themselves cleverer" just by thinking a lot.

It was much more a simple matter of cleverer people surviving, because they were the ones who could deal best with the complex pressures that they encountered in their alien environment. These survivors would then have children who on average were as intelligent as they were, and thus the average intelligence of humans would increase (in the same way that the average colours of the moths described earlier became closer to that of tree bark).

Other creatures weren't in situations where being more intelligent would be a definite advantage, as they were already well adapted to their environments. They already had their own means of surviving, such as by reproducing in large numbers or by staying out of harm's way in their own ecological niches.

Higher Curiosity

When our early ancestors wondered about what was making the savannah's grass rustle (predator or prey?) they were exhibiting a degree of curiosity. It was a relatively primitive manifestation of the quality, as its only concern was "What's that?" (Is it a lion or a warthog?) However, this was definitely a sophisticated response when compared to that of most creatures, for which the response to a rustle was much closer to a simple "There's something there!" (which, you may notice, carries no question mark: it isn't a question).

Our ancestors' "What's that?" response, while being very much a question and thus the result of curiosity, was however only the result of a limited type of curiosity that seeks the acquisition of useful facts – facts of a very static kind (It's a lion. It's a warthog). It was a form of curiosity that didn't call for any degree of analysis to be undertaken.

This is a type of curiosity that's possessed in some degree by many higher animals.

You can see it in action (I think) when a dog inside a house hears someone approaching the door. The dog pricks up its ears and becomes alert.

This "What's that?" level of curiosity works fine for dogs, but for our misfit ancestors it wasn't enough, on its own, to ensure survival. However, it was a step in the right direction.

The "What's that?" level of curiosity emerges within a brain that's capable of discerning that there are things in the world that are hidden from view (such as animals on the other side of bushes or people on the other side of doors). Our ancestors must have grasped at some point that if there was a creature behind a bush before they could see it, then the creature was probably there before they could *hear* it. They realised that just because you couldn't see, hear or otherwise sense something didn't mean that it didn't exist: that things didn't just pop into existence when their presence was made known by sight, sound or smell. (This is something like a very early version of the classical puzzle, popularised by Bishop Berkeley in the eighteenth century, about whether or not chairs still exist when you've left the room.)

Armed with this realisation that there are hidden objects in the world, the cleverer individuals amongst our ancestors developed the realisation that there were also hidden *events* going on, unnoticed, behind the scenes too.

This awareness of hidden events, or mechanisms at work behind the surface, allowed our ancestors to develop a form of curiosity that rather than simply asking "What's that?" asked "How's that?" This type of thinking involves the noticing of links between things.

This is a different order of thinking altogether to the simple fact-acquiring "What's that?" way of thinking, as it requires a grasp of consequences – of *cause and effect*.

The ability to be able to think in terms of cause and effect was of paramount importance in the development of our mental capabilities.

As a result of their enhanced ability to cope with what the world threw at them the members of our ancestors' groups who could think in terms of cause and effect survived better than their less gifted relatives, and they thus reproduced more profusely, creating future generations of our ancestors who were similarly a little bit more insightful on average – a good example of the process of cause and effect itself.

THE ASCENT OF MAN (TO THE TOP OF THE TREE)

These new generations with their superior brain-power had the intelligence not only to ask "How's that?" but could ask an even more sophisticated question: "Why's that?" They could now ask *why* questions as well as *how* questions.

A typical how question could be: "How do I kill a crocodile?" Answer: "By hitting it on the head with a big stone."

In contrast, a why question would be "Why does hitting a crocodile on the head with a big stone kill the crocodile?"

To possess this "Why's that?" curiosity needs the ability to wonder about the reason that things are the way they are, rather than just accepting that things are as they are. It means not just accepting that for some mysterious reason a crocodile drops dead when it's had its head caved in. Thus the qualities of analytical intelligence were born.

This form of curiosity is so sophisticated that it's possible that only we humans have it (Or perhaps other creatures are just hiding it very well to avoid being subjected to tests).

The concept of cause and effect is something that we tend to take for granted. However, it's not something that we're born with. It takes a few years of growth before the brain is capable of understanding it. I still remember the time when, as a child, I first grasped the concept myself.

It was night. I lay in bed in the dark looking upwards. Every so often, to my perplexity, a rectangular area a few feet wide on one of the bedroom walls would suddenly become lighter than the rest of the wall. This light rectangle would then slide across the wall before vanishing. I was obviously aware enough to think that this was interesting, but I had no idea what it was.

I pointed out this fascinating phenomenon to my twin brother who shared the room with me.

"What do you think that is?" I asked him.

"The lights from the cars on the road outside (stupid)."

Of course!

Suddenly it was all so obvious. Every time the rectangle of light traversed the wall it was accompanied by the sound of a car passing on the road. The shape of the light patch was very similar to the shape of the window, which was another clue.

It hadn't even occurred to me that the light on the wall was being projected through the window. I'd just seen a bright rectangle of wall – perhaps I'd assumed that the wall itself was temporarily lighter for some reason. After all, why not?

Linking two seemingly unrelated phenomena – in this case the sound of a passing car and the appearance of the light on the wall – was a major revelation to me.

I vowed to use the concept again.

Anxiety

Out on the savannah we were ill-suited creatures in a dangerous world, so the only way that we could survive was to live by our wits.

Most creatures slotted neatly into their position in the established animal hierarchy: we however didn't know our place, so we had to literally think on our feet.

Life on the ground was hard for our misfit ancestors. Just imagine it. When a predator threatened they couldn't just climb a tree like the ancestors of the other great apes, nor could they flee at great speed like the ancestors of the antelopes, nor could they scurry for cover down a hole like the ancestors of the rodents or fly off like the ancestors of the birds. For these other creatures the only thing that was necessary when danger threatened was to react and retreat to a position of safety, where equilibrium was restored. They could then disengage their brains and relax in a state of relative thoughtlessness.

Our ancestors didn't have that luxury (although it wasn't really a luxury at all – it was actually the norm). Whenever our ancestors retreated to relative safety from any danger they almost invariably found themselves still in a position that was almost as exposed as ever. They were still on the ground in a hostile environment. They found that they were never in a situation in which they could safely drop their guard. They were in a constant state of trepidation, uncertainty, wariness, alertness and fretfulness (Does that sound familiar?).

Needless to say, amongst the groups of our ground-dwelling ancestors there'd be some individuals who were less fretful and less anxious than others – ones that were reasonably contented with their lot. They'd sit around thinking "Things aren't so bad."

Guess which members of the groups were the ones that didn't notice when the sabre-toothed tiger came creeping up.

With the more laid-back members of our ancestors' groups eaten by tigers, the balance of personality types within the groups would have become heavily weighted towards the fretful, the nervous and the neurotic. The personality trait of laid-backness was largely selected out, while the traits of anxiety and edginess were reinforced.

And so it was that the discontented amongst our ancestors survived and thrived, passing this useful personality trait on to future generations. Such as us.

The Tools for Shaping the Intellect

As mentioned above, under the pressure of having to live by their wits our ancestors started to develop the concept of consequences (The rustling in the grass may be a predator or it may be prey – do we eat or get eaten?). A degree of analysis was called for.

Embryonic concepts of cause and effect began to emerge in their brains.

One of the consequences of this was the development of tools.

Tool use probably started by accident. Our ancestor who invented the first tool didn't pick up a stick or a bone and think "What can I do with this?" The inventor was much more likely to be holding a stick or a bone and noticed that it had useful secondary qualities (such as the ability to poke an annoying neighbour in the eye). Fortunately, our ancestors had developed an awareness of cause and effect by then, so the implications of this were duly taken on board. The concept of using objects such as sticks to achieve particular ends was born. We had grasped the concept of tools.

On the subject of grasping tools, one of the features that made tool use possible was that our ancestors had hands that could literally grasp things. This was a direct result of abilities acquired during their tree climbing past in which holding onto branches was a necessary skill.* We were very lucky in this respect – if a creature such as a zebra was by some chance to be born as clever as a human I don't think it would ever have been able to master, for instance, the bow and arrow.

Our ancestors also walked upright, although possibly with a bit of a waddle. This freed the forelimbs from any role in ambulation, allowing them to be used for holding objects. Originally these objects would have been food, later on, tools.

---

* Our opposable thumbs, which we can fold across the palms of our hands, are often cited as being critical to our development, as they allow us to hold tools in very refined ways. I've got a feeling that this talent may be overstated: a quick, unscientific experiment around my house has revealed that I can do lots of things purely by grasping objects with my fingers alone. Perhaps opposable thumbs are very useful, but not essential.

THE ASCENT OF MAN (TO THE TOP OF THE TREE)

Our ancestors could achieve this bipedalism due to their tree climbing past, where the forelimbs were used for grasping.

If our ancestors hadn't originally been tree dwellers we probably wouldn't be here now. We'd have still been out there with the zebras.

(It's generally assumed that other apes, such as chimps, put their hands on the ground when they are walking – a technique known as knuckle walking. It's sometimes argued that this debarred them from developing significant tool use, and may thus have been a factor in their lack of development. I'm not sure of the validity of this conjecture: although they do indeed use knuckle walking, they are also quite capable of walking solely with their hind limbs, which they do frequently while in the branches. Personally I suspect that they didn't develop beyond their current position purely because they didn't need to, because they were just fine in their trees.)

Many creatures other than humans use tools – thrushes use stones as "anvils" on which to smash snail shells, finches use sticks to poke into holes as a way of extracting insects, and even insects themselves sometimes use tools. This in general is very limited tool use however, chiefly involving the manipulation of a handy object such as a stick or twig. It doesn't involve any significant modification of the object. Exception has to be made for one of the most adept tool users on the planet, the Caledonian crow, which, like all members of the crow family, is far from being bird-brained. (This pun is always used when the Caledonian crow is mentioned, therefore I'm obliged to follow tradition. Sorry.) This crow has been studied by Professor Russell Gray, Dr Gavin Hunt and colleagues at the University of Auckland, New Zealand, and had been found to be capable of sophisticated manipulation of tools in the form of specially chosen and modified twigs. Quite why a bird would need to be quite so extravagantly intelligent is a mystery that only the bird is clever enough to answer.

The great apes use tools in a more sophisticated manner than most creatures, with chimps sometimes even using sticks as rudimentary spears. It's not surprising that apes are capable of this relatively complex tool use, being so closely related to us, but they never took the idea and ran with it to the point where it put a chimp in space.

That's because the chimp's basic arsenal of tools are perfectly adequate for the tasks that are required of them. They do the job. There was never any pressure on the chimps to do better. Their lives didn't depend on it. As a result they were perfectly content with their basic stick idea.

We, however, were never in that privileged position. For us it was more a matter of develop tools or die.

Once we'd developed the use of tools something interesting happened to us. The fossil record seems to show that about 300,000 years after the first significant use of tools by our ancestors we'd evolved noticeably larger brains.

It's postulated that by using tools such as spears and primitive cutting implements our earlier, smaller-brained ancestors could eat more meat. The digestion of meat required less energy than did vegetables, so as a result there was a surplus of energy that was diverted into powering the energy-hungry brain. The appendix shrank and the brain expanded. In modern humans the brain demands about 20-25% of the body's energy.

There's also the possibility that meat contains brain-enhancing nutrients that are unavailable in plant matter. There is some evidence, for instance, that the compound known as creatine which is found in animal tissue and is commonly used as a muscle booster by athletes may increase mental ability.* It's the sort of substance that's nowadays given the name of *super food* (by food company marketing departments). The name creatine comes from the Greek *kreas* (flesh) and its similarity to the word *creative* is purely coincidental, I think, even if the substance does turn out to boost creativity in some way.

In parallel to the development of tools the related acquisition of cooking skills may have had a highly beneficial influence on the brain. It's possible that cooking, by breaking down the chemical constituents of food, makes digestion easier and more efficient, thus again allowing energy to be diverted away from food processing and into brain-building.**

Food for thought indeed.

Raw vegetable food faddists take note.

Combining Things

Chimps have smaller brains than we do.

Consequently the chimp doesn't have the mental capacity to envisage a process whereby it could alter a tool (in the form of a stick) so that it works better – it can only use what is presented to it. Our ancestors however realised that they could improve on things. For instance, they could combine the sticks and the stones that they used as rudimentary tools (for poking and smashing and other generally aggressive activities) to make a much-improved tool: an axe.

This ability to combine two elements, such as sticks and stones, to create one greater thing, an axe, is very important. Once our ancestors realised that it was a useful strategy they

---

* Dr Caroline Rae, University of Sydney, 2003.
** Research on the subject is currently being conducted by Dr Richard Wrangham of Harvard University.

used it endlessly, and not only for creating more complex tools. For instance they used it with language, taking a few simple grunts and related noises and grafting them together in new combinations in order to convey more complex information.

They used the same combining system within their thought processes too, splicing together a few simple concepts in order to create new and intriguing ideas.

All of these combinatory processes conform to the saying "The whole is greater than the sum of the parts".

As a result of our acquisition of the ability to combine things, from tools to language to concepts, we developed in leaps and bounds. But despite these leaps and bounds we were still two-legged animals in a four-legged world. We were fish out of water. Wherever we went we were still in a state of near constant emotional discomfort and general dissatisfaction.

It's probable that our all-pervasive feeling of dissatisfaction was made even worse by our recently amplified awareness of the concept of alternatives and of choice (flee or stay). After all, once you realise that there are alternatives you realise that things could be different – and it soon dawns on you that things could be *better*. And that if you make one choice from among the alternatives there's always the nagging feeling that you may have chosen the wrong one.

This feeling of dissatisfaction is a strong driving force in our development.

You can imagine one of our ancestors sitting looking at the perfectly serviceable axe that he's just made – and being dissatisfied with it. Because he just was.

He'd then try to make an even better one. And would succeed.

But he'd still be dissatisfied with the result. It could surely be better still?

Dissatisfaction of this sort is the fuel that keeps driving us forwards.

Our tendency towards a feeling of dissatisfaction, and the accompanying constant desire to improve things, such as by creating better axes, was a critical factor in our ability to sustain ourselves in a hostile environment. No wonder we've got dissatisfaction as our constant companion, hard wired into our brains: it's a wonderful survival tool.

It was this feeling of dissatisfaction that fuelled the long journey of humanity from misfit to overlord. The underdog finally triumphs – it's a classic dramatic arc.

Unfortunately, as I've mentioned before, our tendency towards a feeling of dissatisfaction has propelled us onwards and upwards to such an extent that we're now at the point where we're dangerously close to destroying most of what we've achieved. So the dramatic arc may all end very badly indeed.

Why are we More Intelligent than is Necessary for Survival?

The development of intelligence was our key to survival, in that it helped us to negotiate the strange and inhospitable world of "the ground", but you may have noticed that we seem to be of an intelligence that's way beyond the needs for that function alone. We seem to be too intelligent merely for the purposes of immediate and stable existence. In fact, judging by the mess that we're making of the world right now, we seem to be way too intelligent for our own good.

Why did we become so seemingly preposterously, unnecessarily clever?

It's possibly the result of a secondary pressure that we were under, beyond that of basic survival. This pressure was the internal pressure from within social groups rather than the external pressure from the surrounding environment.

Pressure from within social groups doesn't automatically encourage the development of intelligence – other creatures live in social groups but they didn't develop in the way that we did. This was probably because (as usual) they didn't need to.

The reason that social pressure meant that we developed higher intelligence may again come back to our position as a misfit species on the ground. We'd had to learn to live as tight-knit packs, where individuals had to pull their weight and help the whole group, such as by keeping a watch out for predators and by seeking out food.

Our ancestors were a bit like the characters in one of those disaster movies in which civilization breaks down and only a handful of people survive (possibly after a nuclear war or a world-wide epidemic of a killer virus): small bands of people roaming around a hostile environment, having to pool their resources and skills, or die.

It was essential that we developed the relatively high intelligence and sophisticated communication skills that would allow us to survive adequately in this situation, and that were necessarily far beyond those of other creatures that were in general hunkered down in their ecological niches. But once we'd developed those skills we didn't stop.

Like the characters in the aforementioned disaster movie, life for our intrepid bands of hominids wasn't just about basic survival. There were internal rivalries and jealousies within the groups that had to be reckoned with too. In order to negotiate these complicated social interactions, the more complex a person's brain, the better.

Needless to say, many of these social interactions would revolve around sex. The males in a group would have their eyes on the females. Just as now. The need to compete with rivals for the affections of the most gorgeous females would be intense, and all of the males who thought they were in with a chance would try to impress these females. Just as now. Up to a point these males would rely on their good looks and strapping physiques, but beyond that they'd try to turn the female heads by using displays of skill and intelligence. Just as now.

According to this scenario our excessively high intelligence is largely for the purpose of showing off with, a bit like the peacock's tail. This is the sexual display theory of intelligence.

I think that this has the feel of at least a certain amount of plausibility to it – after all I'm pretty sure that most of the stuff that men do even today is motivated by the desire to impress women, whether it's driving a car too fast or becoming a professor of cognitive neuroscience. Indeed, a friend of mine who recently had to change careers from being an acupuncturist to a plumber (due to a surplus of acupuncturists in his part of California) commented that the main drawback of his new occupation was that it had a lower cachet with the ladies.

Males don't only want to impress females though – they also want to impress other males. A lot of inter-male interaction is geared towards status enhancement and attempts at dominance – because the dominant males get a bigger share of the resources that are available. Amongst these resources are food, shelter, and sexual partners, so there's still a sexual element involved, which I'm sure doesn't surprise you.

It's sometimes obvious which pursuits are carried out by males specifically in order to impress other males rather than females. In the modern world such activities include for instance – skateboarding. Have you ever seen a young woman who's in the slightest bit interested in the skateboarding prowess of young men? Me neither. Such skills are almost purely for the purposes of (young) men testing themselves against each other.

Over the generations the competition between males to out-perform each other has resulted in an inevitable upwards spiral of intelligence levels (along with increasing skateboarding skills). Intelligence increased as a result of more intelligent males having to compete with more intelligent males.

You may have noticed that I've just described the runaway increase in human intelligence as stemming from competition between males for female approval and between males for inter-male dominance. In other words, I've described the increase in intelligence as being male driven.

A reasonable conclusion to this may be that women should therefore lag behind men in the intelligence stakes, just as women obviously lag behind men in the physical brawn stakes.

However, women aren't on average less intelligent than men – they're exactly the same.

It's notoriously difficult to conduct studies of variations in intelligence between different groups of people, as it's very tricky to separate the culturally imposed variants from innate ones. It's also quite hard finding a representative sample of people to test (rather than the usual group of university students). However, very interestingly, some recent studies into the differences between the intelligence levels of men and women claim to find that at the *bottom* end of the intelligence scale there are noticeably more men than women (with about the bottom 2% being almost exclusively male). Why would that be, if intelligence was male driven?

If you're a woman reading this and you're now thinking "Ah ha – I knew it. Men are stupid!" – not so fast. The same studies also found that men outnumber women at the other end of the intelligence scale too (with the top 2% being almost exclusively male). Essentially, there are more male geniuses and dunces, with the vast majority of the men in between being exactly the same as their female counterparts.*

When human intelligence is likened in its development to the peacock's tail it's interesting to see that for humans the females develop the elaborate "tail" as well as the male. The reason for this is sometimes argued to be that the showy male intelligence needs a similar degree of intelligence in its female audience in order for it to be appreciated.

While many men will happily accept this and jump to the conclusion that it shows that it was primarily the males who were powering the intelligence race and as a result dragging the females along behind them, it could equally be argued that it was the females who drove the intelligence race forwards by demanding that the males perform better in the intellectual prowess stakes.

Indeed, the fact that the average male and female intelligences seem to be exactly the same possibly suggests that it isn't the case that women's intelligence follows or pushes men's in any way. The real mystery is why male intelligence has a wider spread (if indeed it turns out that it actually does).

Let's say that the whole thing was a joint effort.

For anyone who resents the fact that the most intelligent 2% of the population are supposedly all male, bear in mind that high intelligence of the IQ variety isn't everything, and that judging by the personalities of some people who've got it, it sometimes

---

* There have been numerous studies of this subject. While I was writing this section some research came out by Professor Timothy Bates of the Department of Psychology at Edinburgh University, 2007. The areas of competence that were tested were science, maths, English and mechanical abilities, possibly leaving the door open to the claim of too narrow a subject range. This topic and related areas of gender difference are dealt with by Steven Pinker, *The Blank Slate*, Chapter 18.

comes at quite a high cost in terms of other, perhaps more desirable, human characteristics. And while you're resenting those top 2%, don't forget to give a bit of sympathy to those unfortunate people in the bottom 2% - all men.

This whole subject is a minefield of sexual politics of course, so I think I'll move rapidly on.

The Infinite Progression Dilemma.

There are other reasons why we may have become as ridiculously intelligent as we are, on top of the need to survive and the need to impress.

It's possible that our increase in intelligence is partly driven by our innate tendencies towards dissatisfaction and curiosity.

As outlined earlier, all creatures that are capable of emotions are burdened with their share of dissatisfaction. Think of the moose standing in the blizzard.

In our case the trait was reinforced by our descent to the ground, where the feeling was amplified by our total immersion in a hostile environment that gave us no hope of remission.

Also, as mentioned earlier, on the ground our nascent sense of curiosity was heightened due to our need to be very aware of any hidden threats and opportunities around us (Is that a predator or prey hiding in the long grass – a dinner or a diner?).

Due to the fact that our ancestors were constantly in danger on the ground these significant levels of dissatisfaction and curiosity became permanently fused into their psychic make-up. They were like little irritants prodding away, forcing our ancestors to react to them all of the time. Our ancestors just couldn't turn them off. And we still haven't been able to turn them off to this day.

Having become intelligent and aware of the possibility of

alternatives and choices, we now find ourselves not only being dissatisfied because we're discontented anyway but also because we have the sneaking feeling that there may be better alternatives than those that are available – even if such alternatives don't actually exist.

A chimp will be content when it selects a perfectly ripe banana from amongst a bunch of otherwise unripe fruit, but that's because to a chimp a ripe banana's as good as a banana can get, as it's the best on offer – it can't conceive of the alternative of having the banana with maple syrup and ice cream. Unfortunately, we can. What's more, we fret over the idea that there may be an even better way to eat bananas that we haven't thought of yet! Or at least I do.

There's always the nagging and dissatisfying possibility that something can be better still.

This quandary is known as the *infinite progression dilemma*.

Dissatisfaction is like the inverse of the carrot on a pole, suspended in front of a donkey. With the carrot, the donkey moves forwards to grab the carrot, but never reaches it, because the carrot moves forwards with the donkey. Dissatisfaction is like the same pole reversed, and with a spiky ball in place of the carrot: a spiky ball that keeps poking the donkey from behind. The donkey will move forwards to get away from the irritant, but to no avail. The spiky ball just follows it along. The irritated donkey is condemned to keep moving forwards forever, whether it wants to or not. Unfortunately, in reality it's not a donkey that's in this predicament – it's us.

Driven People are Doing the Driving

So it is that the human race has been bequeathed a tendency for dissatisfaction and discontentedness that has had a hand in driving it forwards through the ages. A tendency that we still have today.

Even in our modern age in the western world, where in terms of material well-being we are unarguably more affluent and altogether better off than people of any era that has gone before, we still suffer the constant nag of discontentedness. Even if your life is utterly, totally, absolutely fantastic, the chances are that you're never truly, completely, unequivocally satisfied with it. At least not for more than a day or two at a time, if things are going particularly well. We're just not supposed to be.

Like that donkey, we all have a spiked ball prodding us from behind, making us just that little bit uncomfortable almost all of the time.

The existence of our dissatisfaction tendency has major implications for the trajectory of the human race through history.

Essentially, our innate feelings of dissatisfaction are one of our major motivations to change things (linked to our constant need for status).

Although just about everybody suffers to some extent from this nagging prod of chronic discontentment, not everybody has equally dire symptoms. Different people are born with different discontentment quotients. Some people seem to be able to amble through life as though it's something of a breeze, while others are constantly on the verge of exploding due to the total wrongness of everything (ranging from the decline in the spelling skills of the younger generation to the fact that we're about to destroy our planet).

Generally speaking, the more dissatisfied a person feels, the more motivated they are to change thinks.

As a result, such people have the largest effect on human history.

THE ASCENT OF MAN (TO THE TOP OF THE TREE)

They are the ones who, due to that chronic itch in their heads that they just can't get rid of, get up and shape the course of civilisation, for better or worse.

Contented people don't do much as a rule.

Look around yourself today. You'll notice that a very significant percentage of the movers and shakers on our planet are chronic malcontents, people who are driven by some sort of ever-present dissatisfaction demon that they can't seem to shake off.

These are the people who get up early in the morning, prodded by that pang of discontent.

It's people like them who shape the world. Not the guys who are happy enough to have a lie-in.

It's because of the fact that people were dissatisfied that we have such things as – to pick an example at random from the almost endless list of possibilities – handles on cups (to stop our fingers from getting burned while drinking hot beverages). It's why we have cups at all, so that we don't have to drink from pools of water in the way that many other creatures do. And it's also why we have nice hot beverages rather than cold muddy water to drink from the cups with handles.

Next time that you're sipping a pleasingly hot coffee from a nice mug remember that you can only do so because of people's dissatisfaction with what went before.

The moral of this is that we should treat dissatisfaction as a friend.

In our modern world, where happiness seems to be people's primary goal, the pursuit of which is even written into the United States' Declaration of Independence as a self-evident, unalienable right; where people think that if they're the tiniest bit dissatisfied (perhaps in an unspecific, unresolved sort of a way) then they must be ill and must therefore go and get therapy: in that world I think we need to stand back and see just what an ally dissatisfaction has been to us.

So if you feel vaguely unhappy with your life, don't go and try to snuff out that unpleasantness in the therapist's consulting room – you're trying to destroy one of your most valuable human assets.

Go and write a poem or develop a new way of feeding starving people. Or create an improved design for a coffee cup.

Harness that unhappiness!

Don't be dissatisfied with feeling dissatisfied. Embrace it.

There is, needless to say, a downside to the fact that it tends to be the most chronically and acutely malcontented among us, the most driven and obsessive, who tend to rise to the very top of any scale of human achievement.

The personal commitment, effort, ruthlessness and sheer unpleasantness that's necessary in order to get to the higher echelons of any area of human endeavour debar most of us from those ranks.

As a result, the course that the human race takes through history is more often than not steered by people of somewhat questionable character: at best they're overachievers, at worst they're mentally deranged. Just look at some of our politicians and business leaders. Not to mention religious leaders. Our planet is hurtling through space with a succession of dangerous misfits at the helm.

Part III

Why Are We

?

Chapter 18

Why do We Want to Know?

What Lies Behind the Scenes?

Because we're innately and constantly in a state of dissatisfaction over just about everything that we experience, we're therefore innately and constantly in a state of trying to make things less dissatisfying. In order to achieve this we try to understand things, because understanding things puts us in a position from which we can possibly manipulate them to our own liking. As a result we're innately and constantly curious about everything and about how things work, because we suspect that once we know, we can use the knowledge to make them work better. Knowledge is power.

Our inquisitiveness knows few bounds. We're curious, for instance, about why the Sun rises in the morning – not that we can improve on that, but you don't know that until you know that. We're curious about how aeroplanes stay in the air – a subject that you may find particularly riveting when you're actually sitting inside one of them. We're even curious about the imaginary lives of fictional characters – possibly because they provide safe testing grounds for experiences that we may find ourselves confronted by one day. We're curious about everything. So it's not surprising that we're curious about what we perceive to be one of the biggest subjects of all: the whole point of existence: The Meaning of Life.

If we can be curious about why planes fly we can definitely be curious about the ultimate destination of the creatures that are flying in them.

We're curious creatures, and being alive is just about the most curious thing there is.

This is why we ask "What's it all about?"

Even as you read these sentences you're probably thinking that this is where religion comes in. But that isn't inevitable. It's quite possible to formulate a meaning of life based on purely earthly matters such as serving a community, raising a family or doing something useful. Having said that, people do have a tendency to construct meanings to our lives that are not based solely in the worldly sphere. There are reasons for this.

As described earlier, our brains are capable of realising that there are hidden things in the world, things behind what we can see. We are aware that things happen because other things happen, and we are aware that one thing causes another. We are aware, for instance, that the sound of rustling in the grass means that there is a hidden creature making the noise. (Bear in mind that it's possible that when less sophisticated creatures than ourselves hear a rustling noise in the grass they may correctly associate the noise with an animal, but they won't necessarily know that the animal is there in the sense that we understand it. They may know that an animal is *about* to appear due to the rustling, but for all they know the animal may appear spontaneously out of nowhere, with the rustling being some sort of precursor. All they will know is that the sound of rustling and the appearance of an animal are sequential – they won't necessarily understand why. This may be likened to the way that until relatively recently people didn't understand the causal link between thunder and lightning, only the sequential link.)

Not only do we realise that certain things make other things happen, and that one thing follows another, but we also know that we can make things happen deliberately. We can intervene in things. For instance, if we come across a line of dominoes standing on a table we know that if the first one falls it will knock the next one over onto its neighbour and so on until the whole line has fallen. But we also know that we don't have to just stand there waiting for this entertaining event to occur. We don't have to wait for the first domino to fall spontaneously – we can give it a push.

We know that we can choose to make things happen.

What's more, not only do we know that we can make things happen, but we know that we can make *things*. We can make tools. We can make shelters.

We can make dominoes.

So it is that for every object and occurrence in the world we can imagine that there is an agency at work creating the object or putting into motion the occurrence.

In the case of animals making grass rustle all we have to do is creep round and look at the rustling grass from a different direction in order to see the animal that is the creator of the rustling.

We imagine that, just as something created the rustling in the grass, so something must have created the grass itself, and the animal that's in it. And everything else in the world. After all, *we* create things, so it would seem reasonable to assume that everything else is created too. Just as we are creators of spears and axes, so there must be a creator of grasses and animals and of trees and rocks and clouds. When it comes to catching sight of the creator of these things however it's slightly more tricky than getting a peek at an animal that's making the grass rustle, as we can't simply walk around and look at the whole world from a different direction, giving us a sneaky glimpse of the creator in action.

But our psychological make-up and our knowledge of how things are created by our own hand or by the action of other creatures gives us the definite feeling that there's a creator of some sort (or a whole team of creators) at work, hiding somewhere behind the scenes.

Don't jump to conclusions though. It isn't necessary for the creator or creators to be thought of as existing on a mystical or supernatural plane. It's quite possible for it, or them, to exist at a very matter of fact, down to earth, prosaic level. The hidden forces behind the workings of the world may be thought of as being simply an extension of the natural world – an extension that is simply not visible to us.

The creator could be no more than a grander version of the spirits that we endow on objects around us (You may recall that earlier in the book I described how trees, cliffs and even cars can be imbued with human-like personalities or spirits due to our tendency to imagine that these objects have some sort of consciousness). Different to us, but definitely of this world.

Or perhaps the creator is simply a sort of super-though-still-essentially-human being that sits on a throne somewhere inaccessible such as on a mountaintop beyond the clouds.

(Due to the nature of most of the things that happen in the day-to-day world – thunder, lightning, storms, earthquakes, starvation, disease, death, and the like – it wouldn't be unreasonable to come to the conclusion that any hidden creator at work behind the scenes in our world possesses a few quite unpleasant personality traits – not unlike many of the people of questionable character who often end up running things down here in the day-to-day world in fact.)

However, we're not content to let things rest at that rather prosaic, matter-of-fact level, where even the creator of all things exists somewhere that's nothing more exotic than an invisible or rather inaccessible corner of the normal world. We have to create a special place for that creator to reside, somewhere that's totally divorced from our mundane physical world altogether: somewhere on another plane.

It's here that our ideas about what's behind things start to take on rather grandiose proportions. We get religion as we know it, in its pumped up, inflated form.

There are quite understandable, practical reasons why we do this. One is probably that we simply like to bolster the importance of our concerns and preoccupations. We do this in many areas of our lives.

You can see it in sport, where selected sporting activities such as football, baseball, tennis and cricket are elevated far beyond the importance that should arguably be bestowed on the seemingly pointless activity of kicking, hitting or throwing a ball around. You can see it especially in the acme of sporting events, the Olympic Games, where such feats as being able to run faster or jump higher than someone else have been awarded the status of being virtually the pinnacles of human achievement. The huge amount of time, effort, money and emotion that are poured into the Olympic Games for a mere two weeks of activity that ultimately leads nowhere (other than in circles round a track) is staggering. However, despite the protestations of those amongst us who don't like sport, and despite its total lack of practical use and its astonishingly high expenditure of money, time, resources and effort, sport at this level is for many people, both participants and spectators, a hugely worthwhile phenomenon due to the added value that it gives to their lives. In fact, it mirrors in many ways the pursuit of religion.

The same can be said of my own preferred pointless activity of choice – staring approvingly at paintings on the walls of art galleries. Some of these paintings are thought of as the highest attainment of human endeavour – higher even than the ability to kick a ball between two posts. Art galleries, as you may have noticed, often look and feel uncannily like temples, emphasising the supposedly transcendent nature of their contents.

Quite why sport and art are held in higher esteem than other areas of human activity such as, for instance, brain surgery or fire-fighting, is a mystery to me.

Our tendency towards the aggrandisement of our interests isn't, however, the only reason that we religiously elevate the creator of the world to an esteemed and exalted position. Another reason comes about as a direct result of our very high intelligence.

An Unfortunate Consequence of High Intelligence

Our level of intelligence may possibly have developed by following a very similar evolutionary dynamic to the one that caused the giraffe to develop its long neck.

The primary dynamic was probably basic survival. For the giraffe, a longer neck meant that it could reach higher leaves in trees, while for people bigger brains meant that we could reach higher levels of understanding of the workings of an alien and hostile ground-based environment.

There is a theory that the giraffe's neck is not only a practical survival adaptation however, but has a sexual dimension as well.* Here, by an interesting coincidence, it still echoes the

---

* One theory proposes that sexual selection was the primary process involved in the lengthening of the giraffe's neck, with the ability to reach high leaves playing no part at all (Simmons & Scheepers). If you're wondering why female giraffes have long necks, this may be because "long neck genes" are shared by males and females, so the females' necks extended in tandem with the males'.

development of the human brain. As well as being useful for reaching greater heights the giraffe's neck is also a useful sexual appendage (just like our intelligence): it is used by males for the purpose of impressing the opposite sex (just like our intelligence), and is also deployed by males as a weapon against members of the same sex (just like our intelligence). Male giraffes fight each other by swinging their long necks and using their heads as clubs in very much the same way that male humans use their heads (or at least the brains in their heads) as clubs to bludgeon each other at a psychological level.

As well as being developmentally similar, the giraffe's neck and human's brain share some similar qualities on a metaphorical level too.

Although the giraffe's neck is primarily useful for the purposes of enabling the giraffe to eat leaves high in trees and for impressing/whacking other giraffes (depending on their gender), it also has the side-effect of allowing the giraffe to see further into the distance from its elevated vantage point. Our intelligence has a similar by-product of its own: although it originally developed as a result of the pressure on our ancestors to survive in an ill-fitting environment, our intelligence has allowed us to "see" further, by endowing us with our abilities for conceptualisation and analysis.

And like the giraffe's neck, our intelligence isn't without its down side. The giraffe's long neck makes it very difficult for the creature to sit down and relax (although it's a myth that as a result giraffes have to sleep standing up). Similarly we find it difficult to sit down and relax too, due to our unwieldy intellects.

When the giraffe looks into the distance from its great height it can, quite usefully, see an approaching lion that remains unnoticed by the other, shorter creatures with which it shares its habitat. When *we* look into the distance from our intellectually elevated vantage point we see something unsettling approaching too – something that other creatures don't have an inkling of.

We see our own death.

Now, there's a burden for you if ever there was one!

I mentioned not long ago that it wasn't only the need to survive and the need to impress the opposite sex that drove the advancement of the human intellect, but also the ever-present prodding of our innate dissatisfaction.

It seems that this tendency towards dissatisfaction, by virtue of its agency in increasing our intelligence, has revealed to us the fact that we're all going to die. By a great irony it has revealed to us what seems to be the most dissatisfying thing of all.

Chapter 19

Consciousness, Mind and Soul – and the Escape Route from Death

Our intelligence has led us to the point where we feel that we have some sort of super-brain nestling inside our heads. However, the human brain doesn't only seem to be the depository of our day-to-day mental calculations and associated deliberations, acting as some sort of biological computer – it seems to be the cradle of states that are above and beyond those of mere matter. It is the seat of the strange thing that we call consciousness. Not only that: it is the place that harbours those even more rarefied entities: the mind and the soul.

On the spectrum of varying degrees of awareness that I described earlier (as possessed by sunflowers, houseflies and chimps amongst others) these three states – consciousness, mind and soul – are right up there at the top – a very long way indeed from the awareness of our ancestral single-celled organisms in their primordial pond.

The fact that these supreme mental faculties seem to be in some way *disembodied* has an interesting consequence. As I've just mentioned, it is because of our highly developed brains that we are aware of the existence of death, damn it – but fortuitously the fact that some of the faculties of our brains seem to be non-physical gives us a perfect avenue for side-stepping this seemingly unfortunate fate.

By convincing ourselves that these mental states actually *are* disembodied we can argue that they can be disengaged from the body and can continue to exist when the flesh dies.

Our mental states do genuinely feel as though they are disembodied: we didn't just convince ourselves of that possibility once we'd noticed that it would be a good way to cheat death. Indeed, I remember thinking in my early teens that a quite reasonable model for the mind was that it was a cloud-like entity floating in a different dimension, linked to the physical body via some sort of trans-dimensional umbilical cord (No doubt I was under the influence of Cartesian dualism, although I wasn't consciously aware of Rene Descartes' ideas at the time. And maybe a bit of science fiction too). As a teenager the concept of the mind intrigued me, but, being a teenager, the issue of death didn't exercise my brain in the slightest – so there was no wishful thinking or convenient rationalisations involved in assuming that my mind was on a different level to my body. It just seemed to be so.

Let's look at these three mental states, consciousness, mind and spirit, one by one, in alphabetical order, (and as it turns out, in order of transcendence).

Consciousness

Why is it that we think of our consciousness as being disembodied?

Probably because it patently *isn't* physical.

But then, if it's not physical, what exactly is it?

Consciousness seems to have properties that are probably analogous to it being a projection, or an abstract construction, brought about by the workings of our brains.

Although consciousness seems bizarre and insubstantial, its existence is hardly any stranger or more peculiar than other projections that we create inside our heads – such as for instance the three-dimensional model of the real world that we see through our eyes. As I described in Chapter 1 (The Flaws of Perception), when we use our sense of vision we create a "virtual" model of the world in the brain – something that seems to be external, three-dimensional, coloured, solid and very much "out there", even though the whole effect exists entirely inside the head. In a similar way our experience of consciousness feels as though it's "up there", somehow hovering around the head in a somewhat unspecific place or dimension.

Consciousness is perhaps similar to vision in other ways too, in that it's almost like a sense itself – perhaps one that monitors the brain and its workings (analogous to the way that vision monitors the world and its workings). A sort of sixth sense.

To be able to do this monitoring, consciousness, like vision, is something that had to evolve over time, rather than being an all or nothing phenomenon. It isn't something that suddenly popped fully formed into existence from nowhere, only appearing once the brain reached some critical level of functional sophistication.

Just as our sense of vision has evolved to its current level of intricacy from a few light-sensitive cells that dimly reacted to the presence of light, so our sense of consciousness may have evolved to its present level of awesome complexity from a dim and unfocused awareness of the workings of the brain (or even of the workings of the brainless nervous system in more primitive organisms).

This means that other creatures probably possess a degree of consciousness too, in exactly the same way that different creatures possess a sense of vision (or at least an awareness of light) in varying degrees – meaning that consciousness is not an exclusively human feature.

The complexity of consciousness in different creatures is probably linked to their levels of intelligence. Indeed, consciousness can possibly be described as intelligence looking at itself. As intelligence develops, so consciousness develops too. Consciousness is possibly nothing more than the sensation of the existence of the brain, analogous in some ways to our more down to earth (and thus less meditated upon) sensation of the existence of the body.

Mind

Consciousness may be likened to a form of mental projection, or to a model within the brain, but what about that slightly higher and more complex mental phenomenon – mind?

Does the fact that consciousness is possibly just a projection within the brain mean that mind is just a projection too?

Mind is a tricky beast to put your finger on – even more so than consciousness. It seems to be an interesting amalgam of thought, perception, imagination, memory and emotion that is on some sort of higher level to "mere" consciousness.

While consciousness can possibly be summed up to some extent as being "awareness of being" or "awareness of existence", mind is much closer to the definition of your essential, core self.

Consciousness seems to be a state that is intriguingly aware of bother the "lower" corporeal body and of the "higher" mind: it is a state that can monitor both: a sort of halfway house that mediates between the material and the non-material worlds.

As a result, because consciousness seems to be a strange disembodied thing floating around your head in a different dimension, mind seems to be doubly so.

But then...

But then...

Why should mind be any more strange than anything else that's part of the strange creature that possesses it, in this strange universe?

On the basis that a simpler explanation is more likely to be correct than a complicated one, I think that the concept of the mind as a projection within the brain beats the common concept of the mind as a free-floating entity in a state of otherness (whatever that means).

That's consciousness and the mind brought down to earth somewhat. But there's another component to our mental make-up that needs consideration too. A third element that's altogether more mysterious than – and downright superior to – the other two: the soul.

Soul

If consciousness seems to be floating around outside your head, and your mind seems to be floating above and beyond that, then the soul seems to be floating beyond even that, in a higher dimension altogether. The soul is the most seemingly disembodied and most immaterial of our trio of seemingly disembodied mental essences – indeed it's often though of as being so disembodied that it practically has an independent existence all of its own, in a plane that's far removed from our physical level of existence. It exists in a dimension that's so special that it's often given a special status – the status of the "spiritual".

The concepts of consciousness, mind and soul are necessarily vague things due to the nature of the beasts, and there is a degree of blurring and overlap between the three. They may indeed be different parts of one and the same thing – a sort of trinity – although a lot of people feel that there's some sort of difference between them. For instance, you may possibly be of the opinion that consciousness and mind may be the same thing, or that mind and soul are the same thing, but many people wouldn't say that consciousness and soul are one and the same – they seem to be too far apart. Animals may quite reasonably have consciousness, and some of them may just about have minds – but do they really have souls? (Despite what you may think of your pet cat.)

Keeping the three concepts separate for now, the notions of consciousness and mind can be given a certain degree of other-worldly or spiritual status if you're so inclined, but with the soul there's hardly any argument about the matter. Almost by definition it's the unadulterated spiritual self.

Or so we like to believe.

But then...

I think that we really need to ask ourselves what we think our souls are, and why we think that there's a special spiritual dimension that they happen to inhabit.

Before we actually put our souls under the magnifying glass however, we need to have a look at that special spiritual dimension in which they are said to exist.

Spiritual Dimensions

To look at that special dimension we first need to step back and look again at our mundane, earthly reality. We need to get a bit of perspective.

Not long ago I described how people are never satisfied with things, how we tend to have a high dissatisfaction quotient, how we're always a little bit disappointed with life.

To give a typical mundane and down to earth example, I recently bought a new jacket, which I'm very pleased with except that I've got a nagging uncertainty about the colour of the lining material used in the pockets (which is totally invisible to the general viewer).

This is the dissatisfaction tendency in operation.

In such minor ways as this the whole of life is never quite right. The major ways in which life is never quite right are legion of course, but they don't bear thinking about. However, because we have intelligence and imagination as well as dissatisfaction, we can conceptualise alternatives to life that are better than the life we inhabit – right down to the tiniest, most irrelevant detail such as the colour of jacket pocket lining material.

The sad fact is that we experience the physical world as being imperfect even when it's almost as good as it can possibly get.

Sticking with the jacket, if I were ever by some fluke of chance to find and buy a perfect jacket, with just the right colour of pocket lining, I would undoubtedly only experience the total ecstasy of feeling that the jacket was perfect for a few months at the very most. The jacket would then become too shabby and frayed, due to the inevitable process of entropy, whereby all things move towards a state of disorder.

Even if I arranged things so that the jacket didn't become shabby, perhaps by making it immune to the decaying influence of everyday wear and tear by isolating it in a sealed bag in my wardrobe, it would still gradually attain a state of imperfection due to the inevitable process of becoming unfashionable.

There's also a good chance that I'd just become bored with it.

So it is that the world we find ourselves in is never quite right, never quite good enough. The perfect world is always out of reach and unattainable. Despite this, we have an insatiable desire to strive for a perfect existence in a perfect place. Not simply a better existence in a better place, you understand – a perfect one.

Now, it just happens that the medium through which we analyse our predicament – thought – bears some of the qualities that we seek in our quest for perfection. Obviously our thoughts themselves aren't perfect, but they have at least one redeeming quality – they are not part of the base physical world. They are a strangely immaterial component of our being that seems to float "out there", separate from the body. This is a clue to something, or so it seems. Our thoughts are separate from our base physical world, so they seem to indicate that there are dimensions of existence that are beyond our base physical world. This must be true because that's where our thoughts are.

It seems reasonable to assume that the ultimate thing that our thoughts are considering – the perfect place – is possibly "out there" too, also separate from our base physical world (because that perfect place certainly isn't here on earth).

We can image this "out there" place as being perfect (or what we, perhaps misguidedly, think of as a perfect) because of the fact that it's unshackled by the constraints of physical necessity and it isn't contaminated by the inconvenient messiness of the physical world.

We'll come back to this "out there" place later, but for now let's return to the soul.

The Perfection of the Soul

When we survey our existence here in the physical world, on the corporeal plane, not only do we see that the world around us is imperfect, with its inclement weather, stingy nettles, reality television, dreadful modern music and so on, but we also judge that something else is imperfect too, something a bit more personal. We notice that our *personalities* leave a lot to be desired – all of those questionable emotions, dubious urges and suspect cravings that we are prone to certainly take the shine off our opinions of ourselves.

If only we could partition the imperfect parts of our personalities off and disown them in some way.

But lo and behold, we can!

Because of the way that our thoughts and our consciousness seem to be separate from the physical part of our being we can quite easily throw a conceptual cordon around different aspects of them and segregate portions off from each other, conferring a different status on the different portions. We can partition off the imperfect thoughts and urges that we have and we can convince ourselves that these emanate from a relatively lowly portion of our personality. To excuse this baseness we tell ourselves that these thoughts are somehow anchored to our bodies, in the imperfect, physical realm. This conveniently means that they are thus separate from the rest of our personality, which we like to think of as floating much more freely in an uncontaminated state.

Unsurprisingly we convince ourselves that these uncontaminated parts of our mental selves – our souls – are our "proper" personalities, our authentic, untainted, unadulterated inner essences – our True Selves.

Our souls must, we convince ourselves, be purely virtuous and noble. After all, they exist in the abstract spiritual dimensions that we've created, where all is purity and light, so they must be pure too. It goes without saying.

Unfortunately for us, the fact that the soul seems to be separate from the body is an illusion. The soul is probably nothing more than a projection within the brain. Another one. It's no more a separate entity than are consciousness and the mind. In fact, it's perhaps nothing more than the mind with a rather over-inflated opinion of itself.

The corollary of this is that the higher dimensions in which we like to think that our souls are residing don't exist either. They are just wishful thinking.*

Our feeling that there exist higher dimensions or higher planes in which our souls reside is nothing more than a desire. It's something that's generated within the emotional, aspirational part of our imaginations – something that's created in the part of the imagination that yearns for better things rather than the part that simply thinks about things in a practical, no-nonsense sort of way.

Even if the higher planes of the spiritual world were to exist I think that the following point needs to be taken into account. The spiritual world is given a higher status than "base" reality because it is conceived as being at some level of reality that's physically inexplicable. But let me remind you that the level of reality that we're in at the moment is almost completely inexplicable in itself. We're just used to it and have become extremely blasé about it as a result. We only tend to think that our everyday reality is weird when we contemplate its extremes, such as the core of the atom or the edge of the universe – but in truth the place is weird all the way through.

Some people, perhaps understandably, feel uncomfortable about the idea of consciousness, mind and soul (especially soul) being nothing more than projections within the brain, because it has several unfortunate (or at least seemingly unfortunate) implications.

One is that it scuppers our chances of achieving personal perfection.

---

* Other dimensions probably do exist, such as the multiple dimensions necessary for string theory to work. They are, however, part of the "base" physical universe. Just because there are extra dimensions doesn't imply that there are higher ones.

How can a soul that is a mere brain projection be perfect, after all? Our bodies aren't perfect, our brains aren't perfect, so it stands to reason that our brains' projections aren't perfect either. The very fact that our souls may actually be nothing more than mere projections make them sound fairly imperfect to begin with.

Being imperfect isn't such a terrible thing though.

Trying to improve on imperfections gives us all something to do with our time, thus creating a worthwhile life project. (This isn't to be confused with the idea that imperfections or "bad" things are there specifically so that people can strive to overcome them – to become more noble and "good" by battling against them – which is a common idea in some religious ways of thinking. It just happens to be the way things are.)

What's more, perfection has its drawbacks.

Firstly, perfection is only good in comparison with imperfection. For instance, a "perfect" diamond may be a thing of awe and beauty (if you're impressed by that type of thing), but if all diamonds were equally perfect suddenly the whole concept of perfection and imperfection as applied to diamonds becomes meaningless, or at least diamonds become tiresome.

So, can you imagine floating around at a higher level of existence in a sea of perfect, flawless souls? Where's the fun in that? Where's the point? Where's the gossip?

It'd be tedious.

Perfection is boring. In fact it's perfectly boring.

Perfection is boring in a similar way to the way that a pure, perfect, flawless single musical note, as generated by a suitable electronic machine, is boring. The reason that the same note as produced by a violin, a piano or a human voice is wonderful (or awful, depending on taste) is because of the imperfections inherent in the sources, as they can't help but create extraneous notes in the process (which is why a violin doesn't sound like a trumpet which doesn't sound like a guitar).

On top of this, and to trump everything else, perfection doesn't actually exist. It's an idea that we've thought up, that sounds reasonable, but that has no existence in reality. It's an abstract concept that we've had to create in order to put a top end to the scale of the "rightness" of things. It's a bit like the concept of infinity. Is infinity out there somewhere? No. The concept exists, but the thing itself doesn't.

Consequently, it's probably best not to get too exercised about the unachievable perfection of things such as the soul.

If the soul is nothing more than a mental projection then people may be forgiven for feeling miffed that it may not be perfectible – but there's another reason why people feel uncomfortable about the idea of the soul being nothing more than a function within the brain: it holds the implication that the soul isn't immortal.

No Soul: no Immortality

The separating off of the soul from the body, and its placing into a higher, abstract and perfect dimension of being has a useful consequence, as I mentioned earlier. It means that the soul is divorced from the physical world of wear and tear that has to be endured by all things corporeal. Wear and tear is a term that has a certain cosiness to it when applied to such objects as old sofas that have been "worn in", but when applied to people the term takes on an altogether more sinister connotation – that of decay and, ultimately, of death.

Due to the peculiar manner in which the soul seems to be separate from the body we are offered a lifeline. On death this lifeline, in the form of the rather interesting and improbable trans-dimensional umbilical cord that joins the soul to the body, is pressed into action as an evacuation conduit to remove any residual spiritual essences that may have taken up temporary residence in the brain. The cord is then cut (or withers away as the deceased body decays). Our souls are thus untethered from our bodies and drift off in the eternal ocean of otherness – at the same time as our appropriately boat-shaped coffins transport our defunct bodies into the sea of history.

The drifting, untethered soul may connect to another body via a new umbilical cord that it sends down to a newly conceived human, or it may not, depending on taste, but whatever happens it will continue to float forever, immortally and eternally.

If the soul is nothing more than a projection within the brain this whole idea is buggered, to put it mildly.

This isn't as bad as it sounds though, as I'll explain now.

Eternal Life: A Fate Worse than Death

We're very dissatisfied about dying. It seems such a waste.

But look at it this way.

If we were to banish death the whole world would, within a few generations, fill up to bursting point as people reproduced. There'd be no room on the planet for more people.

An essential component of the dynamic of life is that a person reproduces (should they feel the urge to do so) and that they then get out of the way by dying.

If people didn't die they'd have to stop reproducing.

If this were to happen it would mean that the people that were alive at the time of the banishment of death would hog existence forever, giving no-one else a look in.

WHY ARE WE?

Imagine what would have happened if the secret of eternal life had by some lucky chance been discovered in your parents' day (before they'd become your parents). Soon after the secret became known people would have been barred from having children, as otherwise the world would have been overrun (The human population problem is bad enough as it is, and all we've discovered so far is how to stay alive for a few extra decades, never mind for all of eternity). As a result you wouldn't have been born. How would you have felt about that? In some ways it wouldn't be a problem of course, as you wouldn't exist to care about the fact that you didn't exist, but it still smacks of selfishness on the part of your parents, the "new immortals".

There are other arguments that can be levelled against the banishing of death – ones that go beyond the confines of this me-me-me perspective.

In truth we've needed death from the very dawn of life on earth.

Over the history of life the dynamic of reproducing and then dying – and therefore of "taking one's turn" – wasn't only polite, it was essential.

One of the consequences of the fact that creatures reproduce is that their offspring are slightly different to the parents. They evolve.

If there were no death there'd be no reproduction and thus no evolution. No creatures would have borne offspring that had longer legs, or legs at all, none would have had fully-functioning eyes, or eyes at all. Imagine if this deathless state had existed from the time of the beginning of life, at the time of our earliest, primordial single-celled ancestors. Life would have remained in a state of arrested development at the level of those organisms – organisms that were so simple that they wouldn't even be aware that they were alive, never mind aware of the fact that they were destined to live forever. Immortality would be wasted on them.

So, reverting once again to the argument from the perspective of self-regard, as one inevitably does, if there were no death, there'd be no us.

You may well say "That was then: this is now." We needed death in order to get to where we are today, but we don't need it any more. It's as redundant as the appendix.

In that case, what would be the implications if by some act of biological conjuring we were to manage to banish death tomorrow, making us candidates for immortality?

Even ignoring the selfish fact that we'd have to stop new people being born due to space issues the implications would be very unsettling indeed.

At a stroke there would be no need for practically every single quality of mind that it takes to be human. There'd be nothing to motivate you to do anything. It could wait. There'd be no need to eat (if you're immortal you can't starve to death, by definition) and there'd be no need to work. There'd be no need to go to bed at night or get up in the morning. There'd be no need to raise a family (in fact it would be banned). There'd be no need to do anything.

Life would lose all of its shape and become a meaningless blob of mush. Lethargy would rule.

People may end up with only one or two concerns.

One would be the fight against mind-crushing ennui.

Eternity is a brain-numbingly long time. If you've ever had to wait half an hour for a bus and found the experience dispiriting you will still not be prepared to even the slightest degree for the truly mind-mangling monotony that awaits you.

You'd be bored to death. Except that you wouldn't be afforded the luxury of having that way out.

Be careful what you wish for…

The other concern that the possession of eternal life would bring would be a novel and particular fear.

If there were such a thing as everlasting life there would be no fear of death, it's true, but that fear may be replaced by another, greater dread. Freedom from death doesn't necessarily mean freedom from injury, illness or suffering. If you were to live forever you would almost inevitably fall prey to all possible injuries, illnesses (of a non-fatal variety of course) and misfortunes. You may start by acquiring the occasional cut and bruise as all people do. These would naturally heal, but with time you'd eventually lose the odd finger in an accident. After a while you'd lose all of your limbs, becoming a quadruple amputee. You'd also lose your sight through accident or illness, and your hearing too. And anything else that's not vital to your continued existence. And this is how you would spend eternity.

You may think that you'd be able to get round such horrors by the use of advanced medical techniques, perhaps somehow involving a process of organ regeneration. You'd certainly have the time in which to develop such technologies. Remember though that forever is a very long time indeed, and therefore during that period there'd be bound to be infinite lengths of time when such possibilities wouldn't be available, perhaps due to economic downturns.

You'd spend a huge amount of eternity thinking that you'd rather be dead.

So, a major problem concerning death seems to be that it's both necessary and it's undesirable.

One way to get round this problem is to have your cake and eat it. Believe in reincarnation.

With reincarnation you die, it's true, but with the benefit of having had the opportunity to indulge in all of the life-enhancing urges and activities that make life worth living in the first place. Equally, you don't die, as you come back again (due perhaps to that trans-dimensional umbilical cord reaching down from your immortal soul and linking with another body).

In many versions of the reincarnation theory what you come back as in your next life is determined by how you conduct yourself the previous life. The better you conduct yourself in one life, the better your next one.

Belief in reincarnation is a good way to believe in some sort of salvation without the need of invoking a god to do it for you. People who express a belief in reincarnation have told me that they hold this belief because "it gives life purpose" or because "life would be meaningless if you just died."

I don't quite understand this stance, as surely life would be no more meaningful if you just went on and on regenerating as a different person or animal forever. What's the point of that? If only having one life is meaningless, in what way is having an endless string of them *meaningful*? It just sounds more meaningless to me. Perhaps the whole concept is nothing more than a delaying device in order to avoid confronting the dilemma, a distancing from the subject.

On top of this, reincarnation as a way of dodging death has an unfortunate downside. It's a fine idea if it's assumed that the world into which your future selves are going to be born is one that will be as good as, or even better than, the current world, especially if you yourself are reborn a rung further up the social ladder – but what's the attraction of being born into a world that's past its best and is rapidly declining into an over-populated and under-resourced hell-hole as is about to happen any day now? The whole concept of reincarnation falls into the same trap as that which befalls the concept of eternal life – that whatever bad things may occur in the future, you will certainly experience them.

When confronted by these considerations some people will say "Okay, let's skip the eternal life option: I'll settle for an extended lifespan. Say four times longer than the present expectation." By today's standards in the western world that would be about three hundred and twenty years rather than the expected eighty. That doesn't sound too bad, but put yourself into the shoes of our primitive ancestors, whose lifespan was probably a couple of decades at best, and imagine what they may have thought on this subject. Their reasoning may have gone along very similar lines – "I'll settle for an extended lifespan. Say four times longer than the present expectation." That would be about eighty years rather than the expected twenty. Eighty years – does that figure sound familiar? Your ancestor may have been under the impression that if such a lifespan were to be achieved surely people would have little to complain about. Unfortunately, as we now know, people are never happy with what they've got. They're not supposed to be.

So it seems that the whole idea of eternal life at a purely physical, earth-bound level seems impractical at best and downright unpleasant at worst. And that's only taking into account the aspects of it that I can think of at the moment. Personally I think that we're lucky if we're able to navigate through eighty years or so of life without it all going to pot, never mind wishing for an indefinite extension.

There is however an alternative option to that of never-ending life here on earth: that of a never-ending life in some other, higher sphere. What might that be like?

Eternal Life in Higher Dimensions

Let's just imagine, for the sake of argument, that when the body dies the soul somehow survives. Perhaps it remains floating in whatever higher dimension it was imagined to be residing in while it was connected to its earthly body, or perhaps, because it is no longer tethered to this body, it drifts upwards into an even higher dimension altogether. Heaven perhaps. Whichever, it doesn't really matter.

Wherever the soul finds itself to be, what does it do when it's there? Does it remember the experiences that it had when it was linked to a body? Does it have thoughts at all? If it does have thoughts, what does it think about for all of eternity? If it doesn't have thoughts, it won't remember its sojourn on earth, so what was the point of that particular earthly episode?

Does it have a concept of time? If it thinks, then it probably does have, because thoughts need a temporal structure to exist within (I think). This presents the soul with a dilemma. It may contemplate the possibility that it's going to be there (wherever "there" is) for all of eternity, and it may therefore worry that it's going to eventually find the going tedious in the extreme. Alternatively, if it thinks that it may not be there for all of eternity it may start wondering just how long it is going to be there for. It may start worrying that it's going to "die" in some sort of higher-order manner. Either way, things are worrying.

One way round the problem of a soul having to deal with the (ironically) soul-destroying tedium of an eternity of existence is for it to conveniently forget things as it goes along – to effectively only be aware of existence in a very narrow time frame. The resulting impoverished zone of awareness, like a car travelling through fog, seems to rather make a mockery of the idea of existing forever, as what's the point of existing forever if you keep forgetting everything? It's as though your past is constantly dying as it fades from awareness. A bit like now.

Another alternative approach to the subject is to speculate that the eternal soul has no concept of time, perhaps because it doesn't "think" (whatever thinking entails at that rarefied level). Perhaps the soul is simply "pure essence". In that case it doesn't really matter whether it's wherever it is for eternity or not, as the concept of eternity has been rendered meaningless, as time has disappeared from the equation. Again, being in eternity and not being aware of the fact seems to defeat the object somewhat. One has to ask, if we yearn for eternal life but don't realise when we've got it, what's the point of it?

There's something else that needs to be considered. As with most things that are (assumed to be) desirable, once you've achieved or acquired eternal existence it becomes normal. It's no longer a big deal. Complacency sets in, and you take the thing for granted. Only when there's a threat that the thing may be taken away from you do you sit up and take notice again. Or, in the words of the old blues song: "You don't miss your water till your well runs dry". The thing about eternal life is that by definition once you've achieved it you can't have it taken away (because if it could be it wouldn't be eternal) so the chances are that you wouldn't appreciate it once you'd got it. So again, what's the point?

At the risk of going on forever on this subject, here's just one last criticism of the concept of an eternal after-life.

You could argue that this talk of the soul thinking or not thinking, of being aware or of not being aware, is all utter nonsense, due to the fact that the state that the departed soul is in is no doubt totally different to any state that we can possibly imagine. It must be a state that's devoid of anything that's remotely related to our earth-bound mental functionings. That would, I assume, mean that it was devoid of our proclivity for seeking point and purpose. If indeed in the sphere in which the soul exists such things as purpose and point are meaningless then I have to say: why are we worrying about the whole thing?

If the soul exists as some sort of pure pointless essence, then, well, even if it exists there's no point in wondering about it, because there's no point in it.

More Theories that Conquer Death

It's often thought that religion came about because of our desire to conquer death, and that that's why we have religious urges that revolve around the concept of everlasting life.

My feeling is that this point is usually overstated.

As long as you don't think about it too deeply the concept of everlasting life can certainly be seen as a consolation when it comes to the subject of death, but everlasting life doesn't need a particularly complex religion, with all of its codes and practices, to allow a person to believe in it.

After all, it's perfectly possible to formulate some sort of scientific, or at least pseudo-scientific, theory that postulates the existence of immortal multi-dimensional souls (possibly attached to the body by those trans-dimensional umbilical cords). Just because there is no evidence doesn't mean you can't think up a theory. Proving it is the problem.

Here's another theory that people have thought up as a way of getting round the problem of dying. It jettisons the concept of an immortal soul and simply states that our problem is that we tend to look at life in the wrong way.

Here's the argument.

All Life is One

All life on earth probably started with one common ancestor – possibly a single-celled organism in a pool of primordial soup along the lines that I described earlier. This individual organism then split and split and split creating numerous copies of itself.

It's possible to think of the status of these copies in several different ways. You can think of each copy as being a separate, individual organism, which is the usual way to imagine them, or you can think of them in the following manner.

You can consider them as all being separate parts of one single *fragmented* organism. In other words, when an organism splits in two it doesn't become two organisms – it becomes one organism that's in two places at once. This option doesn't naturally spring to our minds partly because of our (quite reasonable) preoccupation with physical integrity.

Each fragment of the organism is slightly different to all of the other fragments, due to the very slight imprecision of the splitting process, and as each fragment of the organism splits further the fragments inevitably become more and more different and complex. In other words, they evolve, just as described in Chapter 13. Some eventually grow legs, some grow roots, some grow feathers, some grow leaves. But they are all still part of one single fragmented organism.

The upshot of this is that all of life on earth, in all of its diversity, is actually one single being: a meta-organism that now carpets the planet. The original single-celled organism that first divided never died. It simply split into pieces and became more complicated. Individual fragments of the organism die, of course, just as individual cells in your body die, but the organism itself lives on.

We are part of that organism.

Thus, although we each die as individuals, the organism of which we are a part lives on (until the destruction of the earth that is). We (along with all other life-forms) can be likened to leaves on a tree. The individual leaves drop off but the tree keeps going. The whole meta-organism is the tree of life.

Versions of this concept that "all life is one" have been

around for a very long time (like most concepts, probably longer than we think), with the most recent manifestation being as part of the Gaia hypothesis of James Lovelock.

The general theory that all life can be thought of as one single meta-organism is very appealing, and, despite my usual reticence to believe in anything that has a pleasing ring to it, this particular idea seems to be something that I can go along with, at least for now.

I'm not quite sure what the concept's implications are though, in terms of its affect on the human psyche and the meaning of life.

If you're looking for any form of personal salvation for instance, it doesn't deliver in that department at all (but then, why should it?). The fact that the meta-organism lives on even though you yourself die sounds good, but when you get down to it, it doesn't give you any form of personal immortality (should you want it), so the whole idea isn't much more of a consolation in that regard than the more mundane consolation of knowing that the human race lives on when you expire.

The idea that all of the diversity of life on earth is in fact a single planet-encompassing meta-organism makes nature sound seductively harmonious, it's true, but that's very much only on the macro-level. Down here at the nitty-gritty micro-level things are different. Try explaining the concept of "all life is one" to a penguin while it's being gnawed in two by a killer whale.

There are some species of creature down here at the grass-roots level that exhibit qualities that make them analogous to mini-versions of the meta-organism. One such species is the ant. Ants can only function when a whole colony works together, with separate ants performing different specialised tasks: any individual ant that's separated from the group can't function and soon dies. It's as though the ants aren't individual creatures at all, but are part of one larger organism, sometimes described as a superorganism. Each individual ant is in some ways more like a cell in a creature than a creature in itself. Ants don't even seem to mind dying individually, which they do unhesitatingly for the good of the colony as a whole.

Ant colonies are sometimes presented as being model societies, with each individual within the society striving selfishlessly for the good of the whole community. Why can't we be more like that? Ants do have a dark side however. It's not uncommon for the mobilised battalions of ants in an individual colony to set forth and attack neighbouring colonies with a ferocity and singularity of purpose that looks very much like warfare.

I think that there's possibly a clue there as to the essential nature of warfare. It's one superorganism attacking another one (with, in the case of human warfare, the individual super-organisms involved being nation states or other culturally, ethnically or otherwise controversially defined groups).

The Meaning of Life

With all of this denial of the existence of a transcendent, spiritual reason for life I expect that you're getting the impression that I think that life is a meaningless accident.

It's an easy assumption to make.

But that's not the case. Firstly, life isn't an accident. It's just not deliberate, which isn't the same thing at all.

On top of that I would argue that life does indeed have meaning – lots of it. But it isn't a meaning that's "out there", wherever that may be.

Life's meaning is generated purely by life's very existence. Its meaning comes from within its own internal dynamics.

Put another way, the purpose of life is something that happens to exist simply because life exists. Just as life itself simply developed for no particular reason other than that it's the sort of thing that happens, so it is with the purpose of that life – it just gradually evolved.

In fact, because the whole issue is all to do with internal dynamics, when it comes to the point of life I prefer to think in terms of the relatively down-to-earth concept of "purpose" rather than the more philosophically loaded idea of "meaning".

Personally I think that the essential factors that give life purpose (or meaning) are the pursuit of the simple desire for greater understanding and the desire for things to be better – those old yearning that we've had since the dawn of humanity.

Progress I suppose.

However, I wouldn't want to give the impression that I think that the ultimate purpose of humanity is progress with any specific end – such as the end of evolving into a race of perfect, supreme beings or even (rather ludicrously) post-physical "cosmic" consciousnesses (as is a feature of some non-theological philosophies and of the film 2001: A Space Odyssey). That simply imposes a set of secular goals on us rather than very similar religious ones.

No. I personally think that the main purpose of trying to achieve progress is that it's simply worthwhile in its own right to try to understand things and to make things better. Nothing more complicated than that. It's wired into our brains anyway, so we don't seem to have any choice in the matter.

As I've mentioned several times elsewhere in this book, progress cannot be referred to without the qualification that it has the unfortunate potential of kicking back like a badly handled chainsaw (I was going to say that it was like a double-edged sword, but I can't for the life of me see in what way such an instrument is dangerous in a manner than a single-edged sword isn't). We've been so amazingly successful at progressing recently that the resulting over-achievement, over-population and over-consumption that have come in its wake mean that we're now in serious danger of bringing the whole edifice of our achievement crashing down around our ears. Progress, eh – who needs it?

You may not agree with my personal choice of a meaning of life. You may think that from the array of possible meanings that are available I've chosen the wrong one. You may well be right. My choice was just a stab in the dark in what I feel is the right sort of direction.

Is there a meaning of life that's greater than this – a true meaning of life? I don't know for sure, as I have no inside knowledge, although I suspect that there isn't.

However, for the sake of argument, let's just imagine for a moment that there actually is such a thing. A true meaning of life. I think that there's a problem with the whole process of trying to decide what it is.

Imagine that all of the possible concepts for this higher meaning of life are gathered together and laid out as a display on a tabletop so that the correct meaning can be picked out after a considered comparison of the assembled options (You have to suspend your disbelief for a moment and assume that we're actually capable of making an unbiased judgement on the matter). There are a few secular options on the table, and more than a few religious ones. And somewhere amongst them is the real one. After carefully scrutinising all of the options you make a choice. What you don't realise though, is that no matter which one of the displayed possibilities you pick, you always go for the wrong one. You don't choose the right one for the simple reason that you don't even notice that it's there in the display in front of you. It's similar to the situation involving the choosing of the moth in Figure 54, where you had to decide which one of a number of differently coloured moths resting on a tree was the least likely to be eaten by a predator (and where you couldn't choose the correct moth because you couldn't see it). How can you be expected to make a choice when you're blind to the existence of the correct option, but where there are other options being presented that delude you into thinking that you are weighing up all of the options? With both the moth and the meaning of life you couldn't see the correct choice because your senses and your brain are simply not equipped to detect them.

I'm imagining here that there is indeed a higher meaning of life, and that you couldn't see it because it happens to be inevitably and permanently invisible to us. Alternatively, maybe you couldn't see it because it actually isn't there. Who knows. In either case, most people choose one of the alternatives on offer, because it's wired into our brains to make a choice.

Knowing the Meaning of Life – the Down Side

For people of a religious disposition the concept that our activities here on earth are enough to give life a meaning (or at least a purpose), as described earlier, is not enough: the meaning of life has to be of a higher order and is (usually) projected outwards, with it's main thrust often being the acquisition of eternal life coupled with the process of "getting closer to God" – beyond which little further analysis is needed. The subject of the higher meaning of life is safely corralled within the confines of the religious setting, where to a large extent its implications are left surprisingly unscrutinized, and where it's imbued with a degree of supernatural elusiveness and mystery that results in it (very conveniently) never quite being pinned down.

This is quite appealing, as no further truths need to be confronted. The act of leaving the meaning of life essentially unanalysed is quite comforting because if the meaning were by scientific investigation (or even by some kind of divine revelation) to be somehow actually revealed there's no knowing what the effect would be on the human psyche.

The revelation of any true meaning of life may have devastating effects if it turns out to be bad news, such as that we are nothing more than a food supply for parasitic worms that tap into our brains from a different dimension and eat our thoughts (which is why we keep forgetting things), and that for technical reasons this is a state that it is impossible for us to extricate ourselves from.

If the meaning were to turn out to be really good the effects may be somewhat unfortunate too. Our smugness, complacency and insufferable sense of entitlement may spiral out of control like some gross mutation of the spoilt child syndrome.

Alternatively, if the ultimate meaning of life turned out to be interesting but not all that special, people may be either pleased or disappointed, possibly profoundly so one way or the other (depending on what they were expecting in the first place). Then after a while we'd quite possibly become surprisingly indifferent.

We may simply think, "So that's it."

We rapidly become blasé about our goals once they've been realised.

According to this scenario, our feelings towards actually finding the meaning of life may follow a similar trajectory to that followed by our feelings towards another great goal that the human race set itself – the goal of venturing into space and setting foot on an alien world. Anyone living before the mid twentieth century who pondered on the subject would possibly have decided that to achieve such a goal must surely be well-nigh impossible. If, however, you happened to be alive during the 1960s you may remember the total wonder of the Mercury, Gemini and Apollo space missions, and the incredible awe at the Apollo 11 landing on the lunar surface, when Neil Armstrong and Buzz Aldrin became the first humans to make a giant leap onto another world. The whole enterprise was literally out of this world.

But as soon as the Apollo 11 mission was over public interest in the entire subject of space exploration plunged. Who can remember the name of the third person to walk on the Moon?*

You may even be thinking at this very moment "The Moon – that hardly counts as an alien world, does it? It's just a stone's throw away after all. One small step away. Mars maybe."

How quickly contempt sets in.

Needless to say, the mission to discover the ultimate meaning of life isn't exactly the same as the mission to land on the Moon, because finding the meaning of life is the ultimate mission. Once it's been achieved we can't just divert our attention and move on to the next project as we do in most other areas of human endeavour.

So, let's stop here and take a look at were we've got to so far.

It would seem that, while there's a possibility that we may be surprisingly unaffected by the discovery of the ultimate meaning of life (should we find that it's not as interesting as we'd hoped it would be), the balance of probabilities is that the revelation would have a negative impact, making us either deeply uneasy

---

* Charles (Pete) Conrad. Followed closely down the ladder by fellow Apollo 12 astronaut Alan Bean. In total 12 astronauts have walked on the lunar surface. They all did so between 1969 and 1972.

(if the meaning turned out to be bad) or deeply unbearable (if it was good). Taking things all round, the chances of an incontrovertibly positive outcome would be slight. It sounds as though it may be best not to know.

In fact, I suspect that deep down we don't really want to know anyway. After all, if understanding the meaning of life is truly important why then don't we pursue it even more diligently and with greater vigour than we do? True, you're reading this book because you're interested in the subject to a fair degree, but after you've put it down you may do something totally unrelated, such as watching a bit of sport on the television or going for a walk. If the purpose behind our lives is so significant and pressing why do we waste such a ludicrously large amount of our time on pursuits that are inarguably less than meaningful? Yesterday, for example, I spent at least half an hour doing sudokus. Here I am, with my precious quota of time on earth tick-ticking away at the unreasonably rapid rate of one year per annum, yet I fritter non-returnable time away in doing worthless puzzles rather than in seeking the answer to the ultimate puzzle of all: that of existence itself. Where's the point in that? Surely my brain should be compelling me to do something purposeful with my every living breath?

Of course there are indeed many people who do spend almost their every waking moment doing purposeful things in pursuit of what they see as life's deeper meaning, for better or for worse, but the fact that a very significant proportion of the population don't do so makes me think that the pursuit is far from being an absolute human necessity.

The pursuit is possibly an intellectual and emotional urge similar to the urge to go to the Moon. Most of us are intrigued by the project, but we don't commit much effort to it in practice, simply being content to follow the developments in the media.

Despite the fact that the meaning of life should theoretically be a thing of overwhelming significance I'm surprised by the fact that people who assume that they know vaguely what it is aren't affected more than they are by the knowledge that they think they are privy to, and that as a result they don't act wildly differently. (Obviously, some people, such as religious fundamentalists, act in significantly unconventional ways as a result of their insights, however the fact that not everyone else does suggests that this is more a result of personality or of social, political or similar circumstances than anything to do with any innate effect of the supposed knowledge.)

For instance, if today you were to pop down to the local shops and you came across Richard Dawkins and the Archbishop of Canterbury buying their groceries – that's one person whose philosophy states that life is a stochastic phenomenon that will end in personal oblivion in maybe twenty or thirty years time if he's lucky, and one who believes that we were created by God and that we are destined to spend eternity by his side – you may be hard pressed to tell them apart unless the archbishop happened to be wearing his work clothes. Such different expectations of the future – yet such little difference in manner. You may, needless to say, see other people buying groceries who most definitely stand out because of their beliefs, for instance because they have a certain dress code or because they steer clear of certain foodstuffs, but there's no inevitable link between belief and such behaviour, especially when the complicating factors of cultural and group identity are factored out. Bear in mind that such things as prescriptive dress codes aren't purely the preserve of religious groups. For instance, if you're a man, when did you last go outside wearing a dress? And if you're a woman, when did you last wear a bowler hat? Dietary prescriptions aren't exclusively theologically-based either – my atheistically-inclined partner, for example, disallows me from eating meat in the house for a whole raft of secular political and ideological reasons, much to my frustration.

Of course neither the Archbishop of Canterbury nor Richard Dawkins, nor anyone else for that matter, actually knows what the ultimate meaning of life is, so they are acting purely on the basis of what they feel is right rather than what they *know* is right, which isn't the same thing at all. There's a comfortable nebulously swirling around the topic that means that it never has to be pinned down and confronted too precisely.

The idea of keeping the meaning of life at arms length is useful for all of us. It means that it remains mysterious and allows us to steer clear of the trap of "knowing too much".

Personally I don't want to know too much, because I enjoy the mystery of not knowing what on earth's going on. If I knew everything I'd be at a loss to know what to do with my time, and I'd have nothing to think about.

The problem of knowing too much may not only apply to the subject of the meaning of life in general, but for believers in a god it may also apply to the issue of "knowing" God too. If God were to become truly knowable, rather than remaining the present, rather convenient unknowable – if he were to become effable rather than ineffable – God would lose his mystery and would become in some ways normal, just as everything else in our experience is normal. Believers may lose their awe in him just as, at a more mundane level, people lost their awe (surprisingly quickly) in our ability to walk on the Moon.

When it comes to knowing God, it may be wise to follow the old adage that you should never meet your heroes, for they inevitably disappoint.

At the very least, familiarity breeds contempt.

If God were to be truly "known", God would become normal. But bear in mind that whether God exists or God doesn't exist, ultimately everything is "normal" in the end. Because normal is just how things are – that's its definition after all.

But also bear in mind that "normal" is something that's mind-bogglingly more bizarre than we can ever imagine. From the core of the atom to the edge of the universe, including everything between.

And that's good enough for me.

THE END

Some books that I read before and during the writing of this one

In reverse alphabetical order, so that people who are normally
at the top are at the bottom just for once

Lewis Wolpert, *Six Impossible Things Before Breakfast* (Faber, 2006)

Keith Thomas, *Man and the Natural World* (Allen Lane, 1983)

Colin Renfrew, *Prehistory* (Weidenfeld & Nicholson, 2007)

V S Ramachandran, *Phantoms in the Brain* (Fourth Estate, 1998)

Steven Pinker, *The Blank Slate* (Allen Lane, 2002)

Steven Pinker, *How The Mind Works* (Allen Lane, 1998)

Richard L Gregory, *Odd Perceptions* (Methuen, 1986)

Richard L Gregory, *The Intelligent Eye* (Weidenfeld & Nicholson, 1970)

Thomas Gilovich, *How We Know What Isn't So* (The Free Press, 1991)

Kitty Ferguson, *Measuring The Universe* (Headline, 1999)

Freeman Dyson, *Infinite in All Directions* (Harper & Row, 1988)

Daniel C Dennett, *Breaking The Spell* (Allen Lane, 2006)

Richard Dawkins, *The God Delusion* (Bantam, 2006)

Richard Dawkins, *Unweaving The Rainbow* (Allen Lane, 1998)

Richard Dawkins, *Climbing Mount Improbable* (Viking, 1996)

Richard Dawkins, *The Blind Watchmaker* (Longman, 1986)

Charles Darwin, *On The Origin of Species* (1859: or Penguin, 2009)

Paul Davies, *The Goldilocks Enigma* (Allen Lane, 2006)

Bill Bryson, A Short History of Nearly Everything (Doubleday, 2003)

INDEX

INDEX